SOVIET WOMEN

D1571502

WILLIAM M. MANDEL lectures extensively on Soviet studies and has a radio program on the U.S.S.R. His other books on the Soviet Union include *Russia Re-Examined: The Land, the People and How They Live*, *The Soviet Far East and Central Asia*, *A Guide to the Soviet Union*, and *Soviet Source Materials on U.S.S.R. Relations with East Asia, 1945–1950* (a compilation of documents).

SOVIET WOMEN

William M. Mandel

ANCHOR BOOKS
ANCHOR PRESS/DOUBLEDAY
GARDEN CITY, NEW YORK
1975

The Anchor Books edition is the first publication of *Soviet Women*.

Anchor Books edition: 1975
Copyright © 1975 by William M. Mandel
All Rights Reserved
Printed in the United States of America
First Edition

Library of Congress Cataloging in Publication Data

Mandel, William.
  Soviet women.

  Bibliography.
  Includes index.
  1. Women—Russia. 2. Women—History. I. Title.
HQ1662.M35   301.41′2′0947
ISBN 0-385-03255-2
Library of Congress Catalog Card Number 74-12732

To the memory of Claudia Jones, black interracial leader; imprisoned 1955; deported; died in exile 1965.

Contents

SOVIET WOMEN

Introduction

I have been to the Soviet Union six times, speak Russian, and am familiar with the thinking of Soviet people. They imagine that if a country is technologically advanced and has a high living standard, it has somehow got to be fairly civilized. Therefore they generally think well of the United States. Because of this, there are things about our country that a Soviet woman just wouldn't believe. Things so contrary to the commonplace rights she enjoys, and so obviously the due of any woman in a civilized country, that she takes them for granted.

She would be shocked, for instance, to learn that under the U. S. Supreme Court decision of 1974 a woman is not entitled to sick benefits when she has to quit work due to normal pregnancy.

"Then I'd have an abortion!" Maria Ivanovna might say, with appropriate indignation.

"But what if your husband wouldn't let you?" Mary Jones replies.

"My *husband?* Whose body is it?"

When Mary explains that there are eighteen states in this country in which a woman must have her husband's or parents' permission for an abortion, Maria would probably suggest: "Then just go to another state."

"Lots of women don't earn very much," Mary replies. "They couldn't afford it."

"They can't afford transportation and an abortion? Tell me, how much would it be for the abortion? Not in money —yours is different from ours—but in terms of days' pay?"

Mary sighs. "Not days. A couple of weeks' pay, or a month's, depending on—"

"Oh my God! (Russians use religious exclamations as much as we do). With us it's free if the doctor says you have to have an abortion, or about one day's pay if you just decide that you want it yourself." Maria pauses and gropes for solutions. "Couldn't you borrow the money?"

"That depends," Mary says. "In twenty-eight states the husband has to approve if the wife takes out a loan."

"The husband! What does *he* have to do with that?"

"Well, most women in the United States don't have their own money; they don't work at paying jobs. Even if they do, banks too often are afraid they'll quit the jobs or lose them. Women are considered bad risks."

At this point, if not before, Maria Ivanovna would probably change the subject, because Russian notions of hospitality regard it as very impolite to talk about anything that makes a guest or host feel inferior. But if the conversation was turned to other areas pertaining to women, she'd be even more embarrassed. For the simple fact is that Soviet women, in terms of rights, benefits, opportunities, and general treatment, are far ahead of American women. The foregoing is only one small illustration of this. How Russian women achieved their advantaged position and how they exercise it today is a story that contains many lessons for women in this country as they struggle toward comparable goals. This book aims to tell their story as I have seen it and as they have told it to me.

Had Maria gone on to raise the subject of pensions, for instance, she'd have been appalled. Private pension plans in the United States cover only one woman in ten retiring from jobs in industry; even fewer in the areas of sales, service, and agriculture. In the Soviet Union *every* woman is pensioned as she reaches the age of fifty-five if she has worked a total of twenty successive years at any kind of paid job, or at a younger age if there was a health hazard.

May 1 is Labor Day not only in the communist countries but throughout much of the world (although it started as a celebration in the United States), and on that day the Soviet papers are full of reports of gains made by working people in the previous year. But on May 1 of 1974, the San Francisco *Chronicle* reported that thirty young women had slept all night outside Carpenters' Union Hall in that city in order to get applications to become apprentice cabinetmakers. It has been nearly fifty years since any such news story has been reported from the U.S.S.R., because they have been free of unemployment for that long and because women are freely admitted into just about every conceivable kind of skilled job.

But what Maria might find hardest to believe is that, in some cases, the clock is actually being turned *back* by half a century under the guise of equal rights for women in large areas of the United States. In 1974 the California State Industrial Welfare Commission legalized the ten-hour day without overtime, whereas previously women had to be paid time and a half after eight hours. In the Soviet Union, as you will see in further chapters, workers don't want overtime and don't work any unless on-the-spot union officials agree it's necessary. There is an absolute maximum of twelve hours of overtime a *month,* and all overtime beyond the official seven- or eight-hour day is paid at time and a half or double time, depending on the job. Those are not merely the rules: they are what actually happens. My taped interviews correspond exactly to what the Moscow reporter of the *Wall Street Journal* learned in the same way from "a dozen women interviewed in Moscow from various occupations" (January 6, 1971), and to what Professor Emily Clark Brown says in her book *Soviet Trade Unions and Labor Relations* (Harvard University Press, 1966), based on visits to twenty-four factories there.

If Mary Jones were a Californian and knew the rest of that 1974 Supreme Court decision, she'd shock Maria right down to her heels. Previous requirements for lounge rooms for women employees and for washrooms and other sanitation features were *dropped* from the law. Maria would be stony-faced, but internally the word that would flash in her mind is *"Varvarstvo!"*—barbarism. Such facilities are required in her country. I remember how surprised I was to find, behind the time-worn exterior of a streetcar barn in Moscow, locker rooms in which each worker (most of the drivers are women) has two completely separated lockers side by side, one for street and one for work clothes so that personal clothing cannot possibly be dirtied by that worn at work.

If Maria knew her Karl Marx (lots of people in the U.S.S.R. don't), she'd find the rest of those California labor regulations to be things he could have used in his book *Capital* a hundred years ago to illustrate his argument that "the capitalist state" exists to help business squeeze the maximum profit out of working people, and that the weakest and least organized people are treated most heartlessly. Agricultural and household workers (mostly Chicanos and blacks in California) are excluded from all limitations on hours and overtime pay, even after ten hours. For good measure, the ruling added the millions of workers in retail service establishments (chiefly women and chiefly unorganized) to those not entitled to any overtime pay rates. Maria knows that in the Soviet Union there are absolutely no exemptions from the labor laws.

Recently NOW (the National Organization for Women) has been expanding into small textile, paper mill, and even rural market towns in the American countryside. At its 1974 convention, it learned that bread-and-butter issues like equal work and equal pay are the focal points of its members' activities there. Abortion, lesbianism, terminology ("woman" for girl, "herstory" for history), and self-help health clinics are given little or no attention. For better or worse, Soviet women would agree with that completely, except for abortion, which they regard as an absolute necessity to protect their life plans against disruption by unwanted pregnancy. But these problems are far behind them. As that *Wall Street Journal* report from Moscow said: "Equal pay for equal work, equal promotion opportunities and access to managerial posts are all taken for granted as women's rights here."

The "taken for granted" psychology sometimes has results that Mary Jones would think strange. No Soviet woman visiting this country, of the many I have met, has asked me, "Why don't you have more women doctors?" But I *have* been asked, "How come so many of your doctors are men?" The questioner, a middle-aged female physician who heads Moscow's enormous public health services, grew up in a society in which most doctors are women (72 per cent in 1973) and regards that as normal. That was not true in her mother's day, when the ratio was exactly as low as it is in the United States at present, but, like most of us, she thinks of now, not of history.

The first regional and national meetings of American trade union women in recent times took place in 1974. Addie Wyatt, director of the Women's Division of the Amalgamated Meat Cutters, said in her keynote address at the national conference, "We women have special concerns. We need maternity benefits and child care."

Regarding maternity benefits, Maria's response would be deeply compassionate. Soviet women have a marvelous sense of warmth toward members of their sex everywhere in the world. It is a kind of gut feminism.

Perhaps this is dangerous ground for a man to tread, but prominent Soviet women seem to me much warmer than their American counterparts. I think I know the reason, and it is a reflection not upon those American women, but upon sex roles in our society. We are raised to believe that people in positions of leadership should behave like men. In the Soviet Union both sexes, I am happy to say, take it for granted that a woman has the right to act like a woman and a man like a man, whether the woman is a pilot commanding an all-male crew in handling the heaviest of transport planes (a real case described in Chapter IV), or the man a physician employed in a hospital headed by a woman. The basic reason, I suspect, is that it hasn't occurred to anyone there to run away from the realities of basic female (or male) physiological functions. If a child is to be breast-fed, for example—which Russians take for granted—then it is recognized that the mother pretty well has to take care of it during approximately the first year of its life, and allowances are made without penalty wherever she may be working. Incidentally, the almost universal preference among Soviet women for breast-feeding their babies undoubtedly is itself a contributor to a comfortable, adjusted-to-nature, warmth-producing atmosphere for mother, child, and father, whatever other behavioral patterns may also exist for them. They see no contradiction, as we often do, between obeying women's natural biological instincts and performing well in almost any occupation. That female pilot mentioned above had two children, one still in kindergarten, when she set a battery of flying records.

Which brings us back to maternity leave. *Every* employed Soviet woman gets 112 days off at full pay, half of it before the child is born, and may stay off her job the rest of the baby's first year of life without losing seniority or position. On the matter of child care, Maria could only exclaim, "But what do you *do* with your children while you work?" Mary's answers would probably disturb her more than any other single thing she could learn about this country, except that at least 100,000 welfare mothers were sterilized in 1973, according to the director of the Office of Population Affairs of HEW (San Francisco *Chronicle,* February 26, 1974), largely under the threat that they'd be cut off the rolls if they didn't submit. To Soviet women, their right to bear children is as sacred as their right not to. To them, that is what being a woman, within the larger framework of freedom to be a human being, is all about.

Tell Maria that a private day-care nursery school taking a child nine hours a day, five days a week, costs each month a week's pay for a well-paid American woman, and she would throw up her hands in horror. Then add that it is nearly impossible to place children under two years and nine months old in city-licensed day-care homes, and she'd be entirely bewildered. But she would begin to understand why most American mothers of preschool children do not have jobs, no matter how much they need the money or want to work for its own sake. And she'd have no trouble at all understanding how hard it is for those who do work.

The Soviet Union provides day or even twenty-four-hour care for virtually every urban child whose parent desires it, and for every farm child during the planting and harvesting season. The fee is actually lower than the cost of feeding the child at home (all child-care centers in the U.S.S.R. provide hot meals as a matter of course). Children are accepted from the age of three months, although relatively few mothers place them before one year. You'll find full details as you get into this book.

Mary and Maria would probably never come to an agreement if they discussed systems of government. But Mary would learn, to her surprise, that Maria regards Soviet government as democratic. I once asked a Jewish woman in Leningrad, married to a Russian plumber, if she bothered to vote. She drew herself up—this was in the privacy of her apartment and only her son was there—and said, "Of course we vote! We dress up in our best clothes as for a most solemn occasion and congratulate each other on the elections!" I pressed on: *"Why* do you vote?" "Because the best people are nominated, and they do the best they can for us!"

Nowadays I wish we could feel that secure in this country, despite the fact that we have two or more candidates on the ballot and they have only one. What is important for this book is that very nearly half of those "best people" who become candidates in the Soviet Union are women. According to the *Congressional Quarterly,* if every single one of the 3,000 women running for city, state, and national office in the United States in 1974 had been elected, women would hold only one half of *1* per cent of the 521,000 elective offices in the country. In the Soviet Union they held *47* per cent of public offices as of 1973. Because their system calls for larger legislative bodies than ours, there are over a million female office holders there, or twice as many as the total number of men in office in this country. And anyone who has met such women officials—dozens of them have now visited the United States—knows that they conduct themselves with the sense of authority we expect of persons of office. Their behavior is certainly not that of people who regard themselves as tokens.

However, the higher one goes in Soviet office, the lower the percentage of female incumbents becomes. And for someone with a developed sense of the meaning of fully equal status for women (as distinct from "equal rights," which Soviet women really do have), many things there are far from satisfactory. The degree to which men share or simply help in the home is far lower than it should be. Although crime in the Soviet Union is low, and among women even lower, a

recent sociological study of female prisoners there showed
that some women still break the law due to love or disappointment in love: stealing to buy a man an automobile, for
example. Psychologically such women may regard themselves
as dependent and inferior. (*Literaturnaia gazeta* [Literary
Gazette], Moscow, May 29, 1974.)

An even more depressing situation, because it is more
widespread, exists in the Soviet desert republic of Turkmenia,
just north of Iran. There it is still common to buy a wife
(*Literaturnaia gazeta*, May 22, 1974). Yet, as I make clear
in the chapter on ethnic minorities, it is also the place where
women have made the most enormous progress relative to
the past and, outside the home, occupy a status American
women would envy.

How to reconcile these things?

The answer lies in looking at Soviet women historically.
Neither the Russians, the Jews, nor the Turkmenians there
have the same background of experience as American
women, whether WASP, black, Spanish-speaking, or any
other ethnic group. I would argue that the achievements toward women's liberation in the Soviet Union are even more
extraordinary in light of the background. But Soviet history
also explains why women haven't advanced further, and
helps one understand why Mary Jones, particularly if she is an
upper-middle-class, big-city feminist, and Maria Ivanovna can
in some respects fail to communicate or can even become
annoyed with each other. And so I open the book with chapters on the history of women in Russia.

A word about the facts in this book. I want it to be read
by people who are turned off by footnotes—people without
a college education as well as those having one or even having advanced degrees. So there are no footnotes. As someone
whose writing is often scholarly in style, I'll admit I don't
think they're all that important. For example, a recent article
on women and Soviet politics in a book coming from one of
our most distinguished universities cites me as authority in its
footnotes no less than seven times. That's flattering. But the
professor who wrote the article simply doesn't know how to
read statistics. He writes of Soviet government that "at the
top, there are just 27 women in the Council of Nationalities

and 26 in the Council of the Union" (Senate and House, in our terminology). Actually, those were the *percentages,* and the true figures are 231 and 232! So little numbers indicating where a fact comes from prove nothing unless one checks the original.

The bulk of the sociological statistics used in this book may be found in my translations of recent work in the quarterlies *Soviet Sociology, Soviet Anthropology and Archaeology,* and *Soviet Law and Government,* available in all major American libraries.

For those who want to delve deeply into the subject of women in the U.S.S.R., I provide at the back of this book the most complete and up-to-date bibliography of books on Soviet women in English and Russian that can be found anywhere, with brief descriptions indicating what each of them contains. A bibliography of the articles I used would simply have been entirely too long for a popular book such as I have tried to write.

For women wondering, as you have a right to, whether any male can be relied upon in a book on such a subject, I should like to say what I can on my own behalf.

For some reason, all the published books about Soviet women written by non-Soviet women appeared during the first half of the post-Revolution history of that society; none have appeared since 1945. I knew (know, in the case of those still living) all but one of the authors of those books. Jessica Smith, who wrote the very earliest of them (*Women in Soviet Russia,* 1928), is a person with whom I correspond to this day, and for whom I worked as a research assistant on my very first such job thirty-five years ago. I have seen Ella Winter (*Red Virtue,* 1933) in recent years, and helped her long ago with a book she wrote on the Soviet Union during World War II. *Red Virtue* is still very much worth reading, despite its prissy title. I knew the great Anna Louise Strong (*I Change Worlds,* 1935), about whom movies and TV shows should someday be made. Among Russians who moved to the West, I knew Fannina Halle (*Women in Soviet Russia,* 1933; *Women in the Soviet East,* 1938) and Masha Scott, about whose experiences Pearl Buck wrote (*Talk About Russia with Masha Scott,* 1945). To this day I treasure the fact that

Masha, who had grown up, gotten her education, and worked as a teacher in Soviet Russia before World War II, came to me for information about her own country when she was taking graduate courses at NYU because she decided that my knowledge of the Soviet Union could be trusted.

So I am able to draw not only upon the experience of my visits there over a span of over forty years (I'm a native New Yorker), but also upon the richness of contact with American women who have known the Soviet Union best. I hope this book lives up to that heritage.

These pages are full of conversations with Soviet women, many of them taped, that took place during my many visits. My confidence in my own understanding has been helped by the fact that women of the youngest generations there, down to nineteen years of age in 1973, have been willing to answer my questions about even the most intimate personal matters, in talks arranged through individual contacts outside official channels of any kind.

I am also encouraged by the fact that American women of all generations who have recently had firsthand experience of the Soviet Union have had at least enough faith in my undertaking to share their knowledge with me in great detail and with utmost patience.

It goes almost without saying that when I mention particular Soviet women and the positions they hold, it is as of this writing. Changes are bound to occur as time goes by. Though the faces of particular job or office holders may change, the main points of the book will remain the same.

The manuscript has been read and criticized in part or in whole by Ethel Dunn, Paula Garb, Phyllis Mandel Glick, and Louise Headd, each of whom has special qualifications for offering opinions and suggestions aside from the basic one of being female.

My deepest gratitude goes to my wife, Tanya, and to Laura X of the Women's History Research Library, Berkeley. Tanya accompanied me on two of the visits, one of them specifically planned to gather material for this book. The fact that she speaks Russian, and has suffered through all my attempts to learn about that country for many, many years, enabled her to pose questions while we were there that others possibly could not have, and has also obviously given her an ability to criticize my writing that no one not knowing me as well could possess. She is a remarkable editor, with an exceptional ability to rearrange material in the most logical sequence and to excise occasional lapses into bad taste. She also did an immense amount of filing and organizing of the research data for handiest reference.

Laura is responsible for having shaken me loose, in endless discussions and arguments, from long-established assumptions about what the liberation of women really means, and for having caused me, as I undertook this work, to pose and seek answers to questions that would not otherwise have occurred to me. In terms of finding materials I asked for, volunteering materials I didn't ask for but know now that I damn well had to learn about, writing page-by-page critiques probably not much shorter in all than this book itself, and sharing the perceptions of her own two visits to the U.S.S.R., she was helpful in a manner that is beyond praise. Although each of these women contributed hundreds of hours to this undertaking, neither bears responsibility for the outcome, and I do not shift to the shoulders of any whose help I have acknowledged here the blame for anything I say with which readers may disagree.

I should also like to thank my father, Max, who first took me to the Soviet Union and one of whose recent adventures there is part of this book, and Mandy Bratt, who did the clean typing on very short notice.

Photographs are from the American Russian Institute, Inc., of San Francisco, and are used with its permission.

Chapter 1
Queens, Princesses, Serfs, and Revolutionaries

To imagine that the background of Soviet women is anything like that from which American women have come is to misjudge the level and the attitudes from which Russian change began.

Despite the prejudice against "backward" peoples that colored the writings of the first Westerners to report on Russia several hundred years ago, differences in the status of women emerge clearly. The physician to Tsar Alexei from 1660 to 1669 was an Englishman, Samuel Collins. He wrote:

"The Russians discipline to their wives is very rigid and severe. . . . Yet three or four years ago a merchant beat his wife as long as he was able, with a whip two inches about, and then caused [her] to put on a smock dipt in brandy . . . which he set on fire, and so the poor creature perished miserably in the flames. . . . And yet what is more strange, none prosecuted her death; for in this case they have no penal law for killing of *a wife or slave,* if it happen upon correction," i.e., punishment for an alleged "offense" (my emphasis).

The state church (Russian Orthodox) gave the odor of sanctity to the oppression of women in a Household Ordinance issued over the name of a high clergyman during the reign of Ivan the Terrible in the sixteenth century. It spelled out when and how to beat a wife.

This was still the case nearly half a century later, according to John Perry, a hydraulic engineer who worked fourteen years for Peter the Great. Women fought back. In view of the price exacted, they were heroes: "The wives on the other hand being thus many times made desperate, murther their husbands in revenge for the ill usage they receive; on which occasion there is a law made, that when they murther their husbands, they are set alive in the ground, standing upright, with the earth fill'd about them, and only their heads left just above the earth, and a watch set over them . . . ; which is *a common sight* in that countrey, and I have known them live sometimes seven or eight days in this posture" (my emphasis). So such resisters were not rare exceptions.

The conditions that gave rise to disobedience are suggested by him, if only vaguely, and concern upper-class women: "It had been always the custom of Russia, at all entertainments, for the women not be admitted into the sight of or into conversation with men; the very houses of all men of any quality or fashion, were built with an entrance for the women a-part, and they used to be kept separate in an apartment by themselves."

Although the status of Western and Central European women was probably inferior to that of English, a sixteenth-century ambassador, Baron von Herberstein, was struck by the worse position of Russian women relative to those elsewhere in Europe: "The conditions of life of Russian women are most deplorable. A woman is considered honorable only when she lives at home and never goes out. If in any case she should allow herself to be seen by strangers, her conduct is regarded as shameful. Very seldom is she permitted to go to church, and still more seldom to see friends, except when she is elderly and will not attract suspicion."

While Russia a thousand years ago was on the same plane of civilization as Western Europe, a wide gap had opened by the dawn of modern times, largely due to two centuries of oppression and exaction of tribute by nomadic conquerors from the East, the Tatar Mongols. Russian rulers were aware of the difference and repeatedly tried to pull the country up by its bootstraps through forced imitation of the West. Peter the Great, among his other reforms 250 years ago, brought upper-class women out of segregation and tried to institute marriage by free choice. In engineer Perry's language, "The Tsar [emperor] being not only willing to introduce the English habits, but to make them more particularly pleasing to the Russ ladies, made an order that from thenceforward, at all weddings, and at other publick entertainments, the women as well as the men, should be invited. . . . and that they should be entertained in the same room with the men, like as he had seen in foreign countries; and that the evenings should be concluded with musick and dancing. . . .

"There was another thing also which the women very well liked in these regulations of the Tsar. It had been the custom of Russia, in case of marriages, that the match used always to be made up between the parents on each side, without any previous meeting, consent or liking of one another, tho' they marry very young, . . . sometimes when neither the bride nor the bridegroom are thirteen years of age. . . ." Here Perry described the beatings to death, the women taking revenge, and the barbarous executions for this, and continued: "These sad prospects made the Tsar . . . take away the occasion of these cruelties . . . ; and the forced marriages being supposed to be one cause thereof, made an order that no young couple should be marry'd together without their own free liking and consent; and that all persons should be admitted to visit and see each other at least six weeks before they were married together. This new order is so well approved of, and so very pleasing to the young people, that they begin to think much better of foreigners. . . ."

These reforms did not reach the mass of the people at all, and for that matter their real cultural influence hardly reached beyond the new capital, St. Petersburg (now Leningrad), not even really to the old one, Moscow. But to the tiny upper stratum of women with property, there were lasting benefits. Under Peter's reforms, a married woman remained full owner of her own property and received the right to dispose of it without her husband's consent.

Six empresses ruled Russia during the seventy years following Peter's death. The last, Catherine the Great, personally acquired high culture, played politics as dirtily and cruelly as men, suppressed massive serf rebellions (one in the same year as the signing of the U. S. Declaration of Independence) with the same kind of indiscriminate slaughter, and waged wars of conquest. Some upper-class women achieved a great deal in the face of male prejudice. Seventy women of Catherine's day tried their hands at writing, encouraged by the example of her own perfectly readable stories and articles. Half a dozen would be regarded as people of culture even by the much higher standards of today. One was truly remarkable, a more outstanding personality than Catherine herself, and should be better known. There have been queens who were the powers behind their husbands' thrones. There have been male queen-makers. But how many instances are there of a woman who placed a queen on the throne and then went on to outdo men in their most sacred preserves, including playing a role in early American-Russian relations? This was Princess Catherine Dashkova.

Dashkova was born and grew up in the reign of Empress Elizabeth, Peter's daughter, who, although quick and bright, was so ignorant that she did not know that Great Britain is an island. But at age thirteen Dashkova was reading Bayle, Montesquieu, Grimm, and Voltaire, and conversed with the men of learning, foreign artists, and ambassadors who visited the exceptionally cultured home in which she was raised. Shortly afterward she attracted the attention of a woman fourteen years older, Princess Sophie of Anhalt-Zerbst, who had come from Germany at age fifteen as wife of the heir to the Russian throne. We know Sophie as Catherine the Great. She began to earn that title by learning Russian (the nobility spoke French among themselves) and convincing everyone that she had her adopted country's interests at heart.

Sophie's husband, Crown Prince Peter, wanted to divorce her and marry Dashkova's sister. Knowing this, and convinced that Catherine (Sophie) on the throne would give Russia the liberties preached by the eighteenth-century philosophers, whom Catherine also read and corresponded with, Dashkova, in her late teens, plotted to put Catherine on the throne. While Dashkova won over officials, Catherine worked on the Army. Soldiers in a Guards regiment proclaimed her empress, and the rest supported them. The two women, in officer's uniform and on horseback, reviewed the troops. Catherine's husband, by now the Tsar, abdicated. Dashkova was not yet nineteen.

Shrewd Catherine pushed Dashkova into the background. The latter traveled abroad for years. On her return, she proposed to the new Empress the founding of a Russian academy to organize the grammar of the language, free it of inappropriate foreignisms, and develop rhetoric and the rules of versification. Catherine made her president of this body *and* of the Academy of Sciences, founded by Peter the Great! Dashkova contributed the words under three letters of the alphabet to the dictionary published by the academy she founded, and was editor of its journal. At the Academy of Sciences, she facilitated publication of scientific works and advanced the compilation of an atlas of Russia and the reading of public lectures on the exact sciences. She initiated a periodical, *The Russian Theater*. After Catherine had been in power over thirty years, Dashkova published a certain play, with nuances of republicanism, in that magazine. Catherine, frightened by the French Revolution, which was in its fourth year, had the book burned and put Dashkova on leave, which ended her public career.

While president of the academy, Dashkova again visited Western Europe, where she met Benjamin Franklin, and they corresponded from 1781 on. Nominated by him, she was elected a member of the American Philosophical Society in 1789. Thus a Russian became the first woman in that organization! She also corresponded with an American physicist and an engineer whose work in navigation she had circulated and translated into Russian. Dashkova and Franklin, both sharp diplomats, boosted each other. She got him elected to the Academy of Sciences she headed, and wrote him, in English, about that.

A painting of Dashkova in her middle years shows a powerfully intelligent, serious, and forceful face of very modern cast. She can very easily be imagined as one of the Soviet women heading large scientific or educational undertakings today or, oddly enough, a significant and responsible revolutionary movement. It is interesting that her memoirs were first published in Russian, half a century after her death, by the male radical writer Herzen (Gertsen*), author of the first

* Russian has no *h*, and names of Western origin are not spelled consistently.

novel by a Russian to deal with the bondage of women. At that, the memoirs had to be published outside Russia, in London (1859), where an English edition had been brought out nearly twenty years earlier. In its own way, that is a measure of the difference in status between even the most high-born Russian women and those in the West. Herzen wrote of her: "In Dashkova the Russian *female personality* [his emphasis], awakened by Peter's shake-up of society, emerges from its seclusion, proclaims its capacities, and demands a role in statesmanship, in science, in changing Russia."

Actually he was writing with the benefit of hindsight, because women had begun to move only in the year or two before he set down those words. Nina Selivanova, a Russian feminist of fifty years ago, wrote: "The whole tenor of early nineteenth-century life was meaningless. The women gossiped and flirted and spent their time aimlessly in distractions and pleasures. . . . The Russian woman of that period seldom took a book in hand. . . . Her amusements were her Saturday bath and the slapping of her servants."

In Selivanova's mind the servants clearly did not count as women. This was not true of another Russian feminist, Fannina Halle, who writes of the period of Catherine the Great and the times that followed: "The *jus primae noctis* [nobleman's right to have sex with a serf bride before her husband] was gradually established, and later cases frequently occurred in which masters made the serf girls whom they had violated strip naked and set the dogs upon them." This pertains to the end of the eighteenth century and the first half of the nineteenth.

However, just as circumstances abroad had caused Tsar Peter, a century earlier, to institute reforms meant to benefit propertied women at least, so the French Revolution compelled some thought among a few Russian men and their female relatives (there is no evidence of independent activity by women at this time). In December 1825 a group of young officer-noblemen made an unsuccessful attempt at a coup based on its ideas. In history they are known as the Decembrists. One of them, Ryleev, who was hanged, had written

earlier that year the first poem suggesting that women could
be self-acting political figures:

> She had it in her, she was capable
> Of being citizen and spouse both.

Picturing a wife who shared the hard fate of her exiled
husband, it was remarkably prophetic or perhaps inspiring,
for that was exactly the choice made immediately afterward
by a dozen wives, a mother, and several sisters of the 121
men exiled to Siberia for that uprising.

There were also other individuals who raised the dignity
of women simply by their personal behavior and lives. Alexandra Ishimova's father, a lawyer, had been exiled to the
Arctic for representing in court, in an ordinary property case,
a man swindled by a relative of the general who ran Russia
for the Tsar. At twenty-one she traveled to St. Petersburg to
petition the Tsar for mercy. It was a bad time—1825, the year
of the rebellion—and it took her thirteen more years to win
for her father the right to return. Undoubtedly her success
was helped by the reputation she established in the meanwhile
as the first Russian woman to write professionally for children. She undertook to interest them—children of the wealthy
and the educated only, of course—in the history of their country. Before turning to the pen, she founded a private boarding
school. Russia's greatest literary critics praised her beautiful
language, style, and gift for narration. She was for many years
the editor and principal writer for the only children's magazine of the day, and later for two periodicals at once. Despite
the fact that her audience was accustomed to the services of
serf slaves or paid servants, she sought to instill the idea that
work, instead of purposeless loafing, is good, for that time
and place a most progressive notion. In a time when class division by birth was taken for granted, she preached humanism
in her writings. The Russian literary language was only taking
form in her day, and she shaped it as addressed to children.
But neither her father's experience nor the events of her day
caused her to doubt the merits of tsarism or the society based
on serfdom in which she lived. After all, there are Americans

today who think that war is part of the normal human condition.

The values of that society necessarily carried over to all relationships of subordination, particularly where women were involved. Performing artists of both sexes were raised to absolute obedience from childhood, disciplined by the rod. With respect to women, the heads of theaters and theater schools regarded themselves as owners of harems and disposed of their "inmates" at will, making gifts of them to men in high places.

Anastasia Novitskaya was a leading ballerina of the early nineteenth century. She had the exceptional strength of will to insist upon being treated with dignity, so much so that in 1819 a ballet was written for her that upheld—only by hint, of course—the right of a woman to determine her own personal destiny in accordance with her heart's desire. Despite the fact that the income of a ballerina who depended solely on her own earnings was not high, she supported her mother, sisters, and a woman relative with four young children. But just one year after the staging of the ballet based on her personal qualities, a count who was governor-general of St. Petersburg and had three ballerinas as mistresses insisted that they be starred, with Novitskaya given a secondary role. She refused, and the count told her that if she would not dance the assigned role, he would put her in an insane asylum. Novitskaya took ill, and hallucinated that this had already been done. When she thought her time of incarceration had come, she dashed barefoot into the streets in a snowstorm and wandered until found by policemen. They bound her and delivered her to her home, where she died.

On the day of her funeral, the young women studying at the Theater School carried her coffin out of the house themselves. And at a time when a ballerina was "a dancing girl" with all the innuendo that snobbish term implied, a magazine gave her the kind of obituary normally reserved for very high dignitaries, writing that she "was famous not only for her exceptional talent but for *the qualities of spirit* associated with it."

Cavalry officer Nadezhda Durova (1783–1866) was an exception to all rules. The daughter of an officer, she was married off at eighteen, bore a child, left her husband after three years, begged her way into a Cossack regiment disguised as a man, and fought in wars for eight years, including the defense against Napoleon. She had been made an officer by the Russian Emperor himself when her true sex was discovered. She published memoirs and novels, and is well remembered. A play was written about her in 1942, an opera in 1957, and a film in 1962.

While the names of ballerina Novitskaya, writer Ishimova, and the noblewomen who followed their husbands into exile have come down to us, women of the people are, with one exception, known only as victims of punishment in local rebellions. One third of the seven thousand serfs exiled to Siberia by their masters in the second quarter of the nineteenth century were women. In a Cossack revolt of 1819 for which two or three hundred were sentenced to an incredible number of lashes, twenty-nine were women. When sailors and their families and townsfolk held the naval base of Sevastopol for four days in 1830, courts-martial tried 1,580 people, among whom, according to one source, 375 women were initially sentenced to death. Women were among the leaders in another uprising in the northern city of Novgorod. These were not movements aimed at overthrowing the government or at bettering the status of women, but spontaneous outbursts against various immediate acts of unbearable oppression.

The one woman of the people whom we know as an individual and leader in a revolutionary insurrection has an entry of her own in the Great Soviet Encyclopedia, 1969:

"ALYONA (years of birth and death unknown), chieftain of a peasant detachment during the Peasant War led by Stepan Razin; previously a nun, by origin a peasant of Vyezdnaia faubourg of the town of Arzamas. Her detachment, numbering about six hundred, participated in taking the town of Temnikov (1670). Was captured by government troops and burned alive. Gained wide renown among the people for her bravery and also for her heroic bearing during the questioning and execution."

In 1776 Abigail Adams, wife of John Adams, later the second President of the United States, wrote her husband even before the Declaration of Independence threatening that women "are determined to foment a rebellion" if "the new code of laws" the American revolutionaries would make put "unlimited power into the hands of husbands." In France women raised demands for equality from the very first year of the Revolution, 1789. In England Mary Wollstonecraft wrote *A Vindication of the Rights of Woman* in 1792.

No Russian woman wrote anything of the sort. But when George Sand (Amandine Dupin Dudevant) published, in 1832, the first of her novels advocating the overthrow of the double standard and opposing existing marriage laws, it was read and discussed immediately in Russia by the educated of both sexes, who knew French at least as well as they knew Russian.

Perhaps the reason that feminism, except as a movement for education and charity, didn't appear in Russia until the present century is that the first fervent advocates of equality for women in that country were men. In England John Stuart Mill's work on the subjection of women didn't appear until 1869, while Russians—specifically Herzen and Chernyshevski —put their views into the much more popular form of novels earlier. In Nikolai Chernyshevski's *What Is to Be Done?* (1864), which set the tone for the new morality, Vera Lopukhov dreams one night that she no longer loves her husband, and she tells him that dream. He helps her see that she loves their friend Kirsanov and stages a mock suicide to free her hand. Later she becomes Kirsanov's wife. A typical reviewer attacked all this as "sheer debauchery." Another wrote: "Such a distortion of the idea of married life destroys the idea of the family, the foundation of the state."

But Chernyshevski and the other Russian thinkers of that day saw women's oppression as part of the over-all backwardness of Russian society, with its serfdom, censorship, and simple absence of civil liberties and representative government. They called for revolution to overthrow this situation, urged women to participate, and insisted that the women had to be treated as equals in personal relations as in everything else.

It is a matter of record that, in this first generation of Russian revolutionaries of the 1860s—it was nearly thirty years before the Marxists came on the scene—those principles were adhered to. I believe this was because they were a relative handful of isolated intellectuals. When the revolutionary movement gained the strength that comes from real contact with the people, the new recruits brought their prejudices with them.

Feminism as a political movement makes sense when representative government and civil liberties exist or are in the immediate offing (as in the American and French revolutions), and women either have been excluded (suffrage) or find *their* equality honored more in the breach than the observance. But where no one could vote or speak out, the fact that attainment of these freedoms for all was a prerequisite to liberty for women seemed obvious. Therefore, relatively few Russian women worked on equality in education, while larger numbers entered the general revolutionary movement, actively and bravely.

The revolutionary movement of the pre-Marxist period could not win. In the frank words of Nina Selivanova, one of its members and supporters, written after the Communist Revolution of 1917 about women revolutionaries in the pre-Marxist period: "But she finds that, in spite of all her love for the masses, she fails to gain their confidence." Later, as we turn to the recollections of women workers of the very beginning of this century who joined the movement that did succeed and who participated in making the revolution, we will understand why that confidence was withheld. But the sincerity, intelligence, energy, and extraordinary courage of those women of the nobility, the capitalist and small business classes and intellectual and professional groups who fought tsarism from populist convictions in the late nineteenth century, was something entirely new, not only for Russia but for the world.

In Western countries during the second half of the nineteenth century, politically active women faced insult, ostracism, family tragedy, but very few indeed suffered imprisonment, much less death. In Russia, in a mass trial of fifty in 1877, fifteen were women. Their age range was from eighteen to twenty-five. The movement had not yet become desperate due to failure, and so these were not terrorists but peaceful propagandists doing what would have been perfectly legal in the West. Politically, they were populists (Narodniks) who believed the solution to Russia's problems lay in that country's traditional peasant communes—freed, however, of landlord exploitation. The most brilliant defense of their activities before the court was by twenty-two-year-old Sophia Bardina. With regard to women, she said, with heavy sarcasm:

"Nor do I know whether the family is undermined by that social order which forces a woman to leave her family and turn to the factory where she and her children are inevitably corrupted, that order which compels a woman to become a prostitute because of her poverty and which even sanctions prostitution as a legitimate and necessary phenomenon in every well-ordered state; or whether the family is undermined by us who are striving to eradicate this misery, which is the principal cause of all social calamities, including the destruction of the family."

For such views she got ten years at hard labor. In one case, when a woman political prisoner, mother of two children, died from the effects of one hundred lashes received as punishment in prison for slapping a jailer, three other women committed suicide in protest. This did win from the Tsar abolition of corporal punishment for women prisoners. But it did not cancel such punishments as that suffered when a group of men escaped, and all the political prisoners, including eighteen women, were put into solitary confinement for three years in stalls six feet by five, during which time they never breathed the outside air. Of forty-three persons sentenced to life imprisonment at hard labor in just ten years, 1880–90, almost always for terrorism, twenty-one were women. Of five sentenced to death for assassinating Tsar Alexander II, two were women.

While some sought to overthrow the system, others worked for reforms in the status of women within it. By the middle of the nineteenth century, there were 148 secondary schools for women. This was in a country of sixty million population, largely serfs for whom education of any kind was as unthinkable as for slaves in the American South except, in both countries, for the house servants. Turgenev described the life of a literate woman house serf in his short story "Yermolai and the Miller's Wife." The miller's wife had been

taken from her village and made a house serf at fifteen. Her
mistress refused to employ married maids, and when Arina,
after several years of service, asked permission to marry, her
serf lover was sent into the Army, and her master immediately
ordered that "her hair should be cut off, she should be dressed
in sackcloth, and sent to the country." The miller bought her
because she could read and write and would be useful to him.
Arina, of course, had to accept whatever was decided for her.

Although the serfs were freed in 1861, they remained dependent upon and ruled by their former owners in precisely
the fashion of the black population of the American South
after Emancipation. The reforms in the status of women that
followed affected the former serfs not at all, except for rare
individuals as atypical in the Russian scene as Sojourner
Truth, Harriet Tubman, Phillis Wheatley, and Frances Harper
in the American.

In Russia a women's magazine appeared in 1859, and the
first university opened its doors to them in 1860. The first
woman medical student appeared the next year: a peasant's
daughter. The first kindergartens appeared in St. Petersburg
in 1871, but preschool child care in the entire Empire covered
only 4,550 children by the outbreak of World War I. In 1864
women were admitted to work in the government telegraph
system, but were not made eligible for pensions, as men were.
The first women's club of any kind was organized in 1859,
and three women who were the founders of women's charities
in Russia established their organization in 1861. They were
Maria Trubnikova, Nadezhda Stasova, and Anna Filosofova.
They helped women find work, provided cheap housing, got
wages standardized, later organized societies of women trans-
lators, printers, bookbinders, and the like, and fought for
higher education for women. After a while the universities
were again closed to women as part of a general reaction
against student activism, but feminists won the establishment
of separate university-level institutions for women. Individual
women became distinguished in the sciences, but had to find
employment for their knowledge in Sweden, Germany, and
elsewhere. The first Russian woman to make an original contribution to science was the mathematician Sophia Kovalevskaya, born 1850. She had to go to Germany to get a Ph.D.

and to Sweden to get a professorship. Her work in analytical mechanics received the highest award of the French Academy. But all this must be seen against the overriding fact that, according to the census of 1897, after nearly forty years of these activities, only one woman in six could read and write. Clearly, no significant mass-scale change had occurred.

But among the small minority involved in political activism, new life-style outlooks and practices developed toward the end of the nineteenth century. This was not true of the feminists, who generally lived normal married lives and made use of their husbands' high positions and wealth. The political revolutionaries, however, were another story. They established communes in the largest cities that were, particularly for women, places of refuge for runaways from the patriarchalism of smaller towns or family estates. But these were not "do your own thing" situations like the crash pads in the Haight-Ashbury, Berkeley, or the East Village. The members of the communes were either political revolutionaries or at least women studying for teaching or medical careers with the notion that this was the best way they could help the common people. They were not channeled into but themselves chose these professions, and this example and ideal has a lot to do with the fact that education and medicine were the professions women selected en masse after the Revolution, when the barriers were down.

The members of the communes shared money, food, and possessions. The women particularly expressed their contempt for existing society by violating its rules of dress. They wore their hair straight, their clothing severe and comfortable, glasses whenever they needed them, and particularly violated convention by smoking. A unisex effect was striven for, not in the wearing of trousers, which was unthinkable, but in the abandonment of everything that made for femininity and for regarding women as sex objects.

Sex attitudes as such, however, were very different from those in the West a century later. Sex was looked upon as an unworthy frittering away of time in a world in which there was a great deal to do, all of it more important. The object was not puritanism, but absolute respect for the individuality of every comrade. Realistically, in an extremely male-chauvinist society, this meant respect for the women. As a consequence, men and women had separate rooms in the communes. Fictitious marriage was a device used to liberate individual women. Women could not obtain the internal passport essential to legal residence anywhere unless they had the approval of father or husband. In most families, the very idea that your father would permit you to have a passport to live alone was out of the question. Thus, fictitious marriages to revolutionary men were arranged, sometimes by mail. It was an absolute rule that such "husbands" would not approach the women sexually, and all memoirs agree that this was lived up to. Obviously, some such arrangements became love. Despite the Victorianism of the times, at least one reminiscence says that it was the woman who finally made the sexual approach to the man. They got married and presumably lived happily forever after.

Because of present dissatisfaction with existing sex norms and laws in the West, these communes and fictitious marriages have been given much more attention than their place among Russian revolutionaries warrants. An American study of 379 Russian female activists who were young in the years we are discussing shows that only four entered fictitious marriages, and one of these became a real marriage. Neither was common-law marriage their thing: 70 per cent of them were legally wed (only church weddings were legal) at least once. A couple of Jewish women even underwent baptism so that their relationships with fellow exiles of Christian birth could be formalized, although both parties were probably atheists. More than half the women married other revolutionaries, and the vast majority of the marriages, whatever the politics of the husbands, occurred after the women had become revolutionaries. From this data, based on compilations of biographies published in the U.S.S.R. in 1927–34, when discussion of sexual matters was frank and free, Professor R. H. McNeal concludes: "What is striking, then, is not the inevitable departures from monogamy but its durability as the standard in Russian culture, including the sub-culture of the radical intelligentsia" ("Women in the Russian Radical Movement," *Journal of Social History*, Winter 1971–72). That statement becomes more and more important as one digs into attitudes toward marriage in the Soviet Union today, because the general trend among peasants as they have become urbanized and workers as they have gained education has been to move up—I use the word deliberately—to the all-round standards of morality, attitudes toward women, and attitudes of women toward themselves marking that earlier radical intelligentsia. However, all present Western experience indicates that relations between spouses among the prerevolutionary radical intelligentsia could not have been free of the consequences of illegality of abortion, impediments to divorce, very limited earning opportunities even for educated women, and virtual absence of child-care facilities. It may very possibly have been to deal with these problems that many of the revolutionary women did not marry until quite late, and apparently remained chaste while single. Promiscuity was quite rare.

Except for instances of solitary confinement, revolutionary prisoners lived in large groups. Memoirs left by both long-term inmates and temporary residents in a Siberian women's political jail with a stable population of thirty describe the most loving concern for each other's health and education. They made particular efforts to see to it that sharing by the "haves" not be accompanied by any feelings of condescension or of embarrassment on the part of the "have-nots." There is absolutely nothing to suggest, even by omission, that homosexual relationships occurred. Whatever one thinks of the desirability of other than heterosexual relationships for human beings, it is long established that both individuals and groups have been capable of adhering to particular patterns they regard as moral, on religious or other grounds. The very notion of lesbian relations was simply not part of the mental and psychological framework of these revolutionary women, who were capable of the warmest friendships, as Russians of both sexes very particularly are.

I will leave it to psychologists to argue about sublimation, repression, or whatever, but some familiarity with the individual characters of a few of these women suggests that they had little difficulty in making themselves do whatever they decided was right. Liudmilla Volkenstein, for example, after a year and a half in the dungeons of the notorious Schlusselburg Fortress in St. Petersburg, was finally permitted to take a walk with another revolutionary prisoner, Vera Figner, from whom she learned that other women were not permitted this. Volkenstein persuaded those who had this privilege to refuse the walks until all could go out into the yard. It took them eighteen months to win, and they did not go out into the yard for that period. Of Volkenstein's character otherwise, Figner wrote: " 'We all need compassion,' was her favorite proverb, and so gentle was her soul, so strong her love for all living creatures, that she always stepped aside in order not to crush insects in her path."

Volkenstein, a mother, was allowed no news of her children, mother, or husband during her twelve years in the fortress, and was then exiled to Sakhalin Island off the coast of Siberia. Figner served twenty years in the fortress.

Sofia Perovskaya was the daughter of a general who had been governor of St. Petersburg—and who not only beat his wife himself but also taught his little son to do so. Sofia adored her mother and, in her underground years, risked her life to see her and sent her gifts when she could not. With an education terminated after six years of tutoring at home, she left at sixteen to enter a high school and then the women's courses at the university. Becoming a revolutionary, she lived under a false internal passport. The famous anarchist historian Prince Kropotkin knew her then, and wrote: "Now, in the capacity of an artisan's wife, in her cotton dress and men's boots, her head covered with a cotton kerchief, as she carried on her shoulders her two pails of water from the Neva, no one would have recognized in her the girl who a few years before shone in one of the most fashionable drawing-rooms of the capital."

Arrested in 1873 with workingmen she was propagandizing, she was released on bail and studied nursing. In 1877 she was acquitted in a trial of 193 and spent the next year in unsuccessful attempts to organize escapes for them. She was caught, exiled, escaped, and in 1881 was the actual organizer of the successful assassination of Tsar Alexander II. She made no attempt to disappear, was arrested, and tried. "Quiet, modest, serious, without a trace of pose or fear, she won the respect of her judges." She asked to share the fate of her comrades and was hanged at the age of twenty-six. She had written her mother that she had lived according to her convictions and was facing the end with a clear conscience. She asked, "Buy me a collar and cuffs with buttons, for I should like to tidy my dress for the proceedings. . . ."

Most famous of the pre-Marxist women, and most significant for us because she was later a leading supporter of the Provisional Government Lenin overthrew, was Catherine Breshkovskaya, known in pre-World War I America as the "little grandmother of the Russian Revolution." Born in 1844, daughter of a serf-owner, she joined the revolutionary movement at its very dawn in 1863. Hers was a good father, and so she accepted his pleas to come home, where he helped her open a boarding school for girls. She then made a "proper" marriage to a liberal nobleman. Together they established a co-operative bank and agricultural school for peasants. They were regarded in much the same way as "nigger-lovers" in the post-Civil War American South, and some of the local peasants were deported to Siberia. This repression, and threats to her father, convinced her that revolution was Russia's only hope. She left her child with relatives, later writing: "The conflict between my love for the child and my love for the freedom of Russia robbed me of many a night's sleep. . . . I was not the only one called upon to make such a sacrifice."

We will understand better why she felt she had to make that sacrifice if we know what she herself had seen of the peasants' lives. In her reminiscences she describes the "emancipation" of 1861, when she was seventeen, as follows:

The peasant was free. No longer bound to the land, his landlord ordered him off. . . . In dull but growing rage, he refused to leave his plot of land. . . . Then troops were quartered in their huts, families were starved, . . . daughters were raped. . . . Then began the flogging. In a village near ours, where they refused to leave their plots, they were driven into line on the village street; every tenth man was called out and flogged with the knout; *some died*. Two weeks later, as they still held out, every fifth man was flogged. The poor ignorant creatures still held desperately to what they thought their rights; again the line, and now every man was dragged forward to the flogging. This process went on for five years all over Russia, until at last, bleeding and exhausted, the peasants gave in.

Yet she still gave reform a chance for a decade before deciding that revolution was the only way out. But the first time she disagreed with a man at a gathering of revolutionaries, the very same men who would not dream of offending her physical dignity, who shared material possessions and dangers on a basis of absolute equality, looked at her in amazement: no woman had previously dared to participate in the discussion—they had simply listened. *Intellectual* equality was something that apparently had not crossed the minds of the male revolutionaries.

Breshkovskaya was the first woman to be sentenced to the mines as a political offender. She spent twenty-three years in Siberia as a convict and exile. Her term served, she resumed her activity. In 1904 she visited the United States to enlist help. Betrayed some time after her return to Russia, she was again in prison and Siberian exile for nine years until the overthrow of the monarchy freed her.

Marxist revolutionaries first appeared in Russia in 1883. The first woman among them was Celia Gurevich, who was Jewish. By the mid-1890s Lenin, then twenty-five, was active, and the Marxists began to challenge the populists over the direction of the revolutionary movement.

The Marxists had a theory of human history, where it had come from and where it should go, including the history of women. Their objective was complete equality of rights for all human beings, regardless of sex, race, religion, or language. They believed the basis of inequality was exploitation for the making of profit, whether of workers by capitalists, peasants by landowners, or whatever. Equality for specially exploited groups, such as women or ethnic minorities, was held to be impossible so long as exploiters could profit by pitting categories of working people against each other: female workers to replace male, children to replace adults, etc., at lower wages. Real equality under capitalism was regarded as impossible, despite all efforts, because unemployment is built into it. Those holding jobs would be compelled, in their own immediate interests, to try to keep them against the groups hitherto barred or discriminated against. But the struggle for such genuine equality was to be used for two purposes. One was to better the conditions of doubly and trebly exploited groups such as women and ethnic minorities as far as possible for the present. The other was to educate them to the reality that their oppressed status could only be ultimately ended by the replacement of capitalism by socialism.

The Marxists were conscious of the oppression of women by men within every economic class, including the workers. This was set forth in the writings they studied and adhered to, primarily in Friedrich Engels' *Origin of the Family, Private Property, and the State* and later, in August Bebel's *Women and Socialism*. They were deeply concerned with prostitution, which was regarded, in its mass aspects, as a product of poverty among women, and the fact that it is virtually nonexistent in the Communist-led countries today indicates that they were both right and sincere in their determination to end it.

They did not think that revolution in the economic system, in the class politically governing, and in the social structure of society would automatically eliminate age-old evils such as the oppression of women, but they were convinced that *without* that socio-politico-economic revolution full equality for women would be impossible. Marxists support the struggle for equal rights for women, and for liberation in personal rights, provided that it teaches that only socialism can open the door to full equality. But they oppose as mis-leaders, however unconscious, those who direct women's wrath against men as a whole rather than against the capitalist system that makes mass-scale equality impossible. It is these latter they characterize as feminists.

Because the Marxists had a keen eye for distinctive forms of oppression, one of the writings they (men as well as women) risked their freedom and lives for to smuggle into Russia was a pamphlet, *The Woman Worker,* by Nadezhda Krupskaya, who had married Lenin. She regarded him as the leader of her party as well as spouse. However, in an action quite unusual for women revolutionists who married, she always used her own surname, not even hyphenating it with his.

The matter of Krupskaya's pamphlet is important. Students of the Russian Revolution all know about *Iskra* (The Spark), Lenin's organizing newspaper smuggled into Russia. But

Krupskaya's American biographer has discovered, in recent research, that her pamphlet was one of the three other publications that were regularly part of all the packages. Krupskaya herself was in charge of the smuggling operation. Theirs was a disciplined organization and not a personal venture. Actually, what it testifies to is that Krupskaya, a greatly underrated figure in history, was both a first-rate propagandist and an executive of incredible patience and capacity.

While Krupskaya wrote directly on and to women, Lenin was assembling the hard facts *about* them for his book *The Development of Capitalism in Russia*. From that book we learn that in the 1890s, when he was writing, one quarter of the factory workers were women, and they numbered 210,-000. Women working at home winding cotton earned five cents per day, and there were 37,500 doing this work or home knitting jobs in Moscow Province alone. They started to work at the age of five or six, often worked eighteen hours a day to fill orders when they had them. The average annual pay was $13.10, because there was no work much of the year. In the same period, commenting upon a proposed platform for the Marxist party, Lenin noted at one point: "Here it would be well to add: 'complete equality of rights for men and women.'"

The Krupskaya pamphlet was based on the Communists' early experience in organizing and educating factory workers in St. Petersburg (now Leningrad) in the 1890s and the first years of this century. Krupskaya was one of the two leading women in Lenin's very early group. The other was Helena Stasova. It is something of a measure of how short the period the Soviet Union had in which to change both women's real conditions, and men's (and women's) heads, that virtually the entire scope of this book is encompassed within a single long lifetime: Stasova was born in 1873, and in 1966 she wrote a preface to a book by a Moscow friend of mine!

Like all the revolutionary women of their generation (Krupskaya was born in 1869), they were of upper-class origin. Krupskaya came from the impoverished nobility, Stasova from a family of renowned cultural figures. The measure of their success is that they persuaded women of the working class to act on their own behalf. What it meant to be such a worker is described by one such woman. She was brought to town from a hungry village at age twelve, and her mother persuaded a dressmaker to take her on as an apprentice by offering that she'd also run to the store, help with the housework, and mind the children: "Don't pay no attention that she's small: she can do laundry and wash floors." Having learned the trade, she moved on to a clothing factory, where she worked eight hours a day and then took work home for another eight. Greedy? She doesn't specify her earnings, but women textile workers were then getting thirty cents *a day*. Rubber workers regarded themselves as so superior because of their daily earnings of forty and fifty cents, thanks to overtime, that when labor won the right to organize mutual insurance societies, they tore up the blanks when offered. That is, until they came down with mass cases of chemical poisoning.

Home? Married men, if they were skilled workers, could afford half a basement room per *family* in a private home, a curtain separating the two families. Ordinary manual laborers were not as lucky. Krupskaya describes a visit to management-supplied housing at the Thornton Broadcloth Mill (much industry was foreign-owned): ". . . a huge building with an endless number of rooms, the partitions *not* up to the ceiling. . . . The din was ear-splitting. The walls were green with damp. There were two families in each of the rooms, which were not large. . . . They dried their laundry in the room, and it was so stifling the oil-lamps sputtered. . . . Dormitory rooms were terribly crowded. . . . The working day was incredibly long (12–14 hours at the textile mills). We saw some of the women workers lying on the cots in exhaustion, their faces in their pillows."

Yet some such women found the energy and made the choice to spend Sundays at the schools conducted by the Marxists, where they learned to read and write—and organize and propagandize. The sixteen-hour-a-day factory-plus-home worker I have quoted entered such a school when she was sixteen. At twenty she was arrested and served three years in exile. In early Soviet times she was sent to the Industrial Academy and worked as a management executive until retirement, after having helped build Soviet government at the grass roots.

Poverty, overwork, and monstrous living conditions were simply routine. But *Iskra* carried letters describing the special suffering and humiliation of women workers: "We bore our children beside our machines"; at the Makarov Bros. Flax Mills the manager "forces his odious attentions on pretty women workers"; at the Pavlov Factory the owner "has a harem"; at the Filippov Confectionery the foremen beat the women, slapping them in the face.

Yet these factory women were relatively free, sexually, by the very fact of having incomes of their own, however poor. They did not face the harsh patriarchalism of the countryside, where sexual exploitation by the father-in-law in a three-generation family was sufficiently common to be described by a special Russian word. The writer Maxim Gorky was beaten nearly to death by Cossacks in one of their villages for trying to save an "adulteress" who was being dragged naked behind a horse. That practice did not exist in town.

In 1903 the founding convention of the Russian Social-Democratic Labor party (including both the communist and socialist wings of Marxism), basing itself on eight years of contact with women workers through the earlier Sunday schools and letters to *Iskra*, put a series of special demands in its platform. Women "should not be employed in industries noxious to the female organism," they should get ten weeks' paid maternity leave, there should be child-care centers at all enterprises employing women, nursing mothers should be permitted half an hour off to suckle their infants every three hours, and male government inspectors of labor conditions *should be replaced by women* in industries employing women. This protective legislation was made law immediately after the Revolution and is now more strongly in effect than ever before; child-care centers exist today in the country as well as in town, women have longer maternity leave than earlier, and there are fewer women in heavy work.

The notion, elevated by Marxists to a principle, that working for a wage gave a woman both a sense of her own dignity and a level of respect from men that upper-class women dependent on men did not acquire, was strikingly borne out in 1905, when revolutionary ferment swept Russia. In May, two communist weavers, one of them a woman, Matryona Sarmentova, led a textile mill walkout which began a general strike in the one-industry town in Ivanovo.

The next day she and at least two other women workers spoke at a rally of thirty thousand. This was the first time in Russian history that any woman *of any social class* had had an audience of thousands for speeches against tsarist autocracy. The elected soviet ("council," but it has become an international word because these councils took on full powers of government) that headed that seventy-two-day strike included 23 women among its 151 members. This was unprecedented. Women had been leaders in tiny self-constituted groups of revolutionaries, but never in a democratic body of both sexes resting upon mass grass-roots support. The memory of such events is not permitted to die. A New York *Times* correspondent who visited Ivanovo in 1973 reported: "Strike leaders such as Olga Vorontsova are local heroes."

The Communists had not won support easily. One of them, Natasha (Concordia) Samoilova, a priest's daughter (priests in the Orthodox Church are permitted to marry), was an organizer in the oil town of Baku at that time. A pamphlet published at a time when obscenities could not be spelled out says of her, "On her way to a workers' circle some women accosted her with curses: 'You ——, you want to take our husbands away from us!'" Another, Dora Lazurkina, Jewish, smuggled out of Russia as a peasant emigrant the previous year at the age of nineteen, told Lenin in Switzerland, "The workers' wives receive us coldly, sometimes say outright they don't like our visits. That's understandable, for we're drawing their husbands into party work, and that nearly always means either prison or exile." She recalls: "It was clear that this troubled Lenin. . . . He looked at me very seriously, and said: 'Now, if you showed more concern for the workers' wives and for women workers themselves, and helped them with their difficult burden of housework, they would have a better attitude toward you. . . . If you see a woman rushed from feeding the children, doing the wash and other housework, who doesn't have a chance either to eat or sit down for a minute, offer to do things for her, help her!'"

Lazurkina says he practiced what he preached. She describes his wife, Krupskaya, and her mother whispering in the front room, so that he wouldn't hear, about something that needed doing while he sat writing. "But Vladimir Ilyich has already set aside his pen and rapidly crossed the room. 'Don't argue with me,' he said, 'I also have got to take part in keeping house.'" His mother-in-law thought highly of Lenin, according to a noncommunist friend, because he sewed on his own buttons, "and better than Nadya [Krupskaya]."

Marxists and feminists contended for women's support for twelve years: 1905 to 1917. It was in the former year that the Tsar was compelled by revolutionary turmoil to allow at least a consultative parliament (Duma), with elections, certain rights of organization, and a freer press. Feminist organizations came into being to demand that women fully share those rights.

In December 1908 feminists organized a Russia-wide congress. Over a thousand delegates attended, but there were only forty-five workingwomen and *not a single peasant woman*—Russia's majority class. The small number of women of the working class reflected lack of time and money, as well as lack of interest in the feminist program, rather than the ratio of influence of Marxists and feminists among women. For the maximum measure of feminist strength was the twenty thousand signatures for women's suffrage they had been able to gather for presentation to the "parliament" in 1907.

At the congress, the approach of the few working-class delegates was similar to that of black women on welfare when they bother to attend predominantly white middle-class women's liberation groups in the United States today. They presented minority reports from all four of the congress' committees undertaking to demonstrate that the first step toward the liberation of women on a mass scale was the abolition of economic class oppression. Their spokesperson was an individual best able to overcome the psychological barrier between them and most of those present: Alexandra Kollontai, a general's daughter and engineer's wife. Her speech concluded with the demands for women summarized in the Social-Democratic platform of 1903. The response was a fifteen-minute storm of jeers from the audience, with cries of "Shut them up! Throw them out!" Class snobbery had triumphed. The St. Petersburg chief of police was in the audience but at a loss over what to do: this disorder was not a village revolt; it involved the flower of "society."

An incident identical even to the language used occurred in San Francisco sixty-five years later. The San Francisco *Chronicle* reported on February 12, 1973: "The preponderance of delegates, who had paid $12 each to attend, were well-groomed, middle-aged business and clubwomen. Corporations like Standard Oil and Pacific Telephone were well represented, as was the Junior League and the American Association of University Women. . . . Protestors said they represented . . . groups . . . such as Welfare Rights, the Women's Switchboard, the Women's National Abortion Coalition. . . . They objected to the $12 fee, which they said they could not afford, and to what appeared to them to be a conscious effort to keep them out. . . . Miss Brush, who is a member of the National Organization for Women, and Helen Little of Welfare Rights, who also tried to speak to the conference, were shouted down with cries of 'shut up' and 'get out.'" Social class is thicker than sex.

That was the burden of a four-hundred-page book by Kollontai, *The Social Foundations of the Women's Question,* published in 1914. It was one long argument against the feminists, who, she said, were more interested in suffrage for privileged women than with freeing women as a whole. The most important feminist society did, in fact, imitate European feminists in accepting the idea of a privileged suffrage limited to the propertied. Another group, the Women's Progressive party, could never bring themselves to an alliance with workingwomen or socialists, and relied for their suffrage bill on the Constitutional Democrats, who might be compared to the machine Democrats in the United States. A populist group founded by women professionals and intellectuals spread to eighty towns in the revolutionary years 1905–7, and appealed to factory workers and even peasants, offering social and labor reforms, but was also centered on suffrage to such a degree that it fell apart when the first two Dumas failed to pass a suffrage bill. The 1908 women's congress was organized by the most conservative of the three feminist organizations.

In 1912 a suffrage bill was passed, but the Cabinet turned it down: the "parliament's" will was not binding under the new so-called Constitution that was the Russian people's first chance to form an opinion of electoral democracy. Minor reforms were gained in educational opportunity, in equalization of inheritance laws, and in ending the lack of legal identity for Russian wives and lack of freedom of mobility or employment under the old internal-passport system.

Meanwhile, the Bolsheviks (the communist wing of the Social-Democratic party) had pushed successfully for a workers' social insurance law, but as passed it covered only workers in large enterprises, of whom the government was most afraid. Women were employed chiefly in domestic service and farm labor, not to speak of prostitution. As a consequence, only 9 per cent of women workers were covered by the law. Nonetheless, they did gain six weeks' maternity leave at from half to full pay, to be decided by representatives of workers' sick-benefit societies, in the election of which women received equal rights with men.

Several events merged to make 1913 a particularly noteworthy year for women. In January a congress on women's education was called by liberal intellectuals, to which only handpicked women workers were admitted. Its theme was the struggle against "male domination." The Bolsheviks decided to respond by organizing the first celebration, in Russia, of International Women's Day, March 8. It had originated in New York in 1908 as a parade organized by socialists for suffrage and an end to sweatshops and child labor, as a demonstration of the independence of women workers from the official suffrage movement, which believed that women could be free under capitalism. Under the political conditions of Russia in 1913, a dramatic situation was inevitable. A police permit for a demonstration was out of the question, so they obtained the Grain Exchange for a "learned symposium." Police were officially present at all meetings, with the power to disperse them when the commanding officer heard words going beyond the terms of the permit. The two front rows of seats in the hall were packed with gendarmes (federal police). One of the chief speakers (all were women), a weaver then twenty-five years old who had been a member of her union executive board for six years, recalls it as follows:

"No matter how poor the workingwomen were, on 'their day,' the first holiday of women in Russia, they put on the very best they had, and the packed hall looked like a meadow in May from the brightness of the colors. . . . [The police] didn't succeed in spoiling our holiday, although every speaker had to get her most private thoughts across to the audience as though breaking through the alert silence of the first rows."

She had prepared her speech carefully, with repeated help from Lenin's sister, but the large audience threw her completely. She forgot it entirely, and ad-libbed:

"The law provides an 11½ hour day, but some stand at the looms 18 hours for 10 or 12 rubles a month [$5–6]. . . . The foremen make young girls sleep with them. And sometimes they do it, they do it out of fear, out of fear to lose even this work which is like that of a prisoner at hard labor, even these miserable pennies. *Bourgeois ladies who are so strong for equal rights for women accuse us of immorality. Untrue! It isn't that the poor classes have no morals. The thing is poverty. It isn't immorality but bitter need that compels some of the workingwomen to engage in the shameful trade!*"

She recalls the speech of another, apparently an educated woman:

"This word [prostitution] brought pain to the hearts of women. A terrible product of capitalism, it caught poverty-stricken women in its mire, *and among them were sisters and friends of those now sitting in this hall*. The speech was unusual in style. It carried its message chiefly through figures . . . and the figures moved us, because *for nearly every one of those present* the figures called living individuals to mind."

The similarity between the attitudes of Russian workingwomen then and ghetto women in America today is striking. To women living at the very edge of starvation, prostitution is the one real immediate alternative, and those who engage in it are regarded with sympathy, not as sexual competitors, much less criminals.

A plaque in the wall of the onetime Grain Exchange in Leningrad now commemorates the fact that the first International Women's Day celebration in Russia was held there.

The emphasis on prostitution at that meeting was because there was a depression, textile workers were being discharged, wages cut, and the women were cynically told to "make up the extra money on the streets." *Pravda,* the Communists' newspaper, covered all this, but its limited space made it impossible to give women's issues the treatment they needed.

The priest's daughter we had mentioned earlier, Concordia Samoilova, had long dreamed of a magazine to be called *The Woman Worker* (Rabotnitsa). Separately, so had Krupskaya.

While Krupskaya is known throughout the world, chiefly (and unfairly) because she was married to Lenin, and Kollontai is famous for her far-out views on sex, Samoilova is undeservedly forgotten.

Born in eastern Siberia in 1876, possibly of part Mongolian heritage, Samoilova was twenty-one and studying in St. Petersburg when a woman political prisoner, Maria Vetrova, burned herself alive. Rumor had it that she had been raped by guards. Samoilova urged a demonstration by the students at her women's college. After four years of activity, she was arrested and jailed for three months. Released, she went to Paris to study under liberal Russian professors in exile. The revolutionary Lenin competed with them there for the adherence of these students, and she was won over. Under the pseudonym "Natasha," she was an underground worker in Russia from 1903 on. When she was betrayed to the police that very year, workers killed the informer. After being jailed for fourteen months, she went to Baku in the Caucasus, where she encountered the hostility to revolutionaries by workers' wives described earlier. This turned her for the first time to an interest in organizing women, but only after seven years of general party activity.

As an editor of *Pravda* from its founding in 1912, she displayed a remarkable human understanding for workers who caved in under the pressure of hunger and went back to work during strikes, and even for those who had been informers but came to the paper to apologize and promise never to do so again. Considering that she had served a jail term because of one such informer, this was all the more striking.

(Samoilova married a revolutionary lawyer in 1905. Their marriage endured till his death from epidemic disease in 1918, after the Revolution, in a remote fishing area at the mouth of the Volga, to which he had been assigned as organizer. She was in Petrograd organizing women at the time.)

In December 1913—just one year after *Pravda* itself had been established—Lenin agreed that the time to found *The Woman Worker* had come. He wrote to his associates in Russia about this, and Samoilova was an editor of the new magazine from the outset. Of the six editors, all women, only one escaped arrest, but the first issue appeared anyhow. The plaque on Moscow's main street that now honors her identifies her for her achievements alone. No mention is made of a blood relationship that might overshadow them: she was Lenin's sister. Despite the magazine's formal legality, the impact it made brought the police again, and all thirty women in the office on this occasion were arrested. They celebrated International Women's Day 1914 in jail so vigorously that the noise was heard in the streets. A magazine of the same name, founded in 1923, had a circulation of twelve million in 1972, ranking third in all the world, behind only *Reader's Digest* and *TV Guide*.

World War I came in 1914. A researcher in Denmark, Richard Stites, writes of Russia: "The War found most feminists and socialists on opposite sides once again. The feminists were rhapsodic about the great possibilities of serving the [Russian] fatherland and, in return, gathering political dividends for themselves. They showed no subtlety in connecting their 'sacrifices' to eventual payment in the coin of women's suffrage. Ironically, most of those who did sacrifice were not feminists at all. Thousands of young women became nurses . . . at the front; thousands more filled places in industry left vacant by their mobilized menfolk. Women began to appear in all sorts of new roles: as streetcar conductors, truck drivers, pilots, administrators—foreshadowing on a smaller scale the great variety of jobs that women would perform a decade later under the Soviets. Tales of female soldiers appeared in the press long before anyone had ever heard of Bochkaryova, the founder of the Women's Battalions of 1917. All over Russia, feminists who, before the War, had warned that only women's suffrage would end the scourge of war were now singing hymns for victory" ("Women's Liberation Movement in Russia 1900–1930," *Canadian-American Slavic Studies,* Winter 1973).

The Russian feminist Nina Selivanova, writing in 1923, said the same thing. Catherine Breshkovskaya, in Siberian exile, rediscovered loyalty to the Tsar, writing an American friend, Helena Dudley, in 1915: "From patriotism as well as from indignation against the ferocity of the Germans, I am hoping for the victory of the Allies." (The Allies were England and France, later joined by the United States.)

It was at this time that Lenin wrote a French-born comrade, Inesse Armand, two letters on "free love" that have recently received wide publicity from the women's liberation movement. But under the circumstances of World War I, the subject was overwhelmed by other concerns, and Armand's proposed pamphlet, which prompted his comments, was never published. Nor were his letters, until 1939. Armand's views, and his, are dealt with in the next chapter.

Women workers encountered ferocity closer to home. Overtime became compulsory, night employment of female and child labor was again permitted, as was work by them in mines and noxious industries. Alexandra Rodionova, a wage worker from the age of eleven, was nineteen at the outbreak of the war. To her it meant that women, who had hitherto been allowed to be conductors only on horsecars, could now hold the same job on the new streetcars. They worked twelve to fourteen hours without a dinner break, starting at 4 or 5 A.M. (Long after the Revolution she had the opportunity to go to college, and was a physician for twenty-two years!) Melanie Savchenko, a factory worker, distributed antiwar leaflets to fellow workers so exhausted they were sleeping on the concrete floor of the mill at midnight, unable to go on. She was arrested in 1916 and spent a year in prison. In the winter of 1916–17 the prison was not heated—in northern Russia, where winter temperatures always go below zero. Amazingly, only one woman died. Rodionova describes the bitterness between pro- and antiwar women: "At Easter lady philanthropists brought rolls and sweets. They offered them through the food-window, but we all refused them." (To Savchenko, the Revolution ultimately brought attendance at

Russia's equivalent of MIT, followed by a career in industrial management.)

Most women workers, however, responded to the war as did Matryona Dvoretskaya, a clothing worker who was twenty-nine when it broke out. "My husband was drafted. . . . There were many like me in St. Petersburg. At first each of us lived our sorrow and hardships alone. For before the Revolution women were the most downtrodden, the *least aware* section of the population." Another woman worker, arrested for distributing *The Woman Worker,* describes a visit made to her in the police station: "My mother dashed toward me with tears in her eyes and began to scold me because no one in our family had ever been in jail and I was bringing shame upon them all."

But the network of police spies was surprisingly sensitive to women's increasing desperation. The Secret Police reported to the Interior Ministry in January 1917: "Mothers of families, exhausted by endless standing in line at stores, distraught over their half-starving and sick children, are today perhaps closer to revolution than Messrs. Miliukov and Rodichev [the liberal opposition] and of course they are a great deal more dangerous because they are the combustible material for which only a single spark is needed to burst into flame."

Chapter II
Women in the Revolution

The number of women employed in factories had increased from 25 per cent of the total when Lenin investigated this in the 1890s, to 30 per cent on the eve of the war, and 40 per cent—two in five—by 1917. Strikes broke out that February, with political overtones from the outset. Demands included an end to the war and to the monarchy. International Women's Day came at the height of this, and the organizers paraded under banners reading "Peace and Bread," "Our Husbands Must Return from the Front." The government called out troops, but they refused to act against the women. The streetcar conductor Rodionova describes her emotions in these terms: "With all the others, I shouted 'Down with the Tsar!' but when I thought, 'how will we get along without a tsar?' it was as though a bottomless pit opened before me, and my heart froze."

Soon after this, Rodionova was elected, with two men from her car barn, to the city-wide committee of streetcar workers. In her reminiscences forty-five years later, she wrote, "Just a short time ago I had been marching with the demonstrators through the city, shouting 'Down with the Tsar!' and it seemed to me that I had lifted off from the ground and was flying into a dizzying unknown. . . . The former illiterate working girl had been transformed into a person, powerful with the knowledge of her own rights, a consciousness of responsibility for everything happening in the country."

The Tsar abdicated four days later. *Pravda,* the Bolshevik paper, which had been suppressed, resumed publication and editorialized: "A week ago, on February 23 [March 8 by our calendar] the authorities in Petrograd hindered working-women from marking their day. That led to the first clashes at the Putilov Works, clashes which grew into a demonstration and revolution. . . . The first day of the revolution was Women's Day. . . . The women of Moscow in many cases decided the destiny of the troops: they went to the barracks, spoke to the soldiers and the latter joined the revolution. Women, we salute you!"

The new Provisional Government consisted of parties favoring liberal capitalism. A woman, Countess Panina, the most noted philanthropist of public cultural activities, was named a deputy minister. The government promised women the vote, and the feminists gave full support to its policy of continuing the war. They "warmly patronized" but did not themselves staff the battalions of female soldiers organized by a peasant woman, Bochkaryova. On May 13, 1917, "Little Grandmother" Breshkovskaya, free and lionized after thirty-two years of prison and Siberia, wrote American friends, "We women have all the rights we wanted."

Her half century of hopeless and heroic work for the common people deprived her of, or never instilled in her, confidence in their ability to rule themselves. And so, one month before the Communist Revolution, Lenin, urging such a revolution and insisting that his party had the capacity to take power and would be able to maintain its government, wrote of the liberal democratic government that had succeeded the tsars, and which Breshkovskaya supported:

We are not utopians. We know that an unskilled laborer or a cook [the Russian word means female cook; only fancy chefs were men] cannot immediately get on with the job of running the government. In this we agree with the Constitutional Democrats, with Breshkovskaya. . . . We differ, however, from these citizens in that we demand an immediate break with the prejudiced view that only the rich, or officials chosen from rich families, are capable of *administering* government. . . . We demand that *training* in the work of government administration be

conducted . . . that a *beginning* be made at once in training all
the working people, all the poor, for this work.

We know that the Constitutional Democrats are also willing
to teach the people democracy. Constitutional Democrat ladies
are willing to deliver lectures to [their] domestic servants on
equal rights for women in accordance with the best English and
French sources. And also, at the very next concert-meeting, before an audience of thousands, an exchange of kisses will be
arranged on the platform: the Constitutional Democrat lady lecturer will kiss Breshkovskaya, Breshkovskaya will kiss ex-
Minister Tsereteli [male], and the grateful people will therefore
receive an object-lesson in republican equality, liberty, and
fraternity.

Yes, we agree that the Constitutional Democrats, Breshkovskaya and Tsereteli are in their own way devoted to democracy
and are propagating it among the people. But what is to be done
if our conception of democracy is somewhat different from
theirs?

Lenin sought to bring women of entirely new classes—workers and peasants—onto the stage of history. They were an 85
per cent majority of all women. His language was hardly courteous. The Communists, both men and women, had undergone
the same kind of persecution, varying from individual to individual, of course, as the populists we have been describing.
Records of heroism were taken for granted by both groups.
The Communists were out to abolish a system in which
women had to work as domestic servants. Their opponents
wanted domestic servants to get equal pay for equal work.
However, no men did the same kind of domestic work as
women. Women who employed them had free time, material
possessions, and other benefits neither sex of domestic workers
could aspire to.

Whatever rights had already been won certainly didn't satisfy women workers. The very next day after Breshkovskaya
wrote her letter to America, several thousand women working
in laundries demonstrated that the kind of rights won had not
changed their lives in any way. They broke the bubble of
seeming peace between labor and capital that had existed for
the ten weeks since the Tsar's overthrow by going on strike
for an eight-hour day and a minimum wage. As their repre-

sentatives went from laundry to laundry to urge others to join them, hot irons were thrown at them and boiling water was poured on their heads, to the point at which the Workers' Section of the City Soviet, the self-constituted people's representative body, voted to send protection with them. When they returned to work under a compromise agreement after four weeks—an extremely long strike in Russia, where workers had no financial reserves or credit—some employers sought to move their businesses away. When the union, in retaliation, took over some of these shops, this confiscation was the very first harbinger of the socialist revolution to occur five months later.

On April 9 a hundred thousand soldiers' wives marched to the newly organized revolutionary government of the city. A photo shows their banner demanding higher rations from the overseers of the poor, who were charity ladies. *Never before had women turned out in such numbers.* The social origins of this upsurge were described by Samoilova, whose death of cholera in 1921 deprived the revolution of a significant thinker as well as an activist. The war, she wrote, "had torn thousands of women away from housework and thrown them into the factories in place of their husbands to earn their daily bread. That war undoubtedly gave impetus to the political consciousness of women workers . . . and compelled them to take a more active part in the over-all struggle of the working class for its liberation."

Because the Soviet was then dominated by moderate socialists and populists who supported the Provisional Government and were obviously insensitive to workingwomen, Alexandra Kollontai was the only member to come out to speak to that enormous demonstration. One soldier's wife, an active member of the needle trades' union, recalls, "But the overseers, the patroness-ladies, didn't want to listen to anyone. The soldiers' wives demanded bread and peace, demanded that all the funds of the overseers be turned over to the Soviet and that the overseers be removed."

She was one of a city-wide committee of thirty-five elected soldiers' wives. They agreed with the Communists' proposal that their chief demand of the government should be an end to the war, but the government called that "counterrevolutionary" and would only consider higher welfare payments. "I spoke and said we would not sell out our husbands for higher rations, and demanded an end to the war."

At the suggestion of Lenin, who had just returned from exile, a women workers' conference convened delegates from the whole city, and a Union of Soldiers' Wives was organized by the Communists. The same woman was one of two who carried its resolution to Lenin. Formerly illegal organizations, with no offices of their own, were now using the underutilized space of palaces. "At first I was frightened by its cold, aristocratic luxury. I had been in such places before, but only to deliver dresses. This time my usual timidity overcame me, but Anastasia encouraged me. . . . Lenin, seeing my confusion, came to the door and put out his hand. . . . He inquired about me personally: what front my husband was at, was it a long time since his last letter. . . ."

Women of the poor were by no means united in their political attitudes. It was one thing to turn out for a demand for higher welfare to servicemen's dependents. And it is not surprising that the most conscious were against the war. Many more were still confused: their men were fighting in the trenches. One woman worker, seventeen at the time but already a Communist, reports the bitter hostility of most of the women at the steel mill where she was employed: " 'Our husbands are shedding their blood at the front, and here you are working for the German cause!' [by opposing the war] they yelled at me. One day I was all but thrown into a red-hot forge by infuriated supporters of the Socialist Revolutionaries [Grandmother Breshkovskaya's populist party]." They wouldn't let Lenin speak inside the plant, so he talked from a street corner outside the gates. " 'So that's what that Lenin is like,' the women whispered to each other, 'and they said to us he's a spy.' . . . I saw tears in the eyes of some. One elderly woman exclaimed: 'May God give health to that Lenin! And maybe my son will come home from the trenches.' "

In this period of bitter political struggle, there was a time in July 1917 when the Provisional Government outlawed all the Communists' papers and magazines but one: *The Working Woman*. As a consequence, Lenin's article explaining his party's position was published there. When the government sent a troop of cadets to confiscate the issue, women from the factories who had come to distribute it quickly loaded it onto trucks and got it safely away. The loyalty of women to the magazine is illustrated by the fact that, in April, the women conductors at the streetcar barn levied upon themselves a donation of *three days' pay* to support it.

When the Communists seized power on the night of November 6–7, 1917, there were armed women on both sides. (History knows it as the October Revolution, for Russia was still functioning by an astronomically outdated calendar.) Although the actual fighting that night was minimal, Lenin himself later stated that of the few forces still willing to risk their lives on behalf of the Provisional Government, the best was a women's battalion.

On the Communist side, the streetcar conductor we have quoted, Rodionova, was assigned to make sure that the streetcars kept operating that night. She carried a pistol. When the cruiser *Aurora* fired the shot signaling the uprising, she dispatched two maintenance flatcars with machine guns on them to the scene of the assault. Factory women organized themselves as medics and contacted women medical students to teach them the rudiments of first aid. The women simply took it as natural that this was how they could help best. A nurse in the tsarist army who had been an underground revolutionary among the soldiers, and who was in charge of organizing the factory women's medic volunteers, describes the fighting only four days after the Bolshevik Revolution, when the long and bitter civil war was just beginning. Sailors from the *Aurora*, under fire right outside Petrograd (earlier St. Petersburg, today Leningrad) from an armored train, yelled to these new nurses, "'Little sisters, crouch or they'll hit you!' At first the girls crouched, but soon straightened up again and calmly walked on, heavily pulling their legs out of the mud. Although this bravery was due to their not understanding the danger, I was proud at the behavior of the workingwomen: they were under fire for the first time. . . ."

Meanwhile seasoned revolutionary women were involved in organizing the new society and its government. Helena Stasova had succeeded Krupskaya as secretary (executive organizer, actually) of the Communists' Central Committee. Alexandra Kollontai became the first woman cabinet member in human history, as People's Commissar of Social Welfare, with the responsibility, among many others, of carrying out the policies she recommended in regard to soldiers' wives.

The difficulties she faced were described in John Reed's eyewitness account, *Ten Days That Shook the World*. Kollontai "was welcomed with a strike of all but forty of the functionaries in the Ministry. Immediately the poor of the great cities, the inmates of institutions, were plunged in miserable want: delegations of starving cripples, of orphans with blue, pinched faces, besieged the building. With tears streaming down her face, Kollontai arrested the strikers until they should deliver the keys of the office and the safe; when she got the keys, however, it was discovered that the former [acting] Minister, Countess Panina, had gone off with all the funds. . . ."

The Union of Soldiers' Wives took over the distribution of welfare. The carry-over officials sabotaged their efforts in order to cause dissatisfaction and would not give them the names of those receiving dependents' allowances. The union sent its members from office to office to track them down, and had to compile the lists anew from the information on drafted soldiers. This took two months. Meanwhile rumors were spread that the Communists had confiscated the welfare money. A crowd of women gathered. The situation was tense. The union activists explained that the delay was due to officials dating from the previous government, but then had to find the bank where the money was deposited. Mikhail Kalinin, the ex-peasant workingman who was then mayor (head of the City Soviet), went with them. They emerged with literally a whole sack of money. They were scared to death; this was cash for two months' payments to thousands of people. One of them recalls, "None of us had ever seen that much money, much less had it in our hands." Frightened, they decided to let the bank cashier handle it. Kalinin said the cashier might deliberately foul up to cause dissatisfaction. " 'If you were able to make the revolution, it means you've got to be able to run your government,' he told us. 'Put the sack on your shoulders and learn how to do the job better than the officials.' "

Once that was done, the Union of Soldiers' Wives began spontaneously, because it was necessary, to do the things that have now multiplied into the enormous network of child-care facilities and women's activities for which the Soviet Union is famous. They started simply by organizing a Christmas party. Next they organized one child-care center and took over the town house of some wealthy person for this. Then they set up repair and clothing-manufacturing shops to provide their members with jobs. Next came consumer co-ops. Soldiers' committees helped.

Kollontai listed her other responsibilities taken over from the old regime: "the whole welfare program for the war-disabled, hence for hundreds of thousands of crippled soldiers and officers, the pension system in general, foundling homes, homes for the aged, orphanages, hospitals for the needy, the work-shops making artificial limbs, the administration of playing-card factories [the manufacture of playing cards was a government monopoly], leper colonies, clinical hospitals for women, etc. In addition a whole series of educational institutes for young girls. . . ."

She organized a council to assist her, involving medical, legal, and educational authorities as well as the workers and lower officials of the ministry. Because people's daily needs were at stake, the work had to be kept going, and Lenin's dream of smashing the bureaucratic machinery of government could not be implemented, as he later bitterly admitted in his famous Testament. A major problem in Soviet society today derives from the fact that there is no such thing as starting with a clean slate. This was no less the case as it affected women. The same human beings, the same families that existed before the Revolution, populated the country afterward. And as children and grandchildren have been born, customs and attitudes continue to be handed down, however diluted and modified.

Kollontai regarded her most important accomplishment to have been the founding of a Central Office for the Care of Mother and Child. This "set off a new wave of insane attacks against me. All kinds of lies were related about the 'nationalization of women,' on laws which 'obligated' 12-year-old girls to become mothers and suchlike." Unfortunately, an unrealistic ultra-radicalism that characterized her general stance within the Communist party led her to transform a famous monastery into a home for war invalids, in a country that was overwhelmingly religious in a very fundamentalist way. Although the Cabinet later criticized her for this, the damage was done. The monks resisted, and a shoot-out occurred. The Church organized street demonstrations against her action and pronounced "anathema" against her. Newspapers, of which there was still a broad political spectrum, attacked her.

In a passage she later deleted from her autobiography she wrote, "I received countless threatening letters, but I never requested military protection. I always went out alone, unarmed and without any kind of a bodyguard. In fact I never gave a thought to any kind of danger. . . ." In this regard, the Communist Revolution in November represented no change for her. The previous April, when Lenin shocked his associates by proposing that the overthrow of the Tsar could be followed very quickly by a revolution to put the working class in power, she was the only one to take the floor to support him. This brought such public hatred at that time that "often I had to jump off tramcars before people recognized me, since I had become a topical theme of the day and often bore personal witness to the most incredible abuse and lies directed against me." But love and hate were a matter of class: the soldiers' wives of the April 9 demonstration, the women laundry workers on strike in May, and "the workers, the sailors, the soldiers . . . were utterly devoted to me." She won reluctant admiration even from bitterly anti-Communist women like Nina Selivanova, who wrote, six years later, "Among those who are Communists by conviction there are others who must not be overlooked, educated and cultured women whose hands are clean from the blood shed in the time of Terror. The most prominent of these is Alexandra M. Kollontai. . . ."

The end of 1917 brought the final showdown between organized feminism and Marxist women. Richard Stites understates it: "After the Bolshevik coup in October, the feminists quickly disappeared from history." To the women concerned, their lives and their souls were involved. Those who kept the magazine *The Woman Worker* going, particularly Samoilova and Claudia Nikolayeva, a worker, found that the women delegated from factories to pick up each week's issue had become, with the editorial board, an informal "women's Soviet."

Nikolayeva was the first woman from the working class itself to become a leading revolutionary and later to rise to a policy-making vote in Soviet times. Born in 1893 in St. Petersburg, she was first arrested at age fifteen. She joined Lenin's organization in 1909, at perhaps its lowest ebb after a period of extreme governmental repression. At eighteen she was already regarded as dangerous enough to be exiled, after another arrest. Her term served, she re-entered underground work in St. Petersburg and helped prepare the initial appearance of *The Woman Worker*. She was arrested again in 1914 and 1915, bringing another term of exile, this time to Siberia. It is more than mere poetic justice that her freedom this time was brought by the overthrow of the Tsar, in which women workers in her home city played so large a part. And it is clear from her record that it was no mere tokenism that made her chairwoman of the historic First Russia-wide Congress of Women Workers and Peasants in November 1918, at age twenty-five. In 1924–25 she headed the famous Working Women's Section (Zhenotdel) of the Central Committee of the Communist party, at a time when its work was particularly difficult due to high unemployment among women. Then, after two years of formal higher political education, she was assigned to a series of the typical fire-brigade jobs to which the party's most trusted people would be sent, regardless of sex. The first of these was in the North Caucasus granary during the key year of organization of collective farms. Then for four years she was second in command in western Siberia, where the second largest steel-coal-chemicals complex in the U.S.S.R. was being built during those critical initial Five-Year Plans of industrialization. Next she moved to the same post in a region near Moscow with the largest concentration of women workers (and, by then, executives) in the U.S.S.R. Simultaneously, she was elected to the Central Committee of the party, which decides what direction the country is to take. She remained a member for the remaining ten years of her life. She died in 1944. From 1936 on she had been a top national officer of the central body of the trade unions.

Obviously, it is not strange that someone of her personal background would have been among those who, in 1917, came into head-on conflict with the version of feminism that upper- and middle-class women espoused. On the eve of the Communist seizure of power, Samoilova, an organizer of genius, nearly a generation older than Nikolayeva and with ten years' more experience as a revolutionary, realized the potential of the "women's Soviet" that had sprung up to support *The Woman Worker* of which she and Nikolayeva were editors. Samoilova called the first formal conference of women workers, which met in October 1917. But this coincided with the "ten days that shook the world." It adjourned, reconvened in November, after the Revolution, and this is where a dramatic face-to-face confrontation with feminists occurred, like that a decade earlier at which Kollontai had been hooted down. But this time the positions were reversed, in that now it was the working-class women who were in control.

Alla Arbuzova, a steel mill worker who was a member of the presiding body of the conference and subsequently became a college teacher, recalls: "Who today knows what the League of Equal Rights for Women was? But we knew it well. It was seeking the votes of women of the working class [in the elections to the Constituent Assembly]. Its candidates were women of the bourgeoisie. We called them the 'equal-rightsers.' They would go no farther, of course, than demanding equal rights for women with men in voting and election. . . . At first the women workers wouldn't give them the floor. Comrade Kollontai advised us to hear them out. . . . And so Mme. Doroshkevich, beautifully dressed, wearing a fashionable hat with a little veil, clattered up to the platform in her French heels. Her very appearance called forth a wrathful murmur among the delegates. . . . *Many of the delegates knew such lordly ladies only too well. With what contemptuous mein they had ordered the kitchen help, maids and nursemaids around* [housework was the largest single field of female employment]; *how well they knew how to tyrannize a servant and humiliate her!* . . . Comrade Fyodorova spoke vividly. Red with excitement and outrage, she threw at

Doroshkevich: 'The women of the capitalist class, equal-rightsers, hold us in contempt as black-bones. So get out of our way, you white-bones! Hooray for the black-bones, who are on the way to win a life for themselves.' . . . Mme. Doroshkevich alternately reddened and paled, and wiped her face with a lace handkerchief."

The disappearance of the earlier feminism was not simply a matter of class hostility. In a matter of months, the new government legislated more than the upper-class feminists had ever asked for: suffrage of course, divorce and civil marriage laws which made marriage a voluntary alliance, elimination of distinctions between legitimate and illegitimate children, employment rights equal to those of men, equal pay for equal work, universal paid late-pregnancy and early-maternity leave. Overnight, the status of women in Russia became far and away the world's most advanced.

That status could be protected only if the new government survived. This projected its female supporters into new roles. The Revolution had been made in a single city, then the capital, in the extreme northwest corner of the most immense country on earth (nine days to cross by rail). That it shortly spread to Moscow did not change matters fundamentally. The cities were isolated and had to be fed. Invading armies had to be pacified or defeated. They included the Germans very nearby in the West, forces right outside Petrograd loyal to the ousted Provisional Government, and monarchists.

By early 1918 the food ration in the city was down to four ounces of bread per day, and nothing else. Women were dispatched to the villages along with men to get food being held back by rich peasants (kulaks) for price speculation. They were starving the cities. The food detachments confiscated all grain beyond the kulaks' own subsistence needs. Vera Slonimskaya, a member of one of the detachments, much later a university graduate, Ph.D., and professor, described the kulaks' "standard procedure" with any food collector captured alive: they cut off ears and tongue, gouged out eyes, split the belly and stuffed it with wheat.

In the city, a political debate raged over whether to make peace at the price the Germans demanded, involving the surrender of enormous western and southern territories inhabited by minority peoples. Women as well as men were on both sides of the argument.

In this incredibly tense and confused situation, the fact that the Congress of Soldiers' Wives voted to support the peace treaty gave Lenin desperately needed support in his own divided camp. Women were no one's tools. They participated at all levels in making the most important kind of policy; they exercised some power. Individually, as we have seen, they took and supported whatever point of view they chose. Their influence, however, was in proportion only to their permanently organized numbers: far lower than the number of women in mass outpourings at moments of great crisis. Stasova was the one woman among the Central Committee members in 1918, and the relative handful of women in the Communist party in Petrograd at that time, 354, was but 9 per cent of its membership. Up to that time it was chiefly factory workers and urban soldiers' wives who had newly become active, and for many of them, particularly the latter, that had meant turning out for a single enormous demonstration when life had become unbearable. Peasant women, the overwhelming majority of the female population, had hardly been touched.

The job was to reach out, and preparations began for the First Russia-Wide Congress of Women Workers and Peasants held in November 1918. The hardships and the human warmth of its organizers come through vividly in the reminiscences of Rachel Kovnator, then eighteen. "Behind was a long, hungry day at work. The wind lashed at my face and through my thin dress—made over from an old one of Mama's—as I ran across the bridge to meetings. But there was no way to warm up in the editorial offices [of *The Woman Worker*] either. That large house was not heated. Some of the windows were broken, and a piercingly cold wind blew in from the Neva River."

No men were present at the meetings, held in the confiscated home of a wealthy family. The senior women, the political "heavies," clearly found these gatherings a chance to relax. Alexandra Kollontai, says Kovnator, was a wonderful raconteuse and a talented mime. I imagine the young working-women must have heard some shockinng tales out of school

about the men, particularly as Kollontai personally practiced
the free love that she preached. One day the electricity, unde-
pendable at best, failed completely, and Lenin's considerably
older sister, Anna, the most experienced revolutionary in the
group—she was then fifty-three—took them back to the 1880s,
telling the story of another brother, Alexander, executed for
an attempt on the life of the Tsar, and her own thirty years
of activity.

But the endless crises left little time for this sort of entertainment. Because of the starvation rations, a special committee was set up to send workers' children to places out of town
where food was available. Leaflets were put out with lines
like this: "Be reasonable, loving parents; send your children
to our proletarian centers." Kovnator recalls that at the assembly points "the mothers, like all mothers, were upset,
alarmed, asked the same questions ten times over: where are
the children being sent, what to give them to take along, when
would they return. And the children, like all children, made
noise and frolicked. The little ones squalled and older ones
pulled their mothers' sleeves: 'Mom, go ahead home, the lady
already told you everything.'" One wonders how many of the
little girls went through exactly the same experience twenty-
three years later when they were mothers, with the Nazis and
Finns surrounding Leningrad, rations again down to four
ounces per day, and their own children now to be evacuated.

The work to lift women's heads out of their washtubs went
on in the midst of all this. As one delegate to the First Russia-
Wide Congress of Women Workers and Peasants put it, its
purpose was "to explain their rights to the millions of women
in even the most remote corners of the country, and call upon
them to take an active part in building a new life." The fine
new laws were meaningless unless women knew of them and
would insist that all obey them.

Between three and five hundred delegates were expected.
Eleven hundred forty-seven came. The kind of people they
were emerges from this delegate's description:

"We from Petrograd had grown accustomed to palaces
since the Revolution, and the gilt chandeliers and marble col-
umns [of the Hall of Nobles] did not amaze us. But most
of the women were astounded by the grandeur of the hall.

They touched the smooth cold marble, felt in disbelief the mossy, silky trunks of the tropical palms, gazed entranced at the glistening crystal chandeliers and shrank back timidly from sitting in the plush armchairs."

Kollontai, seeing this, said in her opening speech, "I particularly greet the peasant women for their courage in traveling to strange and distant Moscow." In a special report on the family and the Communist state, she spoke directly to the life expectations of her audience: "Capitalism sucks all the juices out of the woman factory worker and so you dreamed, like Cinderella, of a prince in a golden carriage. But, comrades, we've made an end to princes and have expropriated the golden chariots. Your savior is the worker, but he owns nothing."

To most of the delegates, simply participating in a large meeting was new: "Delegates spoke poorly and often confusedly, but always sincerely and with passion."

In a certain sense, this meeting was the beginning of what has been called "Bolshevik feminism." One speaker called upon women workers "to overthrow the oppression of their husbands," in the description of a Soviet female scholar in 1971. The delegate in 1918 had said, "I went through it all. When my husband came home from soldiering, he forced me out of the committee, and on account of him I had to leave the party. . . . When the elections to this Congress came up, my husband was not around. . . . When he returned I said that I was going as a delegate to Moscow. . . . To him, the news that I had been elected as delegate was reason for cursing. 'What right do you have to mess around with being a delegate without my permission?' he yelled, and saw me out telling me never to return. . . . I have thrown off the oppression of my husband."

It was decided to organize separate bodies of women, while the Communist party itself was urged to set up a department for work among women (Zhenotdel), which it did.

Lenin felt it essential to address this gathering, although he had been wounded only three months earlier (by a female terrorist, Dora or Fanny Kaplan, who was executed), and the surgeons never dared remove one of the bullets. He had a genius for simplicity. An office-worker delegate reports the impact of his remarks: "Some peasant women had come with mandates from their villages to bring home salt, nails, matches, iron from Lenin. And now they understood that Lenin today was not going to give them either matches or nails. But he gave them something much more important—faith: he showed them the road to take."

Most of what the Congress pledged and strove for has long since become reality for Soviet women. But one problem that plagues them to this day was foreseen by the brilliant Inesse Armand, in a report entitled "The Female Worker on the Job and at Her Housework." When one remembers that the eight-hour day had been established only one year earlier, the words of the resolution adopted on that subject are remarkable: "housework is a heavy burden on female workers and peasants and . . . *negating the eight-hour workday for them* [my emphasis], interferes with their becoming revolutionaries. . . ."

Inesse (or Inessa) Armand had a life no scriptwriter could make a producer believe. She is the classic example of the upper-middle-class wife and mother turned politically revolutionary and sexually independent. She was born in France to a French father and English mother, both theater people, in either 1874 or 1875. She was sent to live with her grandmother, a governess with the Armand family, who were Russified French émigrés become wealthy and liberal industrialists. Their home was near Moscow. At eighteen or nineteen she married the family's eldest son, and had four children during her typically bourgeois life with him for a decade. Then she fell in love with and moved in with his younger brother, with the consent of her husband, who remained her friend and continued to support her financially. A fifth child was born. Despite her unconventional personal life, she was deeply religious.

Prostitution aroused her social conscience, and about 1900 she joined a typical do-gooder society to rehabilitate these women. When a fellow member wrote Leo Tolstoi for advice, and he replied, "Nothing will come of your work. . . . Thus it was, thus it will be," she ceased being a Tolstoian and turned to socialism because of its belief that women are not less capable than men. She was arrested in 1907 and exiled to the European Arctic coast. Her lover, the younger Armand brother, actually followed *her* into exile, reversing a century-old tradition. She escaped to Europe, and by 1911 she was a teacher at Lenin's school for revolutionaries outside the French capital. She is the only woman who seems to have ever attracted him except his wife, Krupskaya. A French Communist biographer, given access to unpublished Soviet archive papers, wrote in his book about Lenin in Paris, published there in 1968, "As for Lenin, how could he not be won by this exceptional being who combined beauty with intelligence, femininity with energy, practical sense with revolutionary ardor?"

The Armand-Lenin intimacy ended in 1916, and had been interrupted for a long time by her own assignment to Russia for underground work (the Revolution came first). There was never a ménage à trois, but all sources agree that Lenin's wife, Krupskaya, became a close personal friend of Armand's in 1913, remained so until Inesse's death of cholera in South Russia in 1920, and virtually adopted one of her children thereafter. The three pictures that Krupskaya kept on her desk in the Kremlin were of her mother, Lenin, and Inesse Armand. She also wrote a biography of Armand.

As a revolutionary, Armand participated in preparing the armed uprising in Moscow in 1917. From 1918 to her death she headed the Women Workers' Section of the Central Committee of her party. Where Samoilova had demonstrated the need for a separate organization of women—but led by the party—on practical grounds, Armand did so on the level of theory, but theory based on the visible realities of the day. She wrote that a woman's lack of political rights in the pre-Communist period, her serfdom in the family, and her repression by housekeeping, which kept her locked into a narrow range of interests, "had created certain features in [her] psychology with which we cannot fail to reckon if . . . we wish to involve the woman worker in the movement."

Writing of the 1918 Russia-Wide Congress of Women Workers and Peasants, at which she delivered no fewer than three of the major prepared speeches on different subjects, she said, "If such subjects as the protection of motherhood and childhood were put forward at the Congress, it is not at all because this is all the woman worker should concern herself with. . . . It was vastly easier for the Soviet government to institute complete political and civil liberation of women than to destroy her age-old slavery in the home, for this required a fundamental break with the old. . . . All this could not be done at once, time would be needed. . . . The age-old structure of the family is pretty much the last stronghold of the old system, the old slavery. This fortress must be destroyed. It cannot be destroyed by screaming about how unsuitable and criminal it is, but by creating new forms of public eating arrangements, public upbringing, social insurance and welfare."

In the real conditions of that day, this could be no more than a hope, except for what could be accomplished by self-help. A delegate later recalled how, upon returning from this meeting, she and three other women at her factory set out to organize a child-care center there. They had many volunteer helpers, men and women. They scrubbed and repaired quarters in which soldiers had been housed, put in windows, found furnishings, and opened up within a month with accommodations for 140. Also, "in pursuit of the directive of the Congress to liberate women from household slavery, we organized a workers' cafeteria in the quarter, from which many families took prepared meals home. And thus the women workers learned to live in a new way. . . ."

By this date it began to be necessary to deal with the literally millions of homeless children resulting from the complete chaos of the contending Russian armies and the military forces of fourteen foreign countries, including the United States, seeking to oust this first Communist government. At the factory described, two homes for such children were opened by the women's efforts, one in the former town house of the Englishman Maxwell, from whom the enterprise had been confiscated. The private property of the wealthy was no longer an obstacle to the practical liberation of women. The personal cottages of peasants and those urban wage earners who had them were more secure in their individual ownership than ever before, and remained so.

These first child-care centers already differed from the few existing before the Revolution. The earlier ones, in Lenin's passionate words, were either "commercial undertakings, with all the worst aspects of financial gambles, the goal of profit, deception, and false claims, or 'the acrobatics of bourgeois philanthropy,' which the best elements among the workers had hatred and contempt for."

Activities in this desperate time were not confined to coping with immediate urgencies or organizing to free a little of the time of women within their existing occupations and levels of development. Remarkable beginnings were made toward releasing potential capacities and genius. Today Irina Yegorova is a Ph.D. retired after a long career in agricultural research. In childhood and youth she did not even know what that was. Born into a peasant family in 1901, she was hired out to look after cows at age nine and worked in a laundry for seven years after that. A member of the all-women union of laundry workers, she participated directly in the Bolshevik Revolution and was then elected to a soviet. In 1919, functionally illiterate, she was sent to a one-year "workers' and peasants' university," in which half the students were women. They had no desks, no tables, no chairs. The classes were held in the dormitory-style rooms in which they lived. They sat on the beds. There were no textbooks or literature. The teaching, such as it was, was purely oral. At first there was no discipline: an instructor or the students might not show up. She and a friend convened the members of the Communist party in the group, who appointed monitors, battled loafers and expelled some.

Yegorova described in her memoirs some of the women she personally knew at that time. One, who had been a laundress, became a physician with thirty years' practice behind her; another had been a seamstress who later studied law and came to head the statewide union of court and district attorney staff personnel; a third woman became a factory manager after engineering training; and another laundress, earlier a houseworker, became a Communist party official.

In actual numbers, however, such achievers represented a *microscopic* proportion of the female population, for they had to have qualities far beyond those required to make similar careers in normal times, even with the assistance of that society in opening doors to women. Most important, they had raised their own consciousness to the point of seeing such futures for themselves when the *overwhelming majority* of each sex could not picture females as other than pregnant and literally barefoot in kitchen and barnyard.

Chapter III
Consciousness-Raising and a New Reality

Starting with the triumph of the Revolution November 7, 1917, the future of Soviet women was decided, not in such constructive undertakings in a couple of great cities as have been described, but in consciousness-raising among both women and men to clear the way for women's permanent emergence from their traditional role. In the words of Helen Emelianova, a Soviet scholar writing in 1971, "An acute contradiction had arisen: the participation of female workers in the socialist revolution was considerable, but immediately after the revolution their numbers were extremely few among members of the party, in the soviets, in factory committees, in trade unions." Peasant women (fourth fifths of the total female population), housewives (a majority among urban women), and houseworkers (an extremely large group) had hardly been involved, if at all.

The job, according to Emelianova, was to "develop the conviction among lower-level party personnel of the need for the party to engage in special work among women, and consequently of the necessity to establish special bodies . . . for work among women."

This didn't come easily. Men were quoted as replying, "I am against this work on principle and therefore I refuse." Consciously they thought they were doing so because of opposition to "dividing the working class" along sex lines, just as the Communist party had always refused to do along ethnic lines. Unconsciously deeper problems existed, as indicated by a report describing the difficulties of founding the women's sections: "On the one hand there is the indifference of the masses, and on the other the hostile attitude . . . of comrades, which at best was one of half-ridicule."

Emelianova spells it out: "The party's policy came up against not merely the resistance of individual hapless officials, but the mass-scale carry-overs in social psychology of the old attitude toward women, with which the entire society was infected and which was invisibly present and manifested itself unwittingly in the activities of many, even party leaders." At local levels there was nothing invisible or unwitting about it. One regional report said that, in party committees, "the attitude toward women is negative, and they don't want to organize women."

The sexist attitudes of men were reinforced by women's passivity, the willing acceptance by many women of their traditional inferior and silent roles, and, when they did seek to organize, reflections of their complete lack of experience. The feminist Selivanova, writing of her own experience among soldiers' wives in 1917, says, "It took two months merely to teach them how to conduct meetings and to make them understand that without silence and order they would not accomplish anything. But the way once shown and grasped, the women went on and did extremely well." This education process repeated itself each time new strata were involved. Several years later, a female peasant who became a Communist had the same experience: "At the conference we were like geese, cackling all at once. Gradually we began to make our way. We got to know the laws. . . ."

Six women Communists in a rural county seat, desperate over their own ignorance of how to proceed, did not hesitate to write directly to the Central Committee in Moscow, and were overjoyed to receive a four-page letter of advice Kollontai had been authorized to send them. However, two years after the women's sections were founded, a male delegate at a convention had the honesty to blame "all party members" for their attitude that these sections were "women's work" in the traditional chauvinist use of that term.

Lenin's tremendous prestige was helpful in changing that attitude, for he argued the importance of this work again and again in those years. But the members of the Central Committee's Section on Work Among Women, themselves female, gave the chief credit elsewhere: "The sections of women workers themselves . . . aroused the initiative of the party . . . in all instances in which the matter at hand concerned the position of women in one way or another."

In 1917 the dam of history had burst, and some of its waters carved a new channel. In three years of effort a solid base of organized women was created. Sixty thousand were elected "delegates," assisted tremendously by a decree over Lenin's signature authorizing that they be paid, albeit on the barest subsistence level, which enabled them to be full-time voices for and primarily organizers of women. With each representing about thirty-five others, they had contact with perhaps two million women, about 2 per cent of the female population, chiefly urban. The attitude of the other 98 per cent was observed in 1923–24 in his home village by an ex-peasant, Maurice Hindus, who had emigrated to the United States. The older women simply could neither understand nor accept any change from their traditional way of life: " 'If you whip your own child they send an agent down to investigate you and threaten to lock you up.' . . . 'The devil only knows why they won't let us drink home brew,' protested Ahapa, a middle-aged woman. 'Because,' the girl who had a Communist brother hastened to reply, 'they don't want the men to get drunk and beat up their wives.' They roared with laughter. Such a silly explanation!"

The vast majority of the urban women had similar attitudes. A delegate reminisces that housewives would respond: "Why should I go to a delegates' meeting? I won't understand anything anyhow. I'm hardly literate, and it's too late to learn. My business as a woman is to make dinner, straighten the room, wash the dishes, sew, patch." Housewives with servants slammed their doors in the faces of the Women's Department workers, and wouldn't let them talk to the servants. As a result, delegate meetings with houseworkers couldn't be organized until long after groups had been established at factories and among housewives. The number of houseworker delegates was never large. This was during the period of Soviet life extending to approximately 1930, which some in the West today idealize merely because of the stirring revolutionary films then being made.

In her splendid book *Red Virtue*, Ella Winter, traveling in 1932, wrote of villages in which "the women stood while the men sat down and ate; kept their heads bent and their hands folded, not speaking until they were spoken to. In one hut when I asked the peasant woman a question, the husband repeated it to his wife, the wife answered him, and he returned the answer to me."

In a city "I talked to a buxom woman worker in a candy factory. 'I was a servant,' she said, 'and was beaten by my master. My mistress said I was no good for anything because I was clumsy and broke dishes. I slept in a tiny foul attic with no windows. Nothing I did was right. I ran away to this factory.'" There she did very well, "'And last week I was elected a member of the Moscow Soviet,' added the woman shyly, 'and I used to believe my mistress when she said I was no good for anything!'"

This was fifteen years after the Revolution. Real emancipation had become a mass-scale phenomenon only then, when unemployment was ended forever, thanks to the industrialization program and economic planning free of the chaos of competing private businesses.

By the time this worker spoke, illiteracy was just about gone, thanks in considerable part to the efforts of the early Women's Sections and then the *delegatki*. This made a tremendous difference. In the early years, even factory women, whose daily contact with numbers of others on the job tended to give them a more progressive outlook, were quoted as saying, "What an idea! Elect *me* a delegate? I'm illiterate. You want to make fun of me." Of seven hundred delegates elected from a working-class district of Petrograd in 1919, the first year of that movement, the overwhelming majority could only sign their names, and that with difficulty.

Literacy made a vast difference in women's attitudes, because they became able to learn their rights. Masha Scott, peasant-born, who emigrated to the United States with her American husband in 1941, said that her mother took the

Revolution as her personal liberation. She stopped her husband from beating her—a practice absolutely universal among peasant men, and not a sign that he was worse than anyone else—by saying to him, "I have the same equality you have and I am not afraid," and by threatening divorce. Nothing could have been more revolutionary, or simply out of the question before the Revolution. Masha's mother would wave her collective-farm membership card in her husband's face, saying, "You always said you supported me. Now I earn as much as you. So I have as much to say as you."

In prerevolutionary times, only male peasants had land. In the collective farms, each *individual* is paid for work done. So women automatically were on the same plane as men.

Collective farms and economic planning under public ownership of industry are the hallmarks of the socialist system existing in the U.S.S.R. today. Their liberating effects upon women simply cannot be overstated. They put an end to all three of the occupations that accounted, statistically, for most female earnings before the Revolution: the hired "girl" on the farm (as distinct from the dependent peasant wife), domestic service, and prostitution. Prostitution disappeared as a statistically measurable phenomenon almost immediately after the ending of unemployment. Professional prostitutes lacking work skills, familiarity with job opportunities, and literacy were housed in "prophylactoria" where they were treated for their diseases, given basic education, taught some skill, and, most important, re-educated in their attitudes toward work.

Ending unemployment for women did not happen automatically in proportion to the demand for labor. It was necessary to fight male prejudice, particularly at the management level. This battle was waged, on the one hand, by the top leadership of the Communist party, in making the hiring and promotion of women a policy binding upon all members of that highly disciplined organization. The government, controlled by the party, formulated this into law. The familiar prejudices were argued down in pamphlets. I have one dated 1931, written by a woman, S. Berezovskaya.

In answer to those making the universal excuses for not hiring women, Berezovskaya quotes data presented to the

Soviet Congress in 1930, by unprejudiced executives, showing lower absenteeism on the part of women than men and fewer violations of work discipline. Gross output by women was higher than men's at many enterprises. "You would think that their problems of the home and child care would result in higher ratios of absenteeism, spoilage, etc. . . . . It would be false to ascribe these better indices of female labor to any natural superiority, as was said until recently about men. What we see here, apparently, are the effects of the considerably lower level of alcoholism and smoking among women." In the forty years that have passed since then, there has been virtually no change in these life-style differences by sex.

With respect to skilled work, Berezovskaya pointed to wildly differing percentages of employment of women doing the same jobs but in different industries. "This demonstrates once again that the poor utilization of female labor on skilled jobs is explained by the same prejudices about female labor." A majority of skilled women were being employed at only semiskilled jobs. "And so again and again there is confirmation of the most outrageous attitude toward female labor on the part both of the executives and of the local voluntary organizations," i.e., party and trade unions.

Turning to promotion of women to executive and management posts, she said the Central Committee of the party had ordered this in 1928, but in 1930 had to pass a special resolution recording "extreme indecisiveness by local party bodies regarding the promotion of women to leading posts involving independent authority, and in some cases absolutely open bigotry on the part of certain party organizations and members."

She recognized that large-scale employment of women had earlier been handicapped by lack of child-care facilities, and that illiteracy among women had been very high, but this was no excuse with regard to a problem involving "not millions but hundreds." "The attitude toward a woman who has been so promoted cannot be passed over in silence. Right and left one sees sarcastic attitudes toward her work, lack of assistance to her." This was still going on, despite party and government measures to the contrary.

It must be realized that the question of whether a woman

could operate a machine tool or fill any kind of supervisory position had been a matter of argument among women workers as well as men. Women tended to accept the ancient argument that they were inherently inferior. This was sanctified by religion, and they were religious in a fundamentalist way. When a female became an assistant foreperson in a textile mill in 1924, this was big news in the press. But on the tenth anniversary of the Revolution, in 1927, it was found that three women, formerly workers, were managing large textile mills, one managed a clothing factory, and 448 were assistant forepersons, forepersons, and shop superintendents. In 1928 six women were promoted to high government positions, one as governor of a province, and another was named to a high post in the party.

By 1929 numbers of women could see themselves as potential engineers and, through pressure for a sort of "open admissions" policy paralleled by party pressure from above, they gained mass entrance to the Bauman Institute of Technology in Moscow. Employed mothers were still often hesitant about the use of day-care facilities, but this was partially overcome by arranging for representative mothers to be on duty and to report back on conditions to the neighbors or coworkers.

These early years saw sharp changes in marriage and divorce laws and widely publicized debates over sexual behavior. In fact, as everyone who has ever taken a course in anthropology knows, this is the sphere of human existence in which large-scale, lasting changes come most slowly of all. In retrospect, the things that actually did happen are readily explainable in terms of the social disruption caused by civil war raging over six sevenths of the country and a famine of holocaust proportions along the Volga in 1920, heaped on top of the terrible losses of World War I. Among the people at large, the most important fact is that the wars left the country with four million more women than men, and the imbalance was highest in the sexually most active age groups. Additionally, some millions of children were left homeless or without parents or left home, and involvement in sex with others, both spontaneously and at the instigation of adults, began earlier than usual. Finally, it was young people newly recruited into the Communist movement who were the backbone of the revolutionary armed forces and the subsequent reconstruction. They were assigned back and forth wherever needed, women equally with men, and the time and opportunity for lasting relationships didn't exist, never mind the possibility that one's lover would be killed tomorrow at the front or by hostile grain hoarders.

The sex imbalance left women at an even greater disadvantage than usual. The first postrevolutionary laws, passed under Lenin, abolished the medieval restrictions of the old legislation (wherever a man chose to go, the wife was required to follow; if she ran away she could be returned by force). Adultery was stricken from the law. There was no such thing as an illegitimate child. No double standard in any form. Birth control and abortion were legalized. The laws were enforced, but only insofar as a three-quarters-illiterate population in the pre-radio era could learn of their existence. They did help to begin to change male attitudes, but slowly. With virtually no doctors in the countryside, abortion was solely an urban phenomenon. With hardly any rubber industry in the day of the condom, birth control was nearly impossible.

There is a peculiar myth, political rather than scholarly in origin, that holds that Lenin's brief lifetime after 1917 was a period of progress, followed by reaction under Stalin. The fact is that Lenin died in 1924, and Trotsky, who had been second in prominence, was thereafter in a powerless minority. It was the first decade of Stalin's leadership (1924–34) that witnessed both the flourishing of films and literature, and the kinds of legislation and experiments in living that many young Western radicals and cultural figures of today look upon with nostalgia.

With respect to family law, this was the period of the "postcard" divorce, when a dissatisfied spouse would simply notify the authorities that the marriage was over, and if the other party was not physically present, a form postcard would break the news. The major intent of the law was to free millions of women who had been married off against their will under traditional patriarchal procedures. It proved catastrophically counterproductive. Women lost the protection against abandonment with a child or children that they had formerly had.

One problem with the early experiments was that the very best of the intellectuals who led the Russian revolution had no notion of how really backward the life of the country's four-fifths-peasant majority really was. Soviet scholar Emelianova wrote in 1971 of Kollontai's prerevolutionary book, *Society and Motherhood,* "It must be emphasized that these ideas later underlay many of the changes carried out by the young Soviet republic. And it is absolutely no accident that [Kollontai] was named Commissar of Social Welfare immediately after the Revolution." But while Kollontai had gotten to know the life of women workers to some degree, she did not know that of peasants. In 1920 she spoke of things "no longer done by the women of today: she spun wool and linen; she wove cloth and garments, she knitted stockings, she made lace, and she took up, as far as her resources permitted, the pickling and smoking of preserved foods; she made beverages for the household; she molded her own candles. . . . What housekeeper would now occupy herself in molding candles, spinning wool, weaving cloth? All these products can be bought in the shop next door."

Twelve years later, when I saw peasants selling produce in the streets of Moscow, they were still wearing homespun cloth and birchbark sandals made by hand. The Russian village of the 1930s still had no shop, only an occasional wandering pack-peddler as in pre-Civil War America, and a seasonal fair where some factory goods could be bought. The Revolution gave the woman a piece of land, but the draft animal and equipment remained her husband's property, so it was not until these things became part of collective farms in the 1930s that she came out from under his direct economic control. By the peasants' own insistence, they still retain an acre or so of small garden farm, which in fact proved to be folk wisdom and saved their lives during World War II and the bitter years of reconstruction until nearly the mid-1950s. In 1972 a Soviet scholar reported to a UNESCO conference in Moscow that "under certain conditions, it [the personal garden farm] can strengthen the influence of traditions of the folkways of the past upon the consciousness and psychology of the peasantry . . . and *preserve the sources of social inequality between the sexes*" [emphasis mine]. Young couples, he found, said they couldn't do without the private plot, although they didn't like it. (China has it, too.)

Here is what each family still does by hand for its garden farm, according to that very recent report. The men make wooden shovels, hayforks, garden tools, sleighs, two-wheel horse carts in some parts of the country, and smoothing harrows. They build and repair small barns, sheds, ice cellars, procure feed for the milk cow, the sow and its litter, and the chickens. They slaughter and smoke, dry, and salt the meat. Here is what the women do, today, fifty years after Kollontai's utopian description: they make butter, cheese, curds, sour cream, jam, fruit preserves, and pickles; they raise vegetables, fruits, berries, and honeybees; they feed and care for the animals; and they sell a portion of these products on farmers' markets or to government agencies to increase the family's cash income. They no longer make cloth or footwear, because now there are country stores where they can buy these things, as well as radios, TVs, bread—so baking is no longer necessary—and canned goods of types not grown locally. This actually does leave the farm family with some leisure time, and the study shows that its only *new* function is organization of that time.

The scholar concluded that "conditions of household culture *similar to those of the past* and the *economic* need to preserve the personal garden farm are the basis for preservation in the family of elements of the old social inequality of the sexes and *the traditional division of everyday kinds of work into male and female* [emphasis mine]. The persisting difference between town and country in material and intellectual life and culture leaves a clear imprint upon the peasant family and gives rise to different outlooks on life—even, one might say, to sharply different value systems."

That conclusion must be kept in mind if the rest of this book is to make sense. Endless propaganda failed to change that situation. Only modernization of country life and urbanization can do so. The biggest progress since Kollontai's day is in that last category. The rural population has dropped from four fifths to 43 per cent of the whole. Nearly half of the country people are no longer collective-farm peasants but teachers, doctors, postal employees, bookkeepers, members of co-operative store staffs, agricultural experts, electric-power and communications people, machinery mechanics, movie operators, community-center workers. Few of these occupations existed or engaged large numbers when people were illiterate, had no medical care, farmed as their ancestors had, had no recreational facilities, and lived by candlelight and oil lamps. An extraordinary percentage of this personnel, including a *majority* of the professionals, is female, and both the women and men went to town for educations beyond the high school and usually junior high school level, bringing home somewhat changed attitudes. For example, the number of children in rural families is now very small.

On the other hand, the tens of millions of peasants who moved to town, and are still doing so, carried their burden of traditional psychology with them. It changes sharply in town, in all respects, as sociological studies in the Soviet Union have shown (see the translation quarterly *Soviet Sociology*, 1962 to date), but it doesn't change *completely* in any respect. The changes take decades, some of them generations. A very simple example of the countrified air of Soviet urban life is mushroom-gathering. It is an universal recreation of people in the very largest cities on summer weekends, even when they go by car or motorcycle. A Russian who can't tell the difference between a poison toadstool and an edible mushroom is unheard-of.

This urban-rural cultural mix has a great deal to do with the destinies of Soviet women, legislation with respect to them, enforcement of such laws, and the energy or lack of it with which the Communist party has pursued its policies in this regard.

The progress toward real equality for women—in education, employment, the professions, child-care facilities, posts in local and middle-level government—even under Stalin's rule from 1924 to 1953, was so much greater than that in any nonsocialist country to this very day that it is very difficult indeed to challenge the superiority of socialism for women. In 1938 a woman became manager of the Moscow Circuit Railroad. The next year a female flier was named head of the Soviet's international airlines. Women had been one tenth of the medical profession before the Revolution, but were clearly in the majority by the eve of World War II.

Because of the frank hostility of every other government to the U.S.S.R. in the 1930s, and Hitler's publicly announced intention, long before the war, to seize great parts of the Soviet Union and make it a colony, the Soviet Union became like a city under siege. Every individual's life was subject to control in what was believed to be the interests of the survival of the whole. This led to some steps backward in the position of women. While workers were made subject to a labor draft, women were deprived of the right to abortion for twenty years before, during, and after World War II, in the hope that this would bring a rise in the birth rate. Divorce was made extremely difficult during the same period.

When World War II did come, a law was adopted relieving men of all financial responsibility for babies born out of wedlock, with the government providing financial assistance instead. Women called this "the man's law" and never ceased complaining (although Stalin permitted no organized protest) until its repeal after his death.

Legal abortion on demand and divorce essentially on demand (the interests of minor children being the only qualifying factor) were restored in about 1955. The prior twenty years left a mark, however, because of the incessant propaganda during that time that the antiabortion and antidivorce laws were not expedients, but fundamentally right. Had it simply been argued that compulsory maintenance of family ties was needed to give women and children economic protection at a time when women's recent illiteracy and the extreme difficulties of life made it hard for them to rise above assembly-line jobs to skilled work with higher pay, it would have been possible to go on discussing the Kollontai and Armand views, with strong support in Friedrich Engels, that ultimately the family based on male superiority would have to give way. But the attempt to justify these expediencies as proper resulted in a sanctification of "till death do us part" that any church would envy.

My belief is that there were three reasons for this. One was Stalin's effort to convince a barely literate people by oversimplification in all spheres, supported by murderous sup-

pression of dissent. Another is that the new theorists who
provided his arguments were, because of their social backgrounds, unsubtle and undereducated. The third, to which
entirely too little attention has been paid, is anthropological.
The people running the country, not merely or even particularly the handful at the very top, but the masses of new industrial, educational, mass media, and government administrators and managers required in a newly urbanizing and
industrializing country, simply brought their rural culture with
them. It was rank with male prejudice, and women regarded
it as right and proper that child-rearing as well as generally
nurturing occupations were their functions, in addition to
the hard physical labor that peasant women had always done.
Full access to education, to professions, and to merit upgrading, plus the greater freedom offered by the world's first mass-
scale system of child care, was as much as they could aspire
at that time. That was pretty high. No noncommunist country has yet statistically reached the Soviet levels of thirty-five
years ago in these spheres.

World War II made everything worse. Now, there was no
time to educate and socialize at all. The male and female
populations were virtually separated en masse for four years.

War may bring out qualities of heroism, loyalty, devotion,
and comradeship, but it also brutalizes. Its entire tone is
macho. At the end of the war, in a terribly decimated country, everyone with experience of command at the front was
given an executive position, high or low, in rebuilding the
country, whether an ex-submarine commander managing a
textile mill with an overwhelmingly female staff (a case I
know personally) or peasant infantry officers put in charge of
collective farms. The entire style to which they had been subject for at least four years was that of giving orders and ex-
pecting unquestioned obedience, not reasoning or persuading.
Not only did this naturally reinforce male-chauvinist practices, but women en masse, exhausted from eleven-hour wartime workdays, responsibilities far beyond their prewar training and experience, and a separation from men that they
found unnatural and emotionally tearing, willingly stepped
back into rank-and-file jobs. They welcomed having long-
postponed children and caring for their men. This was said

in print, directly and accusingly, by occasional women who felt differently, particularly during the discussion of the present Platform of the Communist party adopted in 1961.

To me, the marvel of that period is that despite the steps backward the mass-scale advance of women was not fundamentally affected, as the subsequent years have shown.

Chapter IV
Cosmonaut and Milkmaid

In old Russia, a country in which bread was literally the staff of life, there was little dairy farming. A peasant family that had a single cow regarded itself as lucky. As with the few fowl scratching around the hut, and the single pig and its litter a fortunate family would have, care of the cow was regarded as part of the housework—woman's work. Although there are hot countries in which small animals share the peasant cottage, Russia's very cold climate made this actually necessary, in the absence of heated barns.

Milkmaid in a collective (co-operative) or state (government-owned) farm, which involves feeding and care of the animals and their calves as well as milking, is a *new* job arising out of the real history of farming and of culture (division of work by sex) in a real country. Champion milkmaids are awarded the country's highest honor: the title Hero of Socialist Labor. They are elected to Congress. When one such visited the United States, disbelieving Senators asked her to milk a cow: she did not fit their notion of a milkmaid. Back home, she reported with pride and contempt that the U. S. Congress had no farmworkers in its membership.

In old Russia men worked with the draft animals as women did with the producing livestock. So today men are virtually all the operators of farm machinery, despite forty years of real effort on the government's part (a government composed chiefly of men) to involve women in that work, and all sorts of publicity and special benefits for those who do. But milkmaids usually earn more than tractor drivers. This is because animal care is harder work under Russia's present conditions, government policy is to improve the diet by favoring livestock farming, men simply won't do it for reasons of tradition, and women would otherwise move to town for jobs offering shorter hours and better pay. Earnings have a lot to do with one's prestige in interpersonal relations, as well as with one's independence, of course.

In jobs that *did not exist* in the old Russian countryside but do today, including those of highest standing, women are an actual majority. That is, where the Soviet policy of equality of opportunity has not come up against the wall of traditional *practices*, it has won out over traditional *attitudes*. Among people living close to the soil, few stand higher in their neighbors' eyes than the healer. In the U.S.S.R. three quarters of the doctors are women. Among people who were recently illiterate, the teacher is nearly as respected as the physician. That was as true on the American frontier a century ago as it is in the U.S.S.R. today. In old Russia the rare handful of country teachers were (male) priests. Today all children go to school, and the teachers are chiefly women.

In fact and in the minds of the people, the countryside is Russia's past, the city its present and future. Educational, cultural, employment, and social opportunities are far greater, life more varied and richer in the cities. Central city blight is unknown and streets are safe for women as for men. So countrypeople flock to town. If they have "incomplete secondary" education (equal to junior high) or full secondary, they take jobs in factories, offices, and stores. There are as many women factory workers as men. But those who quit school early—and some people always do—take the jobs available to people of low literacy, including heavy physical work such as the peasant woman has always done. And it is such people who are most visible to foreign tourists: janitors sweeping the snow in front of buildings, hotel service personnel, house painters (unskilled work in the U.S.S.R., as the results show), or members of completely mixed crews shoveling hot asphalt on paving jobs. The foreign tourist is not apt to be in scientific laboratories, engineering offices, courts, higher educational institutions, hospitals, or management offices in stores —all the places where one finds the women who constitute a *majority* of *employed college graduates* in the U.S.S.R.

The whole world knows that the only woman to have flown in space at this writing, Valentina Tereshkova, is Russian. But to me, at least, it is more significant that Soviet women routinely do jobs, without any great publicity, few Western women can even dream of. Many don't even dream of them because they have been clearly told that doors are closed to them and they aren't wanted. Some have been brainwashed into accepting the fact that they really can't do them. For example, Colonel Nina Rusakova, recently retired, was a test pilot: a job involving the very highest flying skill there is. She put forty new models of planes through their paces over the years, from propeller-driven fighters to the most tigerish jets. This means seeing what they will do at night, in rain and snow, in fog. In testing an automatic landing system for large passenger aircraft, not only was she blindfolded, but absolutely lightproof blackout curtains were installed over her cabin windows. This was not a stunt, but something she decided on, to determine how the system would work under the most extreme emergency night-landing conditions. She did that dozens of times a day for weeks on end, then herself proposed to the design council the changes necessary to make it foolproof. She is also responsible for working out, in the sky, the particular flying pattern needed in seeding clouds with carbon dioxide to clear fog and permit landings. The mother of two children, she is married to another test pilot. In World War II she was a fighter pilot and rose to command a squadron.

Today flights over the North Pole are routine, thanks to radar location systems and methods of navigation entirely independent of the earth and of visibility. But twenty years ago they were extremely difficult, because lines of longitude converge at the North Pole—there is no east, west, or north—and because the magnetic pole is not at the geographic pole. Arctic ice and oceanographic research requires landing multi-engine passenger craft on ice floes to deposit and pick up parties and their equipment. In 1954 Z. P. Sidorishina was the first woman to fly to the Pole. She was navigator of one of those ice-landing planes.

The most enormous Soviet plane is a fourteen-wheeled, four-turboprop, freight-carrying monster called the AN-22, bigger than anything in scheduled airline service in any country. Major Marina Popovich was the first woman in the world entrusted with the job of chief pilot of a plane in that class. Her crew of four is all male. In 1972 she set ten records with it, including the carrying of fifty tons (equal to over five hundred passengers) over a long route. She, too, has two children, one still in kindergarten, and is married to one of the Soviet cosmonauts. Of seven male cosmonauts in space in two capsules in a linkup flight in 1969, the wives of three were engineers, one was a scientist, one a physician. All had children.

We are dealing with the kind of flying that women in the West simply aren't allowed to do. The prejudice is of the most basic kind: these aren't small planes that a woman with an inheritance can buy or a rich husband can stake her to. And who is going to trust a woman with a new model on which the prestige of a great power rides, or with being the member of a crew whose job it is to make sure that a plane that is part of a complex scientific expedition gets its load to the right place and back? The Soviet Union does. It was 1973 before any scheduled U.S. airline permitted a woman to be even second officer.

The same thing can be found in field after field. A twenty-thousand-ton freighter is not only an expensive, blocks-long assemblage of machinery that has to be brought safely across oceans despite storms and ice and into port without damage to itself, its cargo, the docks, or boats and ships in its path. It is also an enormous business operation. Not keeping to the straightest possible course can run up immense additional fuel costs. Unlike an oil tanker or grain or ore carrier, which often picks up its cargo from one single shipper and delivers to a single buyer, loading and unloading through one type of special pipe or blower or conveyor, a freighter is like a huge department store. A single cargo varies in size, shape, weight, and density. It must be stowed so that it will not shift in a storm at sea, and will not cause the ship to list because of maldistribution of weight. On-time delivery means money to the many different parties at both ends. It also determines whether they will use the same shipping line in the future or take their business elsewhere. In the case of a publicly owned economy, like that of the Soviet Union, the whole country's business reputation is at stake when one of its ships picks up freight in one private-enterprise country and delivers it to another.

Captain Anna Shchetinina is master of a twenty-thousand-ton freighter. On a typical run from Japan, she carries steel, automobiles, and general cargo to the West Coast of the United States and Canada. She is one of the most experienced of Soviet skippers, having captained ships for over thirty-five years, and you don't become a captain your first year at sea. As such, she is able to write her own ticket. She now spends half the year teaching at the Marine Institute in Vladivostok, and "When I tire of being ashore, I am able to bring a ship out for six months or so."

Captain Shchetinina is large-bodied. Captain Valentina Orlikova is petite, almost fragile, with a face that was stunningly beautiful in photos of both the 1940s and the 1960s. On her very first voyage as a junior officer fresh out of school in 1941, her ship, crammed with thousands of refugees being evacuated from besieged Tallinn on the Baltic Sea to Leningrad, struck a mine. The damage was repaired, and they made it. After the war, she captained a whaler for seven years in the fogbound North Pacific off the Kurile Islands. Then they gave her an office job with a resounding title: "Chief Captain of the Ministry." Within two years she was telling the Minister, a cabinet member, "What kind of captain am I without a ship? Let me out into the merchant marine." In 1956 she was given command of a large refrigerator ocean fishing trawler with a crew of ninety. The U.S.S.R. was desperately in need of additional protein foods for its people, and she was one of the first half-dozen Soviet captains to launch transoceanic fishing off Labrador and Newfoundland. This was pioneering: thousands of depth soundings, hundreds of test drags of the enormous high-seas nets. Caught off Iceland in an extraordinary hurricane creating fifty-foot waves, her vessel might have capsized had one of them hit it broadside. She remained on the bridge, sleepless, for forty-eight hours, directing the changing shifts of helmsmen.

In another storm off North Cape, the northernmost point of Scandinavia, an engine went out on a large Norwegian ship. Orlikova put her trawler about and managed to get a towline aboard despite the high seas, and pulled the Norwegian away from treacherous shoals. Next morning, repairs completed, the captain came aboard to offer his thanks. He was taken to a cabin where there was a small woman in slacks and sweater with just a touch of gray in her hair. He bowed courteously and said in English he wanted to see the captain. She smiled, motioned him to a seat, and stepped out. In a few minutes she was back, in glittering braid and insignia. The Norwegian jumped to his feet and apologized, stuttering, then expressed his gratitude in the loftiest language. She replied that coming to the aid of a vessel in distress was the law of the sea. Before leaving, he said, "Miss Valentina, I've been a captain for ten years, but I have never met . . ." "A woman on the captain's bridge?" she finished his sentence. "I have been a captain for twenty, have plied the Atlantic and Pacific and also have never met a woman captain"—she paused—"on ships of what it is your custom to call the free world. But I'm not the only one in our country. Women command vessels on rivers, on lakes, and on the seas. And there are some a great deal more experienced than I."

By now the Norwegian was busily noting this down and reported it to the press on his return.

Today Captain Orlikova commands an enormous tanker that refuels hundreds of fishing vessels in the open ocean on long voyages far from home. And on her jacket is the gold star of a Hero of the Soviet Union, their equivalent of the Congressional Medal of Honor.

Her case and that of Captain Shchetinina help to explain why the number of women in such top jobs is small. There are four sea captains. For that type of responsibility, very rich experience is essential. And when they first went to sea, or when Colonel Rusakova began flying, the number of women with the education to hold such positions was about zero. Such women also had to fight the condescension and skepticism of men, and particularly false notions of chivalry. That fight is not nearly over in the Soviet Union, but vast numbers of women now have the most complex kinds of technical and scientific training.

Probably the most outstanding example of a woman holding a position requiring the very highest level of executive ability and scientific knowledge of the kind that represents rare talent as well as learning is Professor Alla Masevich.

Professor Masevich, an astronomer, commands the network of over a hundred tracking stations that follow the exact position of every piece of space hardware in the sky. In addition to those on land staffed by thousands of astronomers, they include three special ships, one of aircraft-carrier dimensions. Those ships, and their male-directed American counterparts, are the most complicated on earth. In addition to operating crews, they have hundreds of scientists permanently aboard, and radio telescopes so vast that they make the uninformed wonder why the whole ship doesn't capsize.

Professor Masevich has held that job since 1957 and literally wrote the rule book followed by American and all other stations. But she is not merely the administrator type of scientist (however unique among women) of whom experimental and theoretical scientists often joke privately that they don't have the spark for creative research. Before joining the space program, she had been an authority on the sun. And at a world astronomy congress in 1952, years before the first *Sputnik,* she and a male colleague took issue with a German physicist on a major point of cosmogony: how matter was first created. The Soviet scientists argued from the standpoint of Marxist philosophy, dialectical materialism. So she is experimental observer, theorist, and a major executive. She is also the mother of a daughter, a wife, a collector of cookbooks and cosmetics, and an avid athlete who swims, plays tennis, skates, and skis. And she earns more than the head of the largest Soviet factory or a top Soviet film director: that's the status of science in the Soviet Union.

In the West there are a few women who have made important reputations in psychiatry. But to entrust a woman with the direction of a hospital? Particularly a hospital not in obstetrics, gynecology, or pediatrics? The Belorussian Psychoneurological Center, regarded as the best in the U.S.S.R., is headed by Dr. Efrosinia Breus. She has personally worked on the relationship between psychoses and diseases of the heart and blood, is coauthor of *Nervous Trauma in New-Born Infants*, is involved in hypnosis and group therapy, and is so convinced that the mentally ill recover faster if not isolated from their normal surroundings that her institution was among the first in the U.S.S.R. to give shock treatment, when necessary, as part of outpatient treatment, without hospitalization.

Much in the U.S.S.R. is very puzzling unless one knows its history. Dr. Breus's life story illustrates it in very important ways. She was a twenty-year-old medical student when Hitler attacked the Soviet Union. An evacuation train she was on was bombed. Later, she served as a surgeon at the front. Her husband, her child, her brothers, and her mother were all killed in the four years of war. That was not rare in Belorussia, which lost two and a quarter million people: one person in four. Obviously, a great deal of mental illness was generated in those who survived. For this reason, although she had achieved a reputation as a leading surgeon, she started all over again in psychiatry after the war. Soviet people are not neutral or fatalistic about war. They hate it with a passion. Now you know why.

The leading eye hospital in the Soviet Union, chiefly a research institute, is also headed by a woman, Dr. Nadezhda Puchkovskaya. Not only are there 450 beds for inpatients, plus an outpatient clinic handling 120,000 visits per year, but the staff she directs includes 605 doctors, ophthalmologists, opticians, and engineers, of whom 130 hold the highest ranks attainable in their respective professions. She, too, was a doctor at the front in World War II, heading the eye department of a hospital for three years. She has personally developed extraordinary corneal transplantation techniques, particularly for cases in which burns melt the eyelid and weld it to the eye. Despite her administrative duties and research, she still operates about twice a week. Like all the others we have described, she, being a Soviet woman, did not find it necessary to stay single in order to pursue a career that began in the 1930s. And she is aware of her patients as human beings. Because young children were frightened of the "great age" of her seven-year-old dog, she has been describing it to them as four "for a long time now."

It was big news in the United States in 1972 when a woman was named president of Bennington, a small coeducational liberal-arts college which is "special" in its history of educational experiments, and by no means typical.

The Moscow Institute of Economist Engineers is the equivalent of a college of business administration in the United States. A diploma from it is so highly valued that in 1971 there were six times as many applications for the freshman class as could be accommodated. The best are selected by competitive exam, and so the prestige of this school rises even higher. I have not been able to find enrollment figures, but it has nine departments, training executives for the electric power, iron and steel, machinery manufacturing, chemicals, construction, air transport, automotive transport, city utilities, and warehousing fields. There is also a school of graduate studies. The institute operates both day and evening sessions, as well as a correspondence department whose enrollees get time off from their jobs to attend it for tutoring and exams.

It has existed for fifty years. For nearly half that time, since 1950, its president has been Olympiada Kozlova. Like all Soviet college presidents, she continues to lecture and supervise the work of graduate students and to write scientific papers. Her collaborator in her economic research is her daughter Helen, also a professor.

President Kozlova's story is distinctly, perhaps uniquely, Soviet. Born five years before the Revolution, she was the daughter of a Volga fisherman, and in her teens helped her father with the fishing. Then, at the beginning of Soviet industrialization, she got a job in a factory as a lathe-hand. She recalls a couple of scientists visiting the factory: "They were talking Russian, but I couldn't understand what they were saying." Education was available and free, and she took advantage of that, then went on to graduate work. When she was appointed to head the institute, "it was an ordinary college." It is she who has brought it to its present standing.

She is extremely liberal as an administrator. The students allocate all dormitory accommodations and have a decisive say on scholarships. They are represented on the "Learned

Council," which compares to an executive committee of an academic senate in this country. That body is predominantly male, incidentally, corresponding to the makeup of student bodies when these senior professors were themselves going to college.

On one occasion the student government asked her to expel a female student, who was a disciplinary problem. Kozlova urged them to change their minds, they refused, and she acceded to their request. But when the young woman demonstrated self-discipline in a year on a job, the students themselves petitioned for her readmission. Kozlova naturally agreed. On another occasion the students raised a storm of protest against the severe marking practices of a brilliant young math professor, but she "managed to convince them that Professor Sokolov was within his rights. It was his job to give them the mathematical grounding the country's economists needed." But in another case the students opposed a professor who, in a manner quite familiar in the West, read the same lectures from the same notes every year. She sided with the students, and he was dismissed. Despite all her duties, she holds open office hours twice a week, when anyone may see her.

It's difficult to top descriptions of a surgeon transplanting a cornea onto the eye of a burned child, a test pilot landing a passenger plane blindfolded, a sea captain facing down a hurricane with the lives of ninety in her hands, a cosmonaut alone in a capsule hundreds of miles above the earth, hurtling at incredible speed. Yet there is one Soviet woman whose job seems to me to be even further removed psychologically from the female stereotype than any of these.

The power station near Krasnoyarsk in Siberia is by far the largest on earth, generating three times as much electricity as Grand Coulee. This is a measure of the force of the water in the Yenisei River, two thirds of a mile wide and raised four hundred feet by an enormous dam. To build such a dam, the entire river must be temporarily channeled away from its normal bed. This is done when the water is walled in by high cliffs, as in this case, by mighty explosions that must dump the rock precisely where needed. With a river of this type, fed by meltwaters from the Siberian snows in spring, from snowcapped mountains to the south in summer, and frozen over in winter, the explosion must be set off on the particular day in the year when flow has declined as far as can be expected. The quantity of explosives, the number of drill holes, their location and direction, the amount of explosive in each, all have to be calculated for that flow of water and be ready on time.

The physical work on the Yenisei explosion was done by over a hundred drillers and blasters, all men. The day of the explosion the whole of eastern Siberia seemed to have gathered to watch. Photographers, newsreel men, and reporters had come from as far as Moscow. They shoved their mikes and cameras at the blasting boss, Antonina Kalinina, a woman in her thirties, graduate of an industrial high school not far from Moscow, three thousand miles to the west, who had come there at the beginning of construction and worked her way up. Her crew had worked the last three days and nights without rest—literally; Russians are like that—and she waved the journalists away: "No time now. Up the hill, please. The blast will come soon." She herself stepped out over the frozen soil to check one last time the network of cables carrying the electricity to spark the explosion.

That was in 1963. Today the dam stands as though it had been there from eternity. Only on it can one hear the hum of the turbines far below, and the roar of the water escaping from them.

After a river is diverted, the dam has yet to be built. There is one on the Volga four times as long as that on the Yenisei, and containing six times as much material. If you've stood on a dam, you've seen trickles of water leaking out on the downstream side, and wondered how safe it is. And you've read, now and then, of dams bursting or collapsing, and tremendous catastrophes in the valleys below. So what goes into a dam below the water level is of critical importance. And not only to safety. The turbines spun by the falling water and converting it to electric power are balanced infinitely more carefully than a child's top or a gyroscope, yet each is larger than most buildings on a city street. They are beneath water level, and the structure housing them, whether or not it is part of the dam, must not tilt or yield in the slightest to the enormous and changing pressures of the reservoir. In building a dam, one of the jobs of highest responsibility is supervising the quality of construction of everything that will be beneath water level when it is finished. At the Volga site, which was two and a half miles wide and hundreds of feet thick at the base, that post was held by hydraulic engineer Oktiabrina Tretiakova, barely into her thirties, who had started as a lathe-hand in a repair shop of the U.S.S.R. dam-construction authority, and had earned her degree in night school. The Soviet tourist agency misses a bet by not instructing its guides to tell this story to the foreigners who leave the cabins of the huge riverboats, as I have, to gawk at this immense structure as they pass through its canal locks.

The Volga dam was finished in the early 1960s. Nine years later in Colorado a construction crew walked off the job when, for the first time in the history of the industry in the United States, a woman engineer, Janet Bonnema, entered a tunnel on which work was in progress. Superstitions against women are not confined to peasants in recently underdeveloped countries.

New Yorkers, and all who live in cities where power demands soar in summer as everyone turns on air conditioners at once, know that electricity is not something that is always there. Those who have been through power failures, with all they mean to urban life, have learned that often they are not caused by trouble in one's own city or the supply systems built specifically to serve it. The cost of electricity would be unbearably high if each city had to construct reserve sources sufficient to meet its maximum needs. This is avoided by linking systems together over enormous areas through high-tension lines, so power can be shifted from a place where demand is low at the moment to where it is at its peak. The entire European portion of the U.S.S.R. is connected by such a system, and it is gradually being hooked up to Siberia.

Few individuals in modern society have more minute-to-minute responsibility for the welfare of tens of millions and the functioning of industry, transport, and science than the chief dispatcher of such a system. For all the assistance given by computers and automation, the ultimate decisions have to be made by a human being. Again, in terms of male-female stereotypes, it is fascinating that a male reporter describing the work of Maria Volodina, who is in charge, eight hours a day, of all the electricity between Poland and Siberia, thought of a military commander in chief when searching for a comparison: she, too, "has reserve forces, like corps and armies, and moves stupendous power capacities 'into battle.'" For Volodina, the days in the early 1960s when the first human travelers entered space were like those when a commanding general finds his front broken by a major enemy offensive. Every radio and TV set in hundreds of cities and thousands of villages would be switched on at once. She had to find hundreds of thousands of additional kilowatts in a matter of minutes. Before her, on the entire wall of a building in downtown Moscow, is a diagram of pulsing lights of various colors, and lines in white, yellow, and red, the bloodstream of the economy, with hundreds of power plants, substations, and transmission lines. She pushes buttons, and reserve turbines in Tretiakova's Volga dam start to rotate. She picks up a phone and issues orders to Tula and the Ukraine far to the south, the Ural Mountains to the east, the Baltic states to the northwest. And this happens, on a smaller scale, every day, as when a thundershower darkens Moscow on a summer afternoon, and millions of lights go on hours before sunset.

Volodina was the very brilliant type of young person who rises to the top very quickly: she was in her early thirties when she became Europe-wide dispatcher. She also had the advantage of being of a generation educated after the post-World War II reconstruction of the country had ended, and it was possible to move smoothly from school to college to a professional job in the manner we think of as normal.

Much more typical of Soviet women in positions of authority today is the life of one of the people whom Volodina phones to call for more power—or less, as the case may be. Valentina Levicheva is at least ten years older than Volodina. Her father was a peasant who never became more than half literate. He didn't object to her going to high school, which was a big step forward in the thinking of a Russian peasant in the 1930s: his *daughter* would be a much more educated person than he. But when she told him she intended to go to college and become an engineer, he took it badly: "That's not a job for a girl. Better try something easier."

She enrolled in 1939. Two years later Hitler attacked the Soviet Union. Her father died, and her mother, working as an office cleaner, had three other children to care for, two very young. Valentina went to work to help feed the family, getting a job as night-shift control room operative at the one power station in her city, so she could continue day session. She used her experience as the material for her graduation thesis, and in 1944, when she got her diploma, the station management asked that she be assigned there. (In exchange for their totally free educations, Soviet students are required to work where assigned, at normal pay, for the first three years after graduation.) She was soon promoted, first to engineer in charge of a shift, then to chief engineer in three consecutive departments, thus giving her rounded experience. Meanwhile the system for which she worked expanded from a single station to eight, including the monster on which Tretiakova supervised underwater construction. Only a very small part of her job is responding to instructions from Volodina in Moscow. Chiefly it consists of providing for the power needs of Kuibyshev, a city of a million, and a chain of industries and electrically powered railroads up and down the Volga. Two thirds of her engineering and technical staff is male.

Tretiakova is married and has two children, both in college. The college from which she herself graduated, Kuibyshev Polytechnic, in the city in which she works and grew up, has as many female as male students. Another woman graduate, Svetlana Levanova, who got her diploma fifteen years later, is now assistant dean of its chemical engineering department, administratively responsible for its four hundred faculty and nonacademic employees, mostly men. She gained that post at age thirty-one, after nine years as a research engineer in organic synthesis, during which she married, had a child, and took a graduate degree as a correspondence student. Her husband, also an engineer, "helped a lot," as did her mother. She earns over 50 per cent more than her husband, incidentally. That is by no means the general rule, but what is important is that it is not at all uncommon.

Each year the Soviet Union awards what it calls State Prizes. They are roughly equivalent to our Pulitzer Prizes, except that they cover a broader range of endeavor and lean more heavily to the technical and scientific, as might be expected in a country that is still developing. Nominations are published in the national newspapers, so that all persons and institutions with competence to do so may discuss them and offer opinions to the committee of judges. In a recent year I found women nominated as individuals or team members in the following fields: earthquake geography, English literature, archaeology, thermodynamics, automation engineering in the automobile and tractor industry, steel-mill engineering, a compressed-air-driven industrial production system, and computer design and development. A team of geologists, prospectors, and engineers was named for discovering and carrying to production the internationally major natural-gas field in western Siberia from which the United States will be importing gas in liquefied form. Another team was named for converting railroads to electrical traction in place of coal. Both included female names. A woman was listed as *chief* of a team of seven, *the others all male,* who developed an industrial means of producing chemically pure nitrogen and oxygen from the air for fertilizer and other chemical plants. Women also appeared in a team of chemical engineers, in another that developed a fast-setting, high-strength cement, in a team of bridge engineers, in one of architects, and, finally, in a team that developed and introduced into agriculture a growth substance developed from petroleum.

But do women make it where the requirement is simply for executive skill, without scientific or technical talent or the need for a very rare courage? There are forty-six women factory managers on Moscow's City Council (a very large body). Just outside Moscow is a knitwear plant with seventeen hundred employees, producing garments to a value of tens of millions of dollars per year. All four top jobs are held by women: the manager, Lydia Kovarskaya, the production manager, the head of the Communist party branch, and the head of the union local. Because of her age—she was born in 1909 —Kovarskaya is almost a history of women's liberation in the Soviet Union. In 1924, at fifteen, she went to a trade school, becoming one of the very first working-class women to receive job training. When, at the beginning of that year, another woman was appointed assistant foreperson in a textile mill, it was a matter of national comment in the press. Of another mill, women workers wrote in a collective letter to the editor, "By March 8th [International Women's Day], thirty-three women workers became assistant foremen [sic]. At first the men jeered, but now they respect them."

Assistant foreperson was Kovarskaya's first job, and she knows what it was like to be a pioneer in the face of hostility on the part of men, the timidity it causes, and the conservatism on the part of women. Within fifteen years she was manager of the mill, then very much smaller and with outdated equipment. Now she has held the post for more than thirty years. Perhaps her background explains why she doesn't wish to retire, although she could have done so at fifty-five. As a woman in charge of a primarily female staff (not entirely: "Here men can earn as much as the women!"), it is perhaps not surprising that her concern for problems peculiar to women is at a particularly high level. At any given time, there are about thirty women on paid prenatal and maternity leave (sixteen weeks in all, by law). "A woman's job is kept open for her for a year after her baby is born, so you can imagine we do all we can to make our factory a nice place to work in so that they come back as soon as possible. The factory has a kindergarten and nurseries of its own for 250 children. And there's an excellent children's clinic, and the cafeteria will supply ready-cooked meals to take home. And we've told the union, which looks after such things, to be liberal when issuing paid admissions to vacation resorts."

Thinking back on the women presented in this chapter, it should be obvious that they would have differing attitudes on a variety of things. They range in age from early thirties to mid-sixties, in education from trade school to postdoctoral work, in background from peasant (many) to worker (several) to professional or intellectual (few). The youngest know great hardship only by hearsay; the eldest have lived through experiences few Americans have known, because our country has not been the scene of war in this century.

The life of the most famous of all Soviet women, cosmonaut Valentina Tereshkova, is as nearly typical of those of all these generations as one single individual can be, and it is very meaningful for an understanding of Soviet women that someone still under forty should have experienced what she did.

Tereshkova was born March 6, 1937. That year was the height of the bloody terror under Stalin, so she has no personal recollection of it, nor does the great majority of Soviet women, for the median age of the population is twenty-six. Her birthplace was a little village in the woods twenty-five miles from the nearest city. That made her a typical child of her generation, as two thirds of the Soviet population was rural at the time. There were only twenty cottages in the hamlet.

Her grandfather was of the very poorest peasantry. By the time Valentina was born, private farming was long gone, and the collective farm helped her grandmother take down her log house and move it from the neighboring village. That house had been confiscated from a family of kulaks (the word means "fist"), wealthy peasants exploiting farm labor, so Tereshkova's family had a direct stake in the Revolution. She is proud of the fact that her grandparents on both sides were among the first to join collective farms after the Revolution, when that required courage as well as conviction.

Family tradition helps shape anyone's psychology. Tereshkova's background tells us why Soviet people often have a very extreme loyalty to their society, of an our-backs-are-to-the-wall nature. It causes many to support things as they are against possible needs for change. Her mother was one of eight brothers and sisters. Five died of the causes that led to the Revolution, or in upholding it: three starved to death, one was killed in a battle of the civil war in 1920, and one, a member of the Communist party, was killed by a shotgun blast on his way home from a meeting at which he had called upon fellow villagers to join a collective farm.

Tragedy did not cease for Valentina's mother or for tens of millions of her generation when they grew up and married. When Valentina was three, her father was killed in the Soviet-Polish fighting in which Stalin sought to push the frontier farther away in anticipation of Hitler's attack in World War

II a year later. In her autobiography Tereshkova writes:
"Grandma refused to believe that her son was dead and forever awaited his return. She passed on her belief to me, and
more than once when I saw an unfamiliar man on the road,
particularly one in uniform, I quivered and wondered whether
it wasn't perhaps my father coming home. But time passed,
and his dust-covered bicycle stood as before against a wall
in the shed, and his accordion in the chest. . . ."

A brother was born soon after the father's death, and so
Tereshkova's mother was left with three small children. In
World War I that would have meant death by starvation. But
things were different now. The foreman of the tractor team
in which her father had worked would come and fix the roof
or the fence, or plough the land for the kitchen garden.

But life was hardly easy. Her mother left at dawn to milk
cows, and baby brother was left for the sisters to care for.
He picked up splinters from the rough floor and would be
screaming when Mother came home, dead tired and on edge.
She would throw up her hands and break into tears, and all
four sat there and cried. The little girls added to her troubles.
Bored for something to do, they'd cut up a blouse of Mother's
for rag dolls, and she would threaten to abandon them. But
for all her overwork, her mother wove socks, mittens, and
scarves for the village's men at the front, and baked hard rolls
for the gift packages.

The war came to the village in another form. Women and
children from Leningrad, besieged by the Germans, were
evacuated all over Russia. Two such children, living in the
next cottage, would tell Valentina what bombing and starvation were like, and how it is when warships fire and tall buildings collapse and long-range artillery shells a city. Men without arms or legs began to show up.

"And it was in this most fearsome time that Mama became
seriously ill, and was taken to the hospital." Her grandmother
took over. The little girls would go for water down to the
village's only well, at the bottom of a steep hill, hauling it
to the cottage in pails on a yoke. The collective farm chairman, her father's cousin, would come by and put an end of
a loaf of black bread on the table late at night. Their other
food was potatoes from their patch, and milk from the cow.

Valentina, knowing no other life, thought: "What more could we want?"

Her grandmother loved to read the papers, speak at collective farm meetings, kept no religious symbols in the house, and asked that no cross be placed on her grave. For her generation, raised before the Revolution, that was extremely rare.

The little boys played war. Valentina's younger brother, having no toys, was playing with empty cartridges at the age of three. Next door there was another girl her age, whose father had also died in the war. They called each other milk sisters, for whichever's mother was around would suckle them when they were infants.

The woman who for a decade now has been honored guest in most of the world's major cities saw one for the first time at the age of eight, when her family moved to Yaroslavl the year the war ended. Their belongings took up all the space in a truck, and only the two younger children could squeeze into its small cab, so she and her mother walked the twenty-five miles. Three miles outside the city she saw a railroad train for the first time in her life. "'Mama, what's that?' I exclaimed. 'A train.' 'And the man in the cab: who's he?' 'An engineer.' *'Can women be engineers?'* I asked."

That was 1945, nearly thirty years after the Revolution. In fact, there was even a woman heading a Soviet railroad at that time, and women constituted 40 per cent of the students in engineering colleges. But that was in town. Two thirds of the people were rural, where expectations were traditional. A child's socialization was chiefly by her family, actually mother and grandmother in a world without men, and Valentina, hardly old enough to go to school, already had a definite notion of roles. Urbanization has proceeded swiftly since then, and much that may seem old-fashioned in the attitudes of Soviet women has to be thought of in terms of the fact that even the world's female pioneer space traveler was conditioned in that manner.

Tereshkova first entered school that fall. The fathers of *most* of the children were dead. At ten she entered the Young Pioneers (which is like a co-ed Scout organization). "In the presence of longtime Communists from the textile mill, we gave our word always and in all things to be true to the cause of communism. The troop leader tied round my neck the red bandanna which obligated me to study well and be orderly, for after all a Pioneer must be an example to all."

After the four-year elementary school, she entered a girl's junior high school. Sex-segregated education was one of many peculiarities of Soviet life in Stalin's later years. It lasted only a decade, ending nearly twenty years ago, but it will undoubtedly leave some lifetime mark upon the attitudes of those who were girls and boys in the years 1944–54. Obviously, it did not prevent Tereshkova and hundreds of thousands of other women of her generation from entering fields from which they are barred in other societies.

Tereshkova's autobiography provides a curious insight into the mixed picture of foreign countries with which children grow up. On the one hand, from the French Communist newspaper read in her language class, she told her mother about the life of the weavers of Lyons "for she, as a textile worker, was interested in how her comrades-in-work of far-off France lived and struggled for their rights." But otherwise "our picture of France was that of one unbroken orchard, planted with grape-vines and fruit trees, through which wandered our beloved musketeers from the novels of Dumas."

School gave her not only a foreign language, mathematics, "love for the history of Russia and respect for the history of our city of Yaroslavl," an appreciation for classical music, previously entirely unknown to her, but also the distinctly communist attitude of special sympathy for working people of other countries, and a faith in science that foreshadowed her future career. The geography teacher, after telling of great long-distance flights, said, "The time will come when a person will be able to see the entire earth at a glance as we today look at this globe." At this writing, Tereshkova is still the only woman who has done so.

It was the course in literature that affected her most as a woman. And because Russians are people of an extraordinarily romantic frame of mind, the manner in which she remembers her teacher of literature will help us understand many things that may seem unusual to us, a people of somewhat drier spirit: "Literature was taught by . . . a young woman of indescribable beauty, some thirty years of age. Erect, carrying high a head with black braids coiled into a crown, she moved smoothly and noiselessly through the classroom and brought to mind the heroines of the Russian classics. She taught us to read poetry aloud." (*All* Russians recite poetry, and virtually all try to write it.) "Her voice was pure and pleasant. Our attention never wavered when she read Tatyana's letter to Eugene Onegin." This letter, in Alexander Pushkin's novel in verse, *Eugene Onegin,* 1823, is the first time in Russian literature that a woman was allowed to declare her love for a man. Much more important, the novel founded a tradition in that literature of strong women and weak men. But it was a man who wrote it. Tereshkova goes on:

"But the poet she loved best was our fellow north-countryman Nekrasov, and his poems she favored most were those about the Russian woman. Thinking of the beauty and strength of Nekrasov's women, I was reminded of my mother, and wrote this in my diary." She chose as a diary motto a phrase from Maxim Gorky that was most prophetic: "A human being grows by reaching upward." The diary was never shown to anyone.

Upon graduating from junior high, after a total of seven years of schooling, which was the average for her generation, Tereshkova had no marketable skill. Because Soviet law prohibits employment of children under sixteen except part-time, she was unsuccessful in finding a job, entered an evening high school with people of all ages and occupations, and learned from watching them how hard it was to work and go to school at the same time. In 1954, at age seventeen, she found a job in a tire factory. As her skill improved, her earnings rose, and life became easier for the family, which the mother alone had supported all the previous fifteen years. But Tereshkova had to drop out of school, for her factory, working three shifts, rotated its workers frequently from shift to shift.

Later she changed jobs to be in the same factory as her mother. It was a big event when, in the late 1950s, the family could afford to buy a bicycle as a birthday present for her little brother. And so the family's economic status was back up to where it had been nearly twenty years earlier, when her father had a bicycle. In capsule, that is the history of the living standard of the entire Soviet people in that war and postwar period.

Tereshkova's life continued to be a very typical one. She enrolled in evening technical-high-school courses, and spent all her spare time studying. She joined the Young Communist League somewhat later than many, at age twenty. It was her activity there that brought her into a flying club, where she became an all-round sky-diver. She jumped from planes high and low, by day and by night, onto land and water, did precision jumps landing on small targets and delayed jumps opening her parachute at the last moment. She graduated from the evening school as a cotton-spinning technologist, was elected to head the Young Communist League at her factory, became a member of its statewide committee, and was admitted to the Communist party. But now, as she matured, she demonstrated the extraordinary energy, breadth of interests, and self-discipline that doubtless helped in winning a favorable reply to her application to become a cosmonaut. (She simply wrote a letter volunteering, arguing that the program should not be open to pilots alone.)

It was when the first man (Yuri Gagarin, Soviet) flew in space, in April 1961, that she wrote her letter of application. She was not only the first woman cosmonaut but the first nonpilot. Her persistence helped her over the hurdles of complex technical knowledge, and her toughness and courage saw her through the extremely grueling training. After her flight, she married a fellow cosmonaut, and had one child.

As she was whirling through space, a ten-year-old Russian girl rushed over to an American woman correspondent in Moscow to report news of a new baby sister named Valentina. "'All the girl babies born in the hospital except one are being called Valentina,' she explained."

Among those mothers there were undoubtedly residues, in one form or another, of Tereshkova's question to her mother when still a child: "Can women be engineers?" Now they had a final answer.

Chapter V
The Woman Worker

A Soviet women's magazine may contain dress patterns, beauty advice (by a female M.D. cosmetologist), recipes, information on home canning, a guide to children's reading, a story about a baby who was tranquil and responsive at nine months but became "bad" at age two, another about an eleven-year-old girl who steals small change and even bills from home to buy snacks and lend to friends. It may also offer poetry, short stories, interviews with foreign movie actresses, a front cover that is a watercolor splash of wild flowers, a back cover color photo of a three-year-old in the woods, a story on the tenth year of a school for young fathers that two thousand have attended. None of this except the last would be unusual in one of the American monthlies you can pick up in your supermarket. Nor would a feature story on women scientists with post-Ph.D. status at the Institute of Experimental Medicine of the U.S.S.R. Academy of Sciences, except for the key fact that the institute is *headed* by a woman, Dr. Natalie Bekhtereva. Here the resemblance to American women's magazines ends.

The Soviet women's magazine's very name gives status. It is called *The Woman Worker,* a term opinion-shaping media in the United States usually do their best to avoid using for the tens of millions of American women who hold paid jobs. This monthly, now fifty years old, with the largest circulation of any magazine of any kind in the U.S.S.R., deliberately took the name made famous by its predecessor of 1914–18, described in Chapter II.

Of course it is proud of Dr. Bekhtereva, and of hard-hatted, rubber-booted Alla Belashova, chief engineer in charge of construction of a copper mine, whose full-page picture in her underground domain takes page two of a fairly typical issue. But the magazine's chief concern is the woman described in its title. It tells, for example, of the women house painters who worked on the apartment buildings of a mining town that was built from the ground up in 1959. It interviews a team of seven women in their middle and late twenties who work in a refinery processing ore, and carries a picture of two of them. They are blue-collar workers, none with an education beyond technical high school, and they operate what is called a flotation machine, a chemical process in which an emulsion of oils and water is used to separate the ore from worthless rock. They speak of their work with interest, knowledge, and in a completely feminine manner: "Sometimes such good ore comes in, but we're ready to cry: we can't get all the copper out of it. You stand at the selector waiting for them to give you the result of an analysis, and your heart goes pit-a-pat. It's never the same. You're always increasing the amount of reactants added or decreasing them. Zinc has a particularly bad character. Its mood changes a hundred times a day. And so the most thoughtful are assigned to it. Zoya Lavrova here does well with it. It's interesting here. You're always testing yourself—what you can do and what you know."

In 1970 this seven-woman team was awarded a medal at the Permanent Economic Exhibition in Moscow for their display of a "polymetallic refining process employing new reactants." No miracle, just practical knowledge of their equipment, their raw ore, and the different ways in which it reacted to the various chemicals; plus concern, thought, and patient experimentation. There are individual benefits for workers who develop new methods: bonuses and often promotions. There is also the underlying assumption, which Soviet workers take for granted nowadays instead of thinking about it consciously as they did when I first went there, that the benefits from such improvements go to the country as a whole and not to a group of private investors.

The same issue of *The Woman Worker* contains a somewhat similar article about women working in the shoe industry. The quality of their product does not depend upon the caprices of nature but upon the skill and care with which the three hundred different kinds of materials that go into shoes are prepared. "If only one of them is bad, the glue or the thread, the shoe will be damaged goods." A leather cutter complains that the material she is supplied varies in thickness. "It's as though you're trying to stitch paper to cardboard." The emphasis throughout is that these are not just jobs, skilled or otherwise, at which one earns a living, but work essential to the needs, satisfaction, and happiness of others in society. As I read that article, I was reminded that when I first visited the U.S.S.R. in 1931, one could still see birchbark sandals (*lapti*) over leg wrappings; in 1959 foreigners wearing good shoes were stopped by people trying to buy them off their feet; but in 1973 no one looked at your footwear, and even styles were the same as in the West.

Millions of Soviet women work at what are called "women's industries" in this country and the U.S.S.R., which some feminists are inclined to look down upon. It is forgotten that when women first had to seek jobs in industry, it was natural for employers to hire them in fields related to things they knew something about from home: spinning, for example. Such traditions, once established in industry, form cultural patterns. If your mother or sister or girl friend has a job, and knows of an opening in the same place, you are apt to wind up working there and to feel more comfortable because there is a familiar person to show you the ropes.

The reasons for differences in status and prestige among occupations are different in the U.S.S.R. than in the United States. A generation ago, only "heavy industry"—copper refining, for example—got publicity, because the country was still in the stage of emerging from underdevelopment and the ruins of war. Today, it is able to devote approximately equal attention to the fields that directly make living more pleasant, such as consumer-goods and particularly service industries. The story on the copper town opening that issue of *The*

Woman Worker is immediately followed by a page titled, "We Are the Masters of Daily Life." There is a picture of dressmakers and a customer, and a report of a conference of activist women who work in such places and in barber shop/beauty parlors (women and men work side by side, on male or female customers indiscriminately or depending upon training and skill), hotels and service bureaus, repair shops and the like. They discussed how to improve their work: learning to sew double-knit fabrics, providing truck-mounted repair services to villages, mastering the simple courtesies of selling, easing their customers' lives by speeding minor repairs and making advance appointments.

But if any of this begins to look like a pep-talk magazine skillfully edited by a large corporation's labor and public-relations experts, an article, "Encroachment upon Job Classification Rating," removes any such notion. In both its positive and negative aspects, the content of that article is purely Soviet communist. No labor union publication in the West would have the power to handle this complaint about wage discrimination against women as *The Woman Worker* did, and regrettably few would even have been willing to take it up. In the West the law would not always have been on their side (in the U.S.S.R. there is absolutely equal pay for equal work), and women rarely would have access to the jobs the article dealt with.

A young woman worker had written: "Dear Editors: Please help me get back my job classification that they took away from me I don't know why." She had graduated from a vocational-and-technical school with the Class V rating, "pump and compressor operator." These are government schools, and the law requires that *you must get the classification and pay that goes with your diploma.* But when she went to work at a chemical plant, they persuaded her to apply for a rating "temporarily" one grade lower than the very high one the graduation examiners had awarded her.

Here the power of the press went to work. *The Woman Worker* addressed itself directly to the cabinet department in charge of the industry for which this pump and compressor operator worked. It restored her to her Class V rating, and the shop chief who had pressured her to take a lower one had an official reprimand entered in his work record. The order from the cabinet department was read to all shop and section heads at the plant, warning that nothing of the sort was to be permitted again.

The magazine editor to whom the letter had been referred was reminded of a similar instance two years earlier. She had visited a construction site, where she saw young women digging a trench with a shovel. That hadn't bothered her: she thought they were unskilled newcomers who would take upgrading courses and become plasterers, bricklayers like one woman there whose skill she admired, or a crane operator like another woman on the site. But when she had suggested to one of them that they enroll in a trade school, the worker pushed her shovel into the earth in disgust, leaned on it, and said, "We've already been through it! But they won't take girls into the bricklaying team. . . . They took Fialka in only when she put in writing that she was surrendering her Class III rating and would work as a Class II bricklayer."

The woman, Tamara Fialka, had lost twenty rubles a month by this, perhaps 15 per cent of her wage. "But the main thing is, I feel insulted," she said. The reporter was being shown around by a woman officer of the Young Communist League (Komsomol), who angrily called over the young man representing that organization in the team of bricklayers. It is the Communist organizations, party and Komsomol, that are supposed to uphold the principles of the Soviet Union, one of which is the equality of women. But he said quite calmly that he saw nothing wrong with the situation. He also had a Class III rating, but could Tamara Fialka lift a box of mortar on a par with him, or carry the scaffolding when it had to be moved? Of course not. But they would have to be paid equally if she got the Class III rating. What then would the fellows in the crew say? They had gathered round, and supported him unanimously.

The woman who had been first to speak up really laid it on the line: "That bunch of kulaks [tight-fisted employing farmers, hated by the poor—an extreme insult] have found themselves a farm laborer. They had one before Tamara, Valia Suslova. But now she's a dispatcher. She worked for three years below her proper classification! And they're called a team of communist labor!" (Teams of communist labor are supposed to be models in all ways: ethics, self-improvement, assistance to others. But in fact they sometimes win that title purely by output. And that seems to have been the case here.)

Shortly I will be quoting astounding statistics on the number of women holding skilled manual jobs and the fantastic rates of increase in such employment. Those advances were made possible partly by actions like that which immediately followed. The very next day the situation was discussed by the Communist party committee of the Petroleum Industry Construction Agency, and *that same day* a team from its personnel department checked out the facts in this crew. Tamara Fialka was given back her Class III rating. The women with the shovels were transferred to another construction "firm" in their proper capacity as bricklayers. A year later the reporter learned that Tamara had been upgraded to Class IV because of the quality of her work. The reporter's comments should be read in her own words:

And so the story of Valia Lavrova like that of Tamara Fialka had a happy ending. Yet I'd like to talk about these cases, few as they may be, in the pages of our magazine. High skill ratings for Soviet women workers are no less a matter of pride for us than the authority enjoyed by women scientists, design engineers, academicians. Perhaps I didn't feel that really deeply until I attended last year the United Nations Seminar in Moscow on the Participation of Women in the Economic Life of Their Countries. It turned out that not only in poorly developed states but even in large capitalist countries with advanced industry, there are very few women among skilled workers, never mind the technological professionals. In those countries, women are most often regarded as supplementary labor and are used in low-skilled, poorly paid work.

When you see those figures, you understand clearly perhaps for the first time that our great social gain lies not only in the fact that in the Soviet Union every third engineer is a woman, but in the fact that the percentage of women among highly skilled workers is incomparably higher [than abroad].

And that is why special significance must be attached to reports of encroachments upon job classifications of women workers even if, I repeat, they are few [emphasis mine].

It's worth thinking about why such cases still occur.

It's a mistake to think, as some do, that residues of the old attitudes toward women are manifested only in the fact that parents, say, won't let daughters go to the movies. These echoes of the past have many voices [emphasis mine].

And she urges women who have accumulated enough knowledge and skill to warrant a higher job classification to demand exams to demonstrate this and to have the higher rating entered in their work record books. The point is that Soviet law specifies that a worker must be paid at the rating shown in that book and upgrading tests must be given on demand.

Here some statistics are unavoidable. But these are exciting, if one thinks of the human beings behind the numbers. By 1959, one third of all crane, derrick, and forklift operators were women. In their mothers' generation, in 1926, only one such job in a hundred was held by a woman. Because of the tremendous expansion of industry, the actual numbers are even more striking: 1,800 in the former year, but an army of 557,400 females in the latter! Three hundred times as many. Here's another. In the earlier year, one streetcar driver in thirty was a woman, but by 1959 women were a majority of those at the controls of these vehicles, trolley buses, and subway trains. The U.S.S.R. has subways in six cities. (The *first* female subway-train "engineer" in the United States qualified in New York in 1972. In that same year it was still necessary for a California woman to sue for the right to *rent* a high-powered plough to till her garden: "men only.")

In the United States typesetting in the printing trades, its highest skill, is primarily a male job. In the Soviet Union women, who had been one eighth of the compositors in 1926, virtually took this occupation over by 1959, becoming four out of five! As operators of lathes, milling machines, and other machine tools, they rose from five thousand to nearly half a million. No one can talk of tokenism here.

More important, the most rapid *rate* of increase in the employment of women in recent years has been in the top-skilled mechanical trades. In 1926 women were only 1 per cent of machinists and machine adjusters. By 1939, that is, in the thirteen years during which the U.S.S.R. attracted most attention in the world for its unprecedented opening of new doors to women, they had risen to 4 per cent. In the next twenty years the percentage of women in such jobs climbed only to 6. But in the succeeding *five* years, 1959–64, the figure rose to 9 per cent, the fastest rate of increase at any time in Soviet history. In the United States the opposite is the case. A smaller proportion of women workers are "craftsmen and foremen" now than in 1900! In 1950, 1.5 per cent of employed women here fell into that category; in 1970, 1.1 per cent. Women's earnings in this country were 64 per cent of men's at the end of World War II, 57 per cent today, and are dropping every year in that comparison.

Not only Soviet law, but the Soviet Constitution itself, guarantees women equal pay for equal work. Yet their female industrial workers average three quarters of the pay of men. True, that's a higher proportion than here, but why isn't it equal? Only a very small part of the explanation lies in outright illegal discrimination such as is dealt with in *The Woman Worker* article. A larger part lies in the statistics just quoted. Even where they rose to number over half a million (hoisting-equipment operators) or nearly a half million (machine-tool operators), they were still, respectively, one third and a little over one fourth of the total. So the ratio of their actual earnings to men's reflects not only their continuing progress from unskilled, bottom-wage jobs to the top, but also the fact that they are not yet equal in numbers to men in the most skilled categories, above all because the unequal burden of housework (most men do not share equally in household duties) leaves great numbers of them without the time or energy to take available, free upgrading courses.

Actually, a peculiarly Soviet factor having nothing to do with sex accounts very largely for the earnings difference. Seeking to assure the country's economic independence when they began industrializing in the 1920s, the Soviet leaders stressed the "heavy" industries: coal, iron ore, steel, tractors, etc. Given these, they could produce the machinery for "light" industry: consumer goods. To attract personnel to heavy industry, wages were sharply raised there. Both sexes were welcome and vigorously encouraged to enter them. But women tended to go into consumer and service industries, for reasons that I have already discussed, and these industries paid about one-third less. Nevertheless, the gap between men's and women's earnings is less than that because so many women do work in heavy industry.

The differential applies equally to men. I remember expressing my amazement at the comparatively low salary that the manager of a large, modern knit-goods mill told me he was earning. He replied, "We are a 'light' industry."

Because of the increased emphasis today on consumer-goods and service industries, the gap between earnings in chiefly female and chiefly male spheres of employment is being eliminated by great leaps that would be impossible in a privately owned economy. Wages in hotels, public eating places, and consumer-service industries were *doubled in two years,* 1968–70, and *trebled* for those in the restaurant industry with a high school education or completion of special training for this work.* Hotel-and-restaurant-industry wages are now on a par with those of engineers, the highest-paid mass profession.† I can imagine the reaction to this information of the young divorced mothers I know in Berkeley, some college-educated, who have had to look for that kind of work to support their children (a B.A. doesn't mean you can type), and who have been asked to "stand up against the wall and let's see how you stack up" as a preliminary step to getting a restaurant job with earnings depending largely on tips. There are 4,000,000 white and 1,800,000 black female workers in hotel, restaurant, and service industries in the United States.

The largest hotel in Europe and perhaps anywhere, the new Rossiia near the Kremlin, has as assistant manager a former chambermaid, Claudia Ivaikina. Since hotels have the right to send their workers to college while keeping them on the payroll, many of them are now managed by former waiters and chambermaids.

Clerical work, too, is moving up to a par with industrial work in pay. There, as in the United States, this is largely a

---

* One reason tipping persists is because wages in these jobs were so low until so recently.

† High wages are the only way to get enough people for jobs thought of as being servant-like.

female occupation. In 1970 the Central Committee of the Government Employees Union proposed a large increase for about a million of its members, specifically on the grounds that they were earning less than industrial workers. In earlier years that argument would not have been accepted or even made, because the priority for industry was understood by all. Now, however, the government responded with an offer of a 20 per cent raise. The union rejoined that that would still not meet today's improved living standard, and an increase of 25 per cent was agreed on. The contract also included a provision that bank tellers, mainly women, get an additional week's vacation to compensate for the fatigue of counting money for which they are held personally responsible. Likewise, permissible noise in computer centers was reduced from 85 to 60 decibels, on union demand.

By contrast to the United States picture of employed wives earning only a fraction (37 per cent) as much as their husbands, a survey of Soviet working-class families showed that in one-third both spouses' earnings were just about equal, and in one-sixth the wives were the larger earners, so that in slightly more than half, *the women's earnings either equaled or exceeded their husbands'*. A letter to me from an American woman in a Moscow typing pool clothes this in flesh and blood: "I see the women in my office working very hard to fill the day's norm by 2 or 3 P.M. so that the last three hours is overtime piecework. They bring home an average of 100 rubles a month above their regular pay (100 rubles), which is no less than their husbands can scrape up in extra pay."

In order for U.S. women to achieve the present income status of Soviet women relative to men, they would first have to reverse the long-term trend here widening the male-female earning gap. Secondly, they would have to obtain a 30 per cent raise in pay for every single one of the thirty million wage-and-salary earning women, while not one of the fifty million men got an extra cent! Is that conceivable in our society?

If U.S. women got that 30 per cent raise on the *government's* initiative, as has been the case in the Soviet Union, most of them would obviously be immensely grateful, and for a long time, to such a government. This not only would advance their economic circumstances, but would give them a great deal more leeway and independence in dealing with their husbands, parents, or boy friends. In our chapter on the professions, it will be seen that the same thing has been happening in those occupations. This helps to explain why there is comparatively little dissatisfaction among Soviet women with their position relative to men. In any case, there is not enough to produce a movement for liberation by equalization of the burden at home. This must still be achieved if they are to attain full, real, and not merely legal equality. Legal equality they already possess and Western women don't, of course. (See Leo Kanowitz' book *Women and the Law*.)

The nature of female employment in the U.S.S.R. has been changing, and surveys make clear in what direction women want it to change further. It has declined since 1950 in the physically most strenuous kinds of work: lumbering, transportation (where many did unskilled loading), and the building trades. This is providing a natural answer to such disputes as that reported earlier in this chapter, in which men objected to equal pay for women unable to do the heavy lifting required in some construction work. In a major steel town a survey of workers' children showed that one third of the boys planned to go into manual trades, but *none* of the girls planned to. This, as I know from many conversations with Soviet women, is their way of easing the double load of a job and housekeeping. Also, Soviet women have already shown that they are more motivated to paraprofessional work than men, and equally motivated to professional work, judging by the actual employment figures in both cases.

Most men there would want their wives not to work if they could afford it, according to surveys. The reasons are discussed in a later chapter. However, 70 per cent of wives would work even if their husbands suddenly were to earn as much as both spouses combined do now. And the change in social values that brought this change in attitude continues to be fostered. The 1971 Large Soviet Encyclopedia, which will be the standard reference work there for a generation to come, juxtaposes pictures of equal size of Valentina Gaganova and Yuri Gagarin, who was the first human being to fly in outer space.

Gaganova, a foreperson in a spinning mill, on three consecutive occasions in a four-year period volunteered to take over lagging teams, meaning a sharp pay cut for herself each time, and bring them up to par. She is presented as a model of a communist attitude toward work, and was decorated with the same highest honor awarded to the most outstanding scientists (and dairymaids): Hero of Socialist Labor.

Women's conduct at their jobs differs from that of men, according to Soviet research. It is virtually unheard-of for a woman to show up drunk for work. Among men, that occurs often enough for it to be a matter for discussion in the press. Only one third as many Soviet women quit their jobs as do men, and when they do, it is primarily for family or personal reasons: the husband has been transferred to a different locality, or an unmarried woman wishes to move to a place where there are more single men. Very many, actually, have moved from textile towns near Moscow to Central Asia for that reason. The percentage of young women who desire to go to pioneering construction projects (a common way to get started, among Soviet youth) is considerably smaller than that of young men: 14.4 as against 21.6 per cent. But one in seven still isn't all that few. For example, there's a young couple in Khiva, a thousand-year-old oasis town not far from Afghanistan, who went there from their home in European Russia because *she* had asked to be assigned to the medical facilities of a pipeline-building project in Central Asia when she graduated from nursing school. He found a job driving a pipe-hauling tractor.

A significant difference shown by a 1970 survey is that only one third of women but one half of men wished to upgrade their work skills. This suggests that the difference in earnings will continue into the future. I have no doubt that one reason for the difference in attitude has to do with the significantly smaller amount of time the married woman has after the day's work than does her husband. Another reason, however, is that the employed woman there finds some part of her life-goal satisfaction in raising her children, while the difference in sex-role attitudes causes more men to look elsewhere for that. This point has been made to me strongly by a friend who has had exceptional contact with Soviet women, and is able to see things very much through their eyes because she, an American mechanical engineer and businesswoman who raised her own children to adulthood and maintained her marriage, shares the other values of Soviet women as well.

PROTECTIVE LEGISLATION

At this writing, ratification of the Equal Rights Amendment to the United States Constitution is stalled in the state legislatures. There are two kinds of opposition. One kind is from old-fashioned male supremacists, and women who support them. The other is from representatives of some of organized labor, whose objection is that the amendment's final wording dropped a provision that would have safeguarded protective legislation for female workers won in years of battles through state legislatures. For example, a California judge has declared unconstitutional the state law requiring overtime premium pay for women but not men. The advocates of the amendment as now worded respond that it would require extension to men of the protections won by women. But in 1974 the California State Industrial Welfare Commission used "equality" as the excuse for permitting abolition of the time and a half for overtime for *both* sexes until ten hours have been worked that day!

Soviet protective legislation is based on two realities: physical and sociological. The physical has to do chiefly with pregnancy and childbearing. It is in accord with the findings of a 1964 conference of the International Labor Organization (a labor-management-government body associated with the United Nations) that lifting heavy weights "may affect the pelvis, the abdominal muscles, and the reproductive organs and may lead to modifications and disorders of the mechanism of childbirth." There are other physical factors as well. The sociological reasoning has been very well put, in the context of the United States, in testimony on the Equal Rights Amendment by Myra Wolfgang, vice-president of the Hotel and Restaurant Employees and Bartenders International Union:

"We who want equal . . . status for women know that frequently we obtain real equality through a difference in treatment rather than identity in treatment. . . . Don't talk theory to me, tell me the practice. Don't tell me the man should help his wife. He doesn't. . . ."

The last remark applies to both countries, although men are helping more, also in both countries. The hard facts with regard to the U.S.S.R. are discussed in Chapter XI. As for the United States, one quarter of mothers of children under three are in the labor force. No one will seriously contend that it is the fathers who baby-sit in any significant numbers while the women work, or share nearly equally in child-care when the working day is done. That is the reason for the *federal* legislation in the Soviet Union, and some state legislation here, limiting overtime or the total hours women (and minors) may be asked to work. Regardless of sex, a Soviet person may not be called upon for more than four extra hours in any two consecutive days combined, or 120 hours a year (less than 2½ per week). And the local union must approve each individual management request for overtime.

Some here make the argument that if there were adequate child-care facilities for preschool children, this would somehow eliminate the need for special laws limiting overtime for women. The U.S.S.R. knows better. It has by far the world's largest and longest-established system of child-care centers, including provision for round-the-clock care for those parents who wish it. Nevertheless, cultural inequalities exist in the distribution of work within the family. Women do more of the housework either out of habit or because men simply refuse to do certain things. Law cannot reach into this situation, and therefore law is used to correct the balance as far as possible during paid working hours, a situation in which it can exercise control.

The objections of some women in the United States to protective legislation, such as the limitation on lifting of weights, which results in barring them from jobs, simply don't apply in a socialist society where systemic unemployment is unknown. If there are jobs that are really bad for women, because they bear children, there is an endless variety of others in the U.S.S.R., at all levels of skill, where they can find work. In short, a certain category of protective legislation strengthens inequality in a society that cannot provide jobs for all, but strengthens equality in one that can. Think again of Myra Wolfgang's remarks. Therefore such laws cannot be looked at in entirely the same way in the two countries.

Conversely, the demand for the extension of protective legislation to men where it does not relate to real physical or social differences is unnecessary in the Soviet Union, for it has already been done. In the United States there are some state minimum-wage laws protecting only women from notoriously low wages in a number of industries not covered by federal law, in which men are usually not employed. In the Soviet Union there is a single, universal minimum wage applicable to both sexes, with no form of employment exempted. In practice it has helped women more than men. This is because most of the lowest-paid people, i.e., those aided by the steady raising of the minimum wage, are either older women of rural origin who left school earlier than men, or women with children who still regard their jobs as a supplement to their husbands' incomes and who have not sought to upgrade their skills. Often they seek undemanding work because of the fatigue resulting from holding a job and also keeping house. This is the fault of men, and of the society for not pushing hard enough for sharing of household duties.

Fundamentally, Soviet protective legislation seeks to make it unnecessary for women to choose between family and career, in other words to enable them to be complete female human beings in modern society. The specific provisions in the Soviet Constitution of 1936 for aid to *mothers*—provisions actually carried out even before that date as far as the economy could then afford it—meant that for the first time a modern society recognized motherhood to be a social role, and not something to be coped with by the family or the mother alone. The Constitution reads:

Article 122. Women in the U.S.S.R. are accorded equal rights with men in all spheres of economic, government, cultural, political, and other public activity. The exercise of these rights is guaranteed by according women equal rights with men to jobs, in payment for their work, rest and leisure, social insurance, education, and by government protection of the interests of mother and child, government assistance to mothers of large families and to unmarried mothers, maternity leave with pay, and the provision of an extensive network of maternity homes, nurseries, and kindergartens.

That's on paper. Here's the reality. One day in 1973, of 2,100 women employed by a large Moscow department store, 296 were absent, which is fairly typical. One hundred and forty-four were out for reasons that apply equally to men. Half of these were on vacation (not less than three weeks) and half were on leave at full pay, as required by law, to prepare for exams at evening or correspondence institutions where they were enrolled. But 104 were absent for feminine reasons covered by protective legislation. Thirty-one were on maternity leave, which is sixteen weeks at previous normal average earnings (not just base wage). That period is divided, as well as the obstetrician-gynecologist can predict it, evenly between prenatal and postnatal leave. None of this is a matter of union contract. It is law, and applies to every employed woman in the U.S.S.R., with no industry or office exempted for any reason—size of staff or whatever. As a consequence, there is no bargaining or argument over whether a woman must take maternity leave, or may, or when, or for how long, or at what percentage of earnings or none at all. (The situation in the United States contrasts sharply with this. The Bell System, which is the world's largest employer with over a million workers, provides no disability benefits to pregnant women. Government has taken a similar position. The state of Washington had a law until 1973 denying unemployment insurance to pregnant women.)

In the department store we have been discussing, the other seventy-three absentees were new mothers on extended leave because they chose to be with their babies. A new mother must be given her regular annual paid vacation immediately after maternity leave if that's when she wants it, regardless of normal vacation schedules. Then, until the child is a year old, she has the right to unpaid leave with the job saved for her. Moreover, if she returns immediately at the end of the year, her seniority is regarded as uninterrupted—important for length-of-service bonuses, pension qualifications, and the like.

Finally, there were forty-eight women away on sick leave,

all on full pay from the first day of illness, as with men. However, some women on sick leave are actually out to care for a sick child or other family member needing someone in attendance. This is provided by law. While it also applies to men, the cultural reality is that in virtually all cases both sexes presently take it for granted that it is the wife who performs this function, or some other female (rather than male) family member.

It is against the law even to ask a pregnant woman or one with a child under one year of age to work overtime. Those with children up to the age of eight have the right to refuse it. This also applies to being asked to work on swing or graveyard shifts, or being sent on business trips.

Abortion is legal on demand through the twelfth week of pregnancy, later only if medically indicated. However, the female head of a huge gynecology and obstetrics center in Moscow told me that if, for example, a fifteen-year-old comes in pregnant, they always find some medical excuse to permit the abortion even if the twelfth week has passed. For abortion by choice there is a fee of five rubles, just about a day's average pay. (Other medical services for which one pays include certain voluntary dental procedures.) Abortion is free if by medical indication, at any stage of pregnancy. Soviet labor law specifies that a voluntary abortion qualifies a woman to take unpaid sick leave, thus protecting her against dismissal or disciplinary action for unauthorized absence. I'm curious how the advocates of universal extension to men of the protective laws for women, regardless of the physical facts of sex, would handle that one. If a Soviet woman's actual earnings have been below approximately one half the average monthly national wage for both sexes, she receives sick benefits from the first day of absence due to voluntary abortion; if her wage is above that amount, she is entitled to up to ten days' leave without pay. (The physician who performs the abortion decides when she is well enough to return to work. Such physicians are almost invariably women.) The reason for paid benefits in the former case is so that an individual will not feel financial pressure to return to work before she is really well enough to. Benefits are also paid if abortion is spontaneous or medically prescribed, but if the choice is voluntary, the absence from work is also regarded as voluntary.

Violations of all these provisions occur. But the courts and the press and, as we shall see, the executive branch, are on the side of the letter and spirit of the law, and of the women. In 1972 a new Soviet digest-format mass-circulation magazine called *Chelovek i zakon* (The Human Being and the Law) had an article by a female hero of World War II, concluding: "There is strict punishment for stealing government property. For stealing, for thoughtlessly and irresponsibly depriving a woman or a child of the tiniest fragment of their happiness, the guilty should be punished no less severely, for this is a stealing of that which is most basic—the right of a human being. Moreover, such an act must be regarded as stealing not personal but public property for the further reason that ancient wisdom says: to know whether a people is really happy, one must learn whether women are happy in that country."

My own experience is that Soviet people are more demanding of themselves than we would be with them if dealing with their reality. The actual atmosphere of work in a very ordinary place of employment there is quite different from here. My American friend mentioned above, who worked in a Moscow typing pool doing the routine kind of work no society has yet been able to free people from, wrote me about it as follows:

The thirty women I work with are as a whole quite average Soviet young and old women. Most of them don't know the languages they're typing and are not college graduates. On the job, I am gaining many lessons in the art of being aggressive, standing up for rights, etc. For March 8th, Women's Day, some girls brought a record player for the office party. A few days later the girls turned on the music to accompany their work. The boss, a woman, who sits in an adjoining office, came and ordered the records to be switched off because it hindered our work. The girls unanimously agreed that, to the contrary, it aided their work, and wouldn't turn it off. The boss left, but came to repeat the directive. The scene was repeated four times that morning. But the girls remained solid and to this day we still have music. The boss didn't say another word. This just could never happen in the States. I was flabbergasted at how they did it. I asked my friend why they didn't obey their boss. She answered: "No one can be a *khoziaika* [mistress of the household] at work!"

About their attitude toward the male head of the translation department. I'm not fond of this man, find him very distant and I have just a little instinctive fear of his severe manner. When I began work there and was standing in the corridor talking with some women, he passed me, said an automatic "hello" and went on. I made a face and felt inside a twang of fear. I experienced the same attitude I had toward my men bosses in America. Well, I got blank responses from the people I work with. I've never seen one girl (or man) show any signs of fear, dislike, etc., toward him. Possibly one reason is that he doesn't send any stupid memos around like our bosses. In fact he has never sent any authoritative note around, nor do I in any way feel his authority since he's never exercised it in my presence.

An article in the *Harvard Business Review* makes clear that her attitude "toward my men bosses in America" is absolutely typical (see Alfred Vogel, "Your Clerical Workers Are Ripe for Unionism," in the March 1971 issue).

Her office is so typical of Moscow that when one woman who had worked there ten years and decided she wanted a change switched to another, she found pay and working conditions so similar that she switched back in order to be with the old friends she had made on the job.

We've described a department store and an office. I got a look at an industrial-type situation when I visited a streetcar barn in Moscow in 1973, after I realized that most of the drivers of the cars passing the housing in which I lived were women. Arrangements went far beyond the requirements of protective legislation. Drivers who are mothers got Sunday as a day off, when their children would also be home. Whatever their normal shift (the cars run nineteen hours a day), they would be free by 4 P.M. on Saturday and in the earliest hours on Monday so as to pick children up from nursery or kindergarten and bring them in. This is one function Soviet husbands normally either perform or share, but I was told specifically that some of these mothers were living alone. Women with three children (apparently none had more) were given an extra day off per week, on request. They could also work split shifts, if that made things easier: four hours in the morning, five or six free, then another three or four. In such cases the husband would usually be at home during that last part of the day.

Mothers were given their vacations during the summer school vacation, so the family could leave town. Although both spouses in more than a hundred married couples worked for this car barn, it managed to schedule vacations so they could have them at the same time. The manager's words at this point were meaningful: "For us in management that takes a lot of work." The personnel manager, a woman, cut in: "It's difficult." The manager resumed: "We have got to create reasonable conditions for women. And recently our party and the government are devoting particular attention to questions pertaining to women." The management time to work out such arrangements costs money, additional staff, office equipment. When the country was poorer it could only consider mass-scale basics: preschool facilities, maternity leave, paid vacations. Now that it is more prosperous it can pay more attention to individual arrangements like scheduling those vacations to personal convenience.

When I commented that although the streetcar driver, the union leader, and the personnel manager seated around the table were female but the boss was male, the women were as eager as he to set me right. They named another car barn run by a woman and invited me to go visit her. And the personnel manager said, "The chief of our training department here is a woman, the head of our planning department is a woman, our chief accountant is a woman," and the manager picked it up: "The president of the union local is a woman, the vice-president is a woman: I'm surrounded by women!"

I pressed to find out how workers' grievances were handled, but the example given happened to pertain to a male worker in the maintenance shop. I turned to the streetcar driver, a young woman of twenty-four working there five years, who had not been at all reticent or uncomfortable in the presence of higher-ups, and asked her, "When the young women talk among themselves, what are the beefs they have that they don't bring up officially?" She answered, "Generally there aren't any. What we want, we get."

The answer was almost identical to that I'd gotten fourteen

years earlier when I had a day of conversation with two young female clothing workers traveling home for vacation on the same ship I was taking between two Soviet ports on the Black Sea. I said to them, "How do you get along with management?" And one of them replied, "He's a great guy. He does whatever we want."

But labor problems affecting women may arise outside the realm of simple human relations or even of the pressure of publicity in the press. In such cases, the Soviet equivalents of congressional investigations play a major role. Their Committee on Proposed Legislation in each house of the Supreme Soviet ("Congress") is the equivalent of our Rules Committee: the most powerful of all. In March 1973 the Proposed Legislation Committees of both their houses met jointly specifically to examine the manner in which protective legislation is actually being adhered to in industries with particularly high ratios of female workers: textiles, clothing, light consumer goods; chemicals; paper and pulp; and building materials.

In preparation for the meeting, the chairman of the committee in the House of Nationalities, Mohammed Ibrahimov, spent two weeks visiting industry in the Bashkir Autonomous Republic. He had been alerted to a situation where several shops in one enterprise were structurally unsafe. He told *Izvestia,* one of the country's largest papers, that people from the government's Building Materials Ministry had visited the place repeatedly, but no changes followed. *Finally the unions shut down the shops.* They think of this not as a strike, but rather as exercise of the provision of Soviet law that unions have the legal last word on whether working conditions are safe, and that their inspectors may order any place closed if found unsafe.

On-the-spot investigations and the discussion before the joint committee meeting led it to conclude that the industries involved were adhering to the major requirements of the law. "Exceptional attention is being given to protection of women's conditions" in the current five-year development plans of many enterprises, said Ibrahimov. In textiles, new spinning and weaving equipment greatly reducing noise levels was being installed. But the committee focused its attention on weak spots. Ibrahimov reported an incident in which a pregnant woman had asked for the transfer to lighter work to which the law entitled her, was ignored, and when she insisted was fired. "Of course, a court reinstated her at once, and compelled members of management to reimburse her in full for the days lost." (Soviet courts work extremely fast in matters that are urgent to the lives of ordinary people, somewhat like small-claims courts in the United States are supposed to.)

The joint committee meeting concluded that it was necessary to be stricter with those who tried to evade the law, and that unions themselves had to be more insistent. It also found that protective laws had to be publicized more widely, a reality of life that Westerners often ignore in thinking of the Soviet Union, which they frequently regard as some sort of social machine in which a shortcoming must reflect a fundamental fault rather than anything as simple as ignorance or lack of initiative in finding out one's rights. The American who worked in the Moscow typing pool told me that she and those women did not know that paid time off to care for a sick child was available not only to them but to their husbands. They unthinkingly projected onto the law their own traditional view that child-rearing was the woman's job. Nor did they know of the support payments available to unmarried mothers. Yet a detailed paperback on the laws protecting employed women had been published by the Soviet trade unions in 100,-000 copies a year before that. And excerpts from the most important of those laws appear in the *Trade Union Official's Handbook*, which is published in half a million copies and updated every two years. The major newspapers carry answers to readers' questions on such subjects about once a week. The women's magazines have them in every issue. But none of this can guarantee that there will be someone on every job employing women whose interests run toward reading such matters and filing them in her memory. A Soviet survey shows that knowledge of the new law on marriage, the family, and divorce is greatest among people in their fifties and almost nonexistent among those in their late teens and twenties, for whom it is most important. The middle-aged people are concerned for their children's marriages. Who on the verge of a first marriage thinks of divorce or child-support payments? Yet as a steady reader of their press I know that the prominence given that law in the daily papers during its drafting stages was far greater than we give to such matters.

In reading their manual on protective legislation, I found that, again and again, it noted that certain practices women took for granted had not actually become law until 1971, i.e., reality was *better* than the law. For example, pregnant women and nursing mothers were not actually being asked to do overtime, although it was not then illegal for them. Now it is. Women with children under a year of age, and nursing mothers, were not sent on business trips, although the law only exempted pregnant women after the fifth month.

You already know that physical jobs done by Soviet women are hardly limited to street cleaning (which in fact has sharply declined as machines have come in, but for which annual earnings equal the male-female average for work in industry). What is most interesting to me is that the Soviet Women's Committee takes pride in having been able to extend the list of jobs from which women are barred for the protective reasons stated earlier! Such a list was originally adopted in 1932, despite the fact that the country was then desperate for additional hands for industrialization and to bring women into types of work from which they had previously been barred by discrimination. Actually, the trend during these forty years has been toward increasing enforcement of the list, except during the terrible years of World War II and the following decade, when the shortage of twenty million men killed compelled slack enforcement of protective legislation.

The American stereotype of the Russian woman street cleaner comes with particular ill grace from a society in which the houseworker is still a mass phenomenon. Our million and a half in that category are barred from the benefits of unemployment insurance, Fair Employment Practices (although most are black), minimum wage, sick pay, paid holidays, paid vacations, workmen's compensation, medical or hospital plans, or even the existing women's protective laws covering overtime pay, rest periods, and meal periods. There are very few houseworkers in the Soviet Union today. A survey of five thousand families in one large city found *one* with a houseworker. An article on the Minister of Justice of the Uzbek Republic, who has five children, describes her as putting her hair in a bandanna on Saturdays to do the big weekly cleaning. Her husband, a scholar who can do much of his work at home, is the child-rearer during the week. I personally know such families there. But for those houseworkers who still exist, as well as for writers' private secretaries and personal helpers who may be hired for whatever reason, the laws instituted in earlier years, before industry provided a better choice of work for farm women come to town, still apply. Everyone doing such work must be provided by her employer, for example, with the same 112-day paid pre- and postnatal maternity leave as women in industry, offices, and the professions.

I think it is clear from this chapter that work in the Soviet Union is neither utopian nor ideal. For a majority—those who work on assembly lines, in typing pools, or even in repetitive skilled jobs—it is dull. Until technology provides the means of eliminating such work, it will be. But it is never degrading. There is no such thing as the Berkeley massage parlor that came into the news recently because the masseuses went on strike to end being "paid according to how many clothes they remove for the massage. A topless costs $15, with the masseuse getting $5; a nude goes for $20. . . ."

Chapter VI
Engineers, Lawyers, Executives, Doctors, Teachers

When I sat down to write this chapter, I had a thorough knowledge of the situation of Soviet women with respect to the professions. But regarding American women, all I really knew was the percentage they constituted in certain major fields, and that this percentage was very small in comparison with the U.S.S.R.

The articulateness and high visibility of the women's liberation movement launched here in the 1960s focused sharply on the scarcity of women in top professions. The U.S. press then magnified out of all proportion tiny token improvements in the status of women while understating all that had yet to be accomplished. As a consequence, I assumed that the role of women in prestige occupations, however limited, had to be significantly better than it had ever been, with the exception of when the men were away in World War II. It certainly seemed that the practical advantages the American woman had at home—appliances, a car for shopping and ferrying children, unlimited electricity and gas, effortless heat and water, ordering by phone (and mail), supermarket shopping, and even a husband who is somewhat more helpful than most in other countries—must somehow be reflected in her abundant placement in respected professions.

As I dug deeper and the truth emerged, I was stunned. My pride in being an American was deeply hurt when I found that the share of U.S. women in the leading professions is just about the lowest in the entire world. Fewer women physicians in proportion to males are found in the United States than anywhere but Spain, Madagascar, and South Vietnam! Very far fewer women physicians exist here than in the West European countries to which most of us trace our general culture and which we think of having left behind, such as France, England, and particularly Finland. Although the 1970s have seen a real leap in female admissions to U.S. medical schools, that will not basically change the sex ratio among physicians until today's male preponderance of doctors has retired from practice. In dentistry the situation is worse: only 3.5 per cent of the dentists in our country are women.

I knew the situation in medicine in the United States was awful: only 9 per cent of all doctors are female. But I hadn't known that it is *better* than in any other prestige professions: the female employment percentage is only 5 per cent in law, under 2 in engineering and architecture. My father, a retired civil engineer, told me that he had encountered only one woman in his nearly fifty years in that profession from graduation in New York to retirement in California in the 1960s. Except, that is, for one year in the Soviet Union under contract in the 1930s, when he had a female engineer as his immediate supervisor and others worked alongside him.

I was shocked again when I examined the tables and graphs on American higher education in *The Annals of the American Academy of Political and Social Science,* November 1972. Women hold a smaller percentage of jobs in colleges than fifty years ago. "Life with Father" is still where it's at as far as the real status of women in the class that can afford a college education is concerned. Nor can it soon get better, because women were getting a smaller percentage of doctoral degrees than in 1920, when you didn't even need one to teach in college, as you do now. The annual earnings of college-educated women in all professions in 1970 were distinctly lower relative to men's than in 1950: 44 per cent, down from 53 per cent. They earn less than a male ninth-grade dropout.

But if women have an unassailable stronghold in any profession, it is in education below the college level, right? Wrong. Men have been a majority of high school teachers since 1957. Administration has been taken away from women. More than half of all elementary school principals were female in 1950, but less than one-fifth are today! I use an exclamation point because that's how it hit me. Among high school principals women have dropped from one in sixteen to one in seventy: 222 in the entire United States. There are 11,000 in the Soviet Union, *fifty times as many*. Moreover, the trends there are exactly the opposite. The percentage of women among Soviet high school principals has doubled since 1940, and that of principals of eight-year schools is two and a half times as high as then. This has not yet brought full equality: one quarter of high school principals are female (in the United States, it is only 1.4 per cent).

Academic women are not only down, they are being put down. President Edward Levi, of the University of Chicago, expressed displeasure in 1972 over the insistence by HEW that there be proportionate representation of certain racial, ethnic, and sex minorities on faculties. But the dean of admissions at the Law School of the University of California in Berkeley, a woman, pointed out that taking that entire university system as a whole, females were so tiny a percentage of professors that there would never be equality in the forseeable future unless every single appointment were given to a woman until 1980, when growth of that university is expected to end. A year later the chancellor reported that only one fourth of new hiring had been female. The gap was growing wider.

Against this background, I am flabbergasted when I run into statements like this one, by Professor Bernice Madison: "Soviet women have achieved just about what might have happened anyway because of industrialization and urbanization." Then why do not women engineers, judges, college teachers, executives, doctors, or high school principals in any industrialized country, indeed in *any* other country, compare to their percentage and level in the U.S.S.R.? And why are the Soviet figures, high as they already are, constantly improving, while in our country, in the words of President Nixon's Economic Report of 1973, "progress [since 1910] has not been sufficient to alter the picture significantly."

Statistics are hard reading. They cannot be avoided, and

I have taken the risk of loading this chapter heavily with them because I assume it will particularly interest professionals and advanced students who want qualified facts more than impressions. Let me begin with comparisons:

There are more women engineers in the Soviet Union than *in the rest of the world combined.* They are nearly equal in number to American *male* engineers and over forty times as numerous as American female engineers.

My wife and I spent a summer Sunday watching the crowds at an international Industrial Chemistry Exhibition in Moscow's largest woodland park in 1970. Not only was half the immense attendance female, but women were a majority of the lecturers explaining processes and demonstrating technologies at the Soviet exhibits. Personnel of the Leningrad Institute of High-Molecular Compounds tell of the world-famous Western chemist who visited it and, after seeing several laboratories, asked in obvious perplexity: "And tell me, please, what are these beautiful ladies doing here?" As of 1962, 180 women in that one institute were graduate chemists or other scientists, of whom 37 were Ph.D.s and 2 had the super degree of *doktor,* which usually takes ten years of postdoctoral work plus a really creative thesis.

What this means in human terms came through when three (male) Soviet astronauts went up in a spaceship in 1971. Their biographies were published, and one got another insight into the pervasiveness of women in technical professions. The pilot's wife had a master's degree in agricultural science and works in the Ministry of Agriculture. The flight engineer's wife also had a degree in technical science, and his mother, holding a degree above our Ph.D., is research professor at the Institute of Physical Chemistry of the Academy of Sciences. The test engineer's mother and father were both railway design and construction engineers, and his wife is senior technician in a machine-tool factory.

By contrast, 99 per cent of the one thousand firms of consulting engineers in the United States reported to a survey that they employ no women engineers. In a space for comments, there were some owners who actually said: "As long as I can hire a man to do an engineering job, I won't hire a woman." "No dames ever." "I hate women." (Beatrice

Dinerman, "Women in Engineering Firms," *Consulting Engineer*, February 1969.)

Ten years ago, when England began full-fledged trade with the U.S.S.R., it sold them a complete nylon factory. The contract called for a staff of British mechanical engineers to go there and work with Russians in installing the equipment and getting production going. When these men were brought to an auditorium to meet their Soviet counterparts, with whom they would be working side by side for a considerable period, they got the shock of their lives: most of them were women. Yet England compares very favorably to the United States in the percentage of engineers who are women. That's how nearly nonexistent ours are. When the fertilizer, gas, and shipping technicians in the huge new American-Soviet long-term deals get to work, Americans will have to make the same adjustment.

Natural gas, the other major sphere of American-Soviet collaboration, begins with geological exploration and, in the area to be developed, depends entirely upon licking the extraordinary problems created by permafrost, the permanently frozen waterlogged soil of the Far North that turns into virtual quicksand from the heat emitted by the usual type of building. Women form a very high proportion of Soviet field permafrost scientists, an occupation physically as demanding as that of the astronaut. On prospecting geology, the New York *Times* recently reported from Moscow: "The hardships that geologists, many of them women, endure in the field have won admiration."

The shipment of liquefied natural gas out of the Soviet Union in special ships will obviously be through a port. In this country, longshoring is a man's world. In one of the largest Soviet ports today, Odessa, 1,200 of the 6,500 port people are women. Helen Kosheleva heads all its construction and repairs, and has 400 workers under her, of whom 360 are men. Zoya Ulyanova is in charge of all passenger-ship handling, and supervises 130 workers, chiefly men.

Sometimes Americans in the U.S.S.R. need medical care. The chances are better than two to one that the doctor will be a woman. There are more women physicians in the U.S.S.R. than *in the rest of the world combined*, even including the other communist countries. Soviet female physicians are about twice as numerous as American *male* doctors, and twenty times as many as U.S. female doctors. Incidentally, there are about two and a half times as many Soviet female engineers as physicians, a point I make because of a myth that women there are channeled into "female" professions. What makes medicine a female profession? It isn't in any other country, and the percentage of women among doctors before the Russian Revolution was about the same as in the United States today. Perhaps the idea arose out of the fact that the percentage of women is much higher among Soviet physicians than engineers, but percentages and *actual numbers* of real people are very different things. Moreover, the sex ratio is moving toward equalization in both professions. Although women are 72 per cent of the doctors, they are only 56 per cent of the medical students. Contrariwise, while women are 30 per cent of engineers, they have risen to 38 per cent of engineering students. Economic motivations play virtually no role. In the 1960s, when engineering still paid much better than medicine, a survey found that only one tenth of engineering students of both sexes had entered that field to make money. That corresponds entirely to my impressions in conversations with young people.

American women still suffer from a psychological barrier. In 1971 the chairman of the Admissions Committee of the University of California Medical School (San Francisco) said of women, "The big question is why only 15 per cent women apply." To which Dr. Barbara Arons, an eminent hematologist at Stanford replied, "They are told it's impossible, that it's not feminine."

In "advanced" Sweden the situation is not basically different: one fifth of doctors are female, and the male dean of the leading medical school said in 1973, "It is still hard for women to enter specialties like surgery and obstetrics, because of the conservatism of some chief doctors." Women are the great majority of Soviet obstetricians and are heavily represented in every branch of surgery.

What the worldwide figures mean is that the status of Soviet women in the professions is incomparably superior, absolutely in a class by itself. While readers associated with particular occupations may want to remember the statistics about doctors or engineers outnumbering those of all other countries taken together, the most meaningful single figure is internal: the U.S.S.R. is the only place where women have attained actual equality in *numbers* with men in professional employment. To be precise, they are 52 per cent of all employed college-trained people, corresponding exactly to their share of the population in the working age groups.

Soviet couples I have personally met bear this out. In one case both spouses are demographers with Ph.D.s. The husband's sister is an earthquake geologist married to a university vice-president. I have met a male physicist of Central Asian nationality whose mother was the first female chemistry professor to emerge from her people. The mother of a female biochemist I know, married to a sociologist, is herself a retired economics professor. Most of the couples I know have school-age children, but grown daughters where they exist are professional people, at least one an engineer. I can count fourteen Soviet couples of my acquaintance in which both spouses are professionals. Except for one whose grandfather's family was prominent before the Revolution, and another whose revolutionary writer father was murdered by counter-revolutionaries, every one of these spouses, of both sexes, came from the poor or even the poorest of the poor in Soviet times, including three who were peasant children, and one whose father carried loads on his back to earn his bread. It is in this up-from-poverty characteristic that these Soviet couples, particularly the women, differ from couples one might find by hard looking on American university campuses. I know one college-educated Soviet man whose wife is still working toward her degree, and one who got his degree late in life and whose wife did not attempt to. But the Western pattern of the male professional married to a housewife does not exist.

In the professions of highest prestige, women outnumber men. Studies of social psychology there show that medicine ranks first in prestige in the public mind among mass-scale professions, and in it women are seven in ten. College teaching is second in prestige ranking, civil and mechanical engineers third, secondary school teachers fourth. These four professions account for five sixths of all professional employment, and women distinctly outnumber men in the four combined. The legal profession there is very small, and accountancy is only paraprofessional in the U.S.S.R., while business administration is just beginning to appear as a profession. In the countryside, where college teaching is absent and engineering is a minor occupation, the professional stratum consists overwhelmingly of women: doctors and schoolteachers. In view of their prestige, this should have a very positive further effect in breaking down remaining attitudes of male superiority where it is strongest, in the rural population.

I have wondered at the origin of a second myth, that medicine in the Soviet Union is a low-prestige profession. Perhaps the reason is that, until the early 1970s, doctors were paid less than engineers, and to the American mind if you earn more you stand higher. However, as in the case of wage differences among Soviet workers, the spread was originally designed to encourage greater entry into the field in which more people were needed. By 1970 there were four times as many engineers as doctors. Management there consists almost entirely of engineers, and is classed in that profession. Medical and educational occupations got raises of 20 per cent across the board in 1972. Actually, differences in earnings are narrowing so rapidly in the Soviet Union that not much can be learned from that.

It is indicative of Soviet values that the shifts toward equalization of students by sex in medicine and engineering occurred before those pay raises. The same thing is true in education: men were 29 per cent of teachers but 34 per cent of teaching majors before the salary increases were announced. What all these figures say to me is that each new entering class is less motivated, in both sexes, by traditional notions that nurturing and healing is women's work, and professions involving mechanical things, mathematics, and science are men's. The same trend exists in the United States, but it is vastly outweighed by the fact that the men go where the money is, and this is assisted by admissions policies as well as parental decisions regarding financial assistance, if one child has to be favored over another.

The practical effect of the 1972 raises has been another

world first: the essential elimination of the pay differential between predominantly male and predominantly female occupations. In practice the difference, in professional and technical and research assistant paraprofessional occupations, had already been quite small. Prior to the 1970s, the number of industrial and clerical workers and salespeople with full high school educations was small. Possession of that much education meant at least paraprofessional employment, and a prominent researcher recently found that *four fifths of Soviet married women with at least high school education are earning as much or more than their husbands*. As people with at least that much education become a majority of the labor force, female real earnings will catch up with male in the population as a whole. In the age group under thirty, women are extraordinarily better educated than men: 50 per cent more college graduates! I have met a locomotive engineer on the Trans-Siberian Railroad whose wife was head of the Department of Mathematics at the University of the Far East in Vladivostok.

In December 1972 two female law students testifying before the Status of Women Commission in San Francisco said that one of the major deterrents in their profession was the lack of women lawyers to emulate. By that date, women were one third of the *judges* in the Soviet Union. More than half of those were added in the preceding twelve months, so there is definitely a trend toward equalization of numbers by sex. In this country, two judges in a hundred are female. The head of the Moscow University Law School was a woman (of Islamic origin at that) as early as thirty years ago.

While there is actual equality in numbers in full professional work, and near equality in earnings, the percentage of women at the very highest levels of achievement is far less than their share in the population. In the creative arts and professions they are only one fifth to one tenth of the members of the guildlike "unions," admission to which signifies that one actually earns a livelihood in that field and doesn't have to supplement it by outside earnings. Actual numbers are impressive: 200 female composers, 700 creative writers (fiction, plays, poetry), 2,500 architects, 2,500 painters, sculptors, graphic artists (a female sculptor, Catherine Belashova, has headed that union since 1968, although only 20 per cent of its members are women), and 4,000 women journalists.

In the first generation to grow up after the Revolution, the women of the pre-World War II era, the breakthrough was from illiteracy clear up to the mass level of professional attainment by college graduates. They climbed from the cellar to the fourth floor. From its windows they could see the penthouse, could arm their daughters psychologically for the next quantum leap. Soviet plant managers in manufacturing industry have had their training in engineering, not business administration. In the mid-1920s, before industrialization began, women were 1 per cent of the engineers. Thirty years later, in 1956, they were over a quarter of the engineers, but only 1 per cent of the industrial plant managers. But in the next *seven* years, they multiplied to 6 per cent of that executive level. Manufacturing industry is where women heads of enterprises are fewest. Include construction, agriculture, lumbering, transportation, and communications, and they are *12* per cent. Now add office administration, and the percentage of women in management doubles again, to one quarter of the total. (These data are chiefly from the last two titles in the Russian-language bibliography at the end of this book. As such figures are published to guide Soviet planners and policy-makers themselves, their reliability is generally accepted.)

In the mass profession of highest prestige, medicine, female physicians already constitute half the heads of all hospitals and clinics, and are closer to their percentage in the field (seven tenths) than in any other. These are appointive posts. In education, where principals are nominated and elected by their fellow teachers, overwhelmingly women, we have seen that only one quarter of high school principals are female. As the central health officialdom is still heavily male, the interesting fact emerges that men have appointed more female doctors as hospital heads proportionately than women have elected female school principals.

There are several significant reasons for the lower number of female administrators. The childless career woman known to us, perhaps because of the tremendous single-mindedness needed to make it in a man's world, simply doesn't exist in the Soviet Union. Researchers have found that over 99 per cent of Soviet women want to bear a child. Every Russian woman executive, official, scientist, and doctor I've ever met was a mother, nearly always with but one child, however. Sociological surveys show that for educated Russians, that is the accepted norm of family size today and for the past generation. Men there don't share equally in the burdens of the home. The time lost in personal and professional development due to the burden of child-rearing being chiefly on women means that fewer of them, native abilities being equal, qualify for higher posts. I know two Ph.D. grandmothers there who have limited their own careers in order to help their professional daughters with child-rearing. Therefore there are women of executive capacity who simply won't take such jobs, or refuse them until their children are grown, which also reduces the percentage.

Further, many women get the ego satisfaction from child-rearing that men seek in management. I was present in a home when a scientist with a completely sharing husband told her sister-in-law, also a scientist, that she had refused an executive post. The other agreed: "It's too much bother." She insists on *directing* their child's upbringing. Her husband obeys.

Soviet studies in social psychology show that women in the mass do not yet have as much confidence in other women as executives as in men. (See, for example, V. N. Shubkin, et al., "Quantitative Evaluations in Studies of Groups," *Soviet Sociology*, Fall 1968.) Also, male-chauvinist attitudes toward working under women are not entirely gone. Many Soviet women, seeing the picture only in the context of their society, would regard that as an understatement. But I cannot help seeing it in a comparative context. You will recall from an earlier chapter that in 1972 male construction workers on a tunnel in Colorado walked out when a female engineer walked in for the first time in history. In Russia the first few women began working as mine engineers and bosses forty years ago. In all fields of Soviet employment combined, there are literally millions of men working under female supervisors. But there are many more millions of women working under male direction. The chief problem of chauvinism there is no longer unwillingness to work under a woman boss, but a subtler aspect that indicates doubts about women's competence. I would say that even that is secondary today, contrary to the situation here. But one carry-over of an earlier era in the U.S.S.R. is what an older generation of Americans would call the bull-of-the-woods foreman and higher executive, in whom toughness of attitude substitutes for executive skills, knowledge of personnel relations is still lacking, and four-letter-word profanity is considered the expression of force of character. With some exceptions, both sexes in the Soviet Union accept the notion that profanity is not for women's ears (or tongue), and unsubtle men don't know how to resolve the problem. After writing these lines, I made another trip to Moscow to settle some questions in my mind, and was very shocked to learn that an extremely high government office consisting of elderly onetime workingmen and peasants "answers" this question by maintaining a 100 per cent male staff! As a couple of female management people said to my wife and me on a previous visit, "Business is conducted in a male atmosphere." They indicated that a great deal of heavy drinking is done in settling business affairs. Judging by the carafe of vodka they had ordered in the restaurant where we ran into them, they had adapted to that atmosphere. They were not drunk or even high, but Russian women did not buy hard liquor in the past and still drink very much less than men, both at home and in public. On my 1973 trip, when I mentioned to women having seen other Soviet women drunk, they literally shuddered. They took drunkenness in men for granted, without approving it.

Despite all the foregoing, there is a remarkable parallel between women's attaining given levels of education and reaching, not many years later, the comparable executive ranks. For example, in 1939 they were 13 per cent of all engineers. And twenty years later, they were 12 per cent of "managers, heads, and chiefs of enterprises" in the producing branches of the economy, the level that it takes nearly that many years to reach. They were one fifth of direct production-level forepersons, for which an engineering degree is not usually required. Let's look at one of them.

Anna Dmitrakovich has worked for twenty years at a plant making Diesel locomotives. The assembly department employs three thousand people, and the crew of sixty women crane operators she heads lifts and shifts all the subassemblies, including such delicate and critical jobs as lowering the immense engines precisely into place within the body. Before each shift begins, there's a five-minute instruction and assignment meeting. At it, she quickly learns who is out sick that day, or absent because of an ill baby, and her first job is to move people around to fill in. She personally knows how to operate any one of the various cranes, including the enormous one mounted on huge steel girders spanning the entire department and running below its ceiling on rails mounted high on each wall. This versatility gives her very high standing with the crew. She is liked because, although her managerial duties free her from the duty of directly running any equipment, she will often fill in for an absent worker and therefore make it unnecessary to call someone in ahead of time to work a double shift or lose a day off. Soviet people don't like overtime, even though it offers premium pay, and women, who bear most of the burden at home, like it least of all.

Russian style, she is called "Aunt Anna" by the younger women, and she deserves the appellation. When a worker is sick, she makes sure that the union sick-benefit delegate visits her. She is herself a member of the union executive board, and workers tell her if, for example, a retired former teammate finding it difficult to live on a pension needs a free grant-in-aid from the union. When a member of the crew, living alone, was sent home for recuperation after an operation and a special diet was prescribed, Aunt Anna organized volunteers who took turns in doing her shopping and helping in the house. As my source puts it, "and sometimes that kind of support from your comrades is no less important than medicines."

As a union official, crew chief Dmitrakovich decides which applicants shall receive union-paid accommodations at vacation resorts. Looking after working conditions is another part of her union duties, along with the chairman of its department committee. They called in a public health physician to measure gas content in the air of one shop, found it poor, and gained the rebuilding of the ventilation system. Because of the immense wall openings to permit locomotives to depart, they secured the installation of heaters, and shields for protection against drafts. They check out the forgetfulness of management up above, as when drinking fountains were removed during reconstruction work and no one ordered them put back afterward.

As foreperson of sixty workers whose direction is supposed to occupy her full working time, Anna Dmitrakovich is today a "brain" rather than a manual worker, and in fact holds a more responsible job than the mass of drawing-board engineers.

As Soviet society becomes more technological and sophisticated, it is holders of advanced degrees who move toward the top, today still largely in science, but increasingly in government and the economy as well. With a million persons employed in science and scholarship at the higher-education level, of whom 400,000 are female, this sphere, too, has its well-educated hierarchy.

While the same factors that slow women's advancement in the "practical" professions apply in the academic world, here too their progress to the higher ranks is closing the gap between them and men. For example, women were 20 per cent of associate professors in 1967 (about three times as high as in the United States), but 25 per cent of the promotions to that level the following year, and 31 per cent of those awarded Ph.D.s that year. While women were 7 per cent of those holding the degree of *doktor* in 1950, this percentage had nearly doubled to 13.3 in 1969.

The attainment of advanced degrees by Soviet women offers a particularly shocking contrast to the United States. Because the history of large-scale education to that level is much longer here, we have nearly twice as many living holders of the Ph.D. (male plus female) as does the Soviet Union. But the *percentage* of women among them here is so small (11) that the *number* of Soviet women of that level is half again as large as here: 68,000 to 44,000.

It is no accident that college teaching and associated professions in the United States are the only field of employment in which an actual majority of women is unmarried. Among factory workers only one woman in five is unmarried. The personal life of the academic gypsy is not easy, and as most women in college teaching are held to the level of lecturer, the tenure-or-out rules force them to move on. There have been many newspaper stories in recent years about married couples, one spouse of whom commutes hundreds of miles. Bonnie Wheeler teaches at Columbia, but her whole salary goes for the upkeep of her New York apartment and air commuting from Cleveland, where her husband teaches. Joan Cadden and Curt Zimansky, who are married, lived sixteen hundred miles apart for a year. Finally, he took a leave of absence so they could spend a year together. Eleanor Heider teaches psychology at the University of California, Berkeley. Her husband gave up his tenured professorship at Brown on the other seacoast to be able to live with her, but found no permanent job nearby in two years. For each of these stories of devoted couples, how many have broken up under the strain?

Soviet law specifically protects against such situations. The only "compulsion" in employment there today is that college and paraprofessional graduates are supposed to take jobs where assigned for the first three years—although the law provides no penalty for violation, and some ignore it. Most, however, are glad to be spared the problem of job-hunting, even though the planning of the economy provides positions for all. Since one is supposed to take a job where assigned (usually a choice of three is offered), the law makes the following provisions. A married couple graduating simultaneously must be given positions in the same locality. A graduating student married to someone previously graduated must be found a job in the same place as the spouse. I cannot conceive of how a go-shift-for-yourself economy could legislate this kind of humanism. And the figure of 55 per cent unmarried faculty women in this country, most of whom no one will claim are adjusted to that state or desirous of it, indicates that this is not something that works out of its own accord.

Soviet professional women are not exempt from chauvinist violations of the letter and spirit of their laws. A woman factory economist was fired in 1970 on the grounds of staff reduction, according to a clipping I have from their press. Dismissal was to occur upon completion of her regular twelve-week vacation (the job was in a pioneering area, where exceptionally favorable benefits are provided), and was to be accompanied by the required two-week severance pay. She went to court. Testimony proved that she had informed both the union and the manager that she was pregnant, thus putting her under the protective legislation prohibiting dismissal of women pregnant or with infant children. She had not been offered replacement work, even though she had offered to take a learner's job operating a power lift, but had been refused. She was reinstated in her position as economist, with pay for the thirteen days lost (Soviet courts act very quickly where people's jobs are concerned), and the court ordered the manager to reimburse the plant to that amount out of his own pocket.

The physiological consequences of being a woman can be taken advantage of by other women. I know of the head of a psychiatric clinic in Moscow who took maternity leave. Others at the clinic took advantage of her absence to write a joint letter to higher authorities complaining about her work. She was removed from her position and is now working elsewhere as an ordinary doctor.

More serious is the report of a senior professor of economics in Moscow that a high percentage of his graduate students of *both* sexes in business administration stated that they would not knowingly hire a pregnant woman, although such a refusal is against the law. They were honestly reflecting the reality that mothers of young children have a higher degree of absenteeism because women and men both regard care of an infant as the mother's responsibility. Obviously, this problem will not be solved until there is an appropriate change in sex roles.

A brilliant high school graduate was turned down for admission to law school (which starts with the freshman year in the U.S.S.R.) on the grounds that she was too young and therefore immature. When tears came to her eyes, the male dean of admissions added, "And try to get along without a hankie." Her older sister, hearing of this, took her to the president of the institution, who accepted her application. The applicant then deliberately took it back to the dean, so that he would have to process it from her hands. That was not many years ago. Today she is a particularly successful staff attorney for a manufacturing enterprise.

Even those who never encounter discrimination of any kind at school or work—the vast majority by every evidence—feel the burden of unfair distribution of work at home. But the figures on women in the professions and their advance into high academic posts, based on equality of opportunity, economic independence, and unparalleled availability of child care, make clear that the position already achieved is one that can only be envied.

Chapter VII
Arts and Sports

The best-known work of art by any woman in the world is the eighty-foot-tall stainless-steel sculpture of a female collective farmer and a male worker by Vera Mukhina, for it is reproduced as the logo at the beginning of every film made by the largest Soviet movie studio. Soviet motion pictures are shown very widely throughout the noncommunist world, despite their infrequent presentation in the United States. The original Mukhina sculpture, which crowned the Soviet pavilion at the Paris World Fair of 1937 and was seen by enormous numbers there, today towers at the entrance of Moscow's permanent fair, where it cannot be missed by the eight million annual visitors. It also gets a full-page plate to itself in the Large Soviet Encyclopedia, which is consulted by endless numbers of people in every library in the Soviet Union and by a great many persons abroad.

For some reason, Soviet female artists have been particularly outstanding in the field of sculpture. Another who gets a full-page plate in the encyclopedia, which reproduces ten of her works, is Sarah Lebedeva, who was best at portrait busts. Incidentally, the Large Soviet Encyclopedia is currently being translated and published in the United States. A number of volumes are already out, and in them one finds more articles about women of accomplishment of all countries than in any similar reference work from any other country. For example, between the French writer Gabrielle Colette and the French sculptor Marie-Ann Collot, there is the Norwegian writer Jacobine Camilla Collett, a feminist. The work of Soviet female artists in the book is not segregated into some special feminine category, nor limited solely to illustrating articles about them.

I wonder if any other general encyclopedia regards a textile designer as worthy of an article. Sulamith Zaslavskaya gets that honor (her first name identifies her as Jewish, incidentally, as does Lebedeva's). While most of her work is abstract, the piece that heads a listing of her best is a batik on cotton entitled "Women of Asia and Africa." From 1944 to 1971 she was staff artist for the Moscow silk fabrics mill called Red Rosa in honor of the Polish-Jewish revolutionary Rosa Luxembourg.

While the inclusion of artists of Jewish origin does not relate to their ethnic identity, because they do not come from any geographic political unit of the U.S.S.R. based on nationality, the encyclopedia carefully includes women representing the *cultures* of such minorities. For example, there is an article illustrated by portrait head sculptor Claudia Kobizeva, who holds the title of distinction, "People's Artist of the Moldavian Soviet Republic." Her portrait subjects are chiefly women.

Female Asian artists of the U.S.S.R. are a story of their own, because Islam forbids images in its art. So while women did and do weave magnificent rugs that are often high art, it was only with abandonment of religion that it became possible for them—as for men of those nationalities—to practice non-Islamic art forms, Third World as well as Western. As early as 1938, Kurt London, in an excellent book, *The Seven Soviet Arts,* found worthy of reproduction the amateur work of an unnamed peasant woman of the Caucasus, "Assembly of Women Workers," in appliqué on silk. He describes it well: "The emancipation of women, who formerly in these countries had had no rights at all, must obviously have made a strong impression on her mind. The aspiring artist (enjoying meanwhile a special training) employs lively colours and natural skill in a kind of folklore style."

But even at that date there were already trained female artists who had learned to work in oil, such as Mamedova, an

Azerbaijani, whose people were the first on the Soviet southern frontier to discard Islam. She, too, was moved by the change in women's status, as is indicated by the title of her painting reproduced by London: "Nomad Women Around the Loudspeaker." There is a strong resemblance between the subject matter chosen at that time by Soviet artists and that of Chinese today: the basic gains of their revolutions.

American women are hungry for material with which to prove, to themselves first of all, that females can create successfully in all fields. Let us, therefore, take note of just a few outstanding Soviet female artists. In sculpture the four already named had a great precursor. Perhaps her example explains female pre-eminence in Russian sculpture. She was Anna Golubkina, a magnificent impressionist who bracketed the pre- and postrevolutionary eras. In 1900 she was the first Russian sculptor to dare to give artistic form to so plebian a subject as a worker. In 1905 she was the first in a reactionary monarchy with the boldness to do a portrait bust of Karl Marx, and was sentenced to a year's imprisonment—she was already forty-one—for distributing Marxist party leaflets in that year's unsuccessful revolution. In 1927, ten years after the Soviet government was established, she did a bust of Leo Tolstoi that renders his surging and restless spirit better than any other portrait of him I have seen in any form.

Leah Davydova-Medene, who works in her native Latvia, is the most recent of Soviet female sculptors to gain U.S.S.R.-wide recognition. Work of hers was purchased in the mid-1960s by the Russian Museum in Leningrad, and in 1971 Soviet Encyclopedia gave her an article to herself. I was struck, while visiting an exhibit on Soviet youth which toured the United States in 1974 under the cultural exchange program, by a sculpture in sparse, clean lines—sandstone, I think—showing a farm woman seated "In the Field" with her face turned to warm in the sun. The signature in our script read "N. U. Karbovskaya." Only someone with a knowledge of Russian would realize that the *-aya* ending meant that the scupltor was female. Also interesting and thought-provoking were the signatures on two watercolors, which told the viewer who knew Russian name-endings that they were both done by a wife-and-husband team! Unfortunately, no explanation of the division of labor was offered.

The outstanding Soviet female easel-painter is Tatiana Yablonskaya, whose work has a tremendous sureness of line and color. Used by her to present predominately female themes, it says "we are women, and proud of it." The work that won her national recognition is called "Grain," done in 1949, when women were, in the most literal sense, feeding the country because there were few able-bodied men to return to the farms after World War II. The central figure is a vigorous young woman rolling up one sleeve as she is about to shovel grain on a threshing floor into sacks. Others are filling and tying the sacks and operating the stationary thresher. Barely visible in the background are a couple of male farmers loading the sacks onto trucks, and a half-grown boy leading a horse. I was struck by the fact that the reproduction of this painting in the encyclopedia was used to illustrate a nearly book-length article on the Ukrainian Soviet Republic, which is as large and as populous as France. In a word, a woman is presented as the leading painter of that republic, and the work chosen was a tribute to the role of women in raising it from the ashes of war.

On a trip to the U.S.S.R. in 1966 I bought a packet of postcard reproductions of paintings by Soviet children. Looking at it as I wrote this chapter, I found that fourteen were by girls and eight by boys. The section of children's art in the exhibit that toured the United States in 1974 was about evenly divided between the work of boys and girls. So one can assume that the future of women in Soviet arts is secure.

The best current art may be seen in fine, large color reproductions in your library's file of the monthly *Soviet Life*. Women may be identified by first names or by surnames that end in *-aya* (*-aia*), *-na*, *-va*.

Today, of course, the most influential of the arts is film. A 1972 directory, *Films by and/or About Women*, put out by the Women's History Research Center in Berkeley, tells us of the current Soviet female directors Vera Stroyeva, Julia Solntseva, Irina Poplavskaya, Larisa Shepitko, Maria Fyodorova, and Maria Slavinskaya. But turn to a serious film magazine like *Take One* and one finds only Olga Preobrazhenskaya and Esther Schub, who worked in the 1920s. No modern Soviet female directors are represented.

Poplavskaya's *Jamilya* is one of the few recent Soviet films that has won a place in the repertoire of foreign movies shown with some regularity in the United States, and which you may therefore have an opportunity to see. It combines still shots with motion film, sepia and color. A crying boy maturing as a painter suddenly sees his world anew because of an emotional crisis, and the scene before him explodes into color, color distorted by the tears in his eyes and his special perception as an artist. When a folk epic of the Asian Kirgiz (the film is by a Kirgiz author anad made in that language in that Soviet republic) is chanted at a celebration, the cutting itself follows the intoxicating rhythm of the verse and the hand motions of those reciting and singing it. Like any significant work of art, the film has many things to say. Perhaps one reason for the immense impact of the cinematic art is that, wielded by a real creator, it can say so much that more limited forms cannot. The film is set in World War II. Jamilya is married in an extremely traditional society which still has a symbolism in which older women strip her of the garments identifying her as unmarried and replace them with others that to her clearly represent a sign of submission. Her husband goes off to the war after they have married. Jamilya is not sure whether he married her mainly because she had beaten him in a traditional Kirgiz horse race. (The race is one of the visually exciting things in the film, the more so because the actors are all Kirgiz, born to the saddle.) One of the many triumphs of the film is that Poplavskaya, a Russian, produced a work absolutely lacking in the condescension that marks Western work even when it is sympathetic to minority peoples (*Little Big Man*, for example, in its treatment of native Americans).

Jamilya falls in love with a wounded soldier, also Kirgiz, invalided out of the Army and sent to her collective farm to work. But he is not a member of the same clan, and when they elope, the entire village (the women supporting the men as a matter of course) sets out to lynch them. In that day, thirty years ago (the film itself was made in the 1970s), she, by her very action of violating the marriage vow, was the only emancipated woman in her village. The improved situation among the Kirgiz today is described in Chapter IX, on ethnic minorities.

The one other feature film by a Soviet woman director shown with some frequency in the United States is Stroyeva's *Boris Godunov*. Certainly no opera has ever been filmed more successfully. While her current fame is for movies of that type (another is *The Grand Concert*), she also made *The Revolutionists*, in 1936. With her husband, director Grigorii Roshal, Stroyeva did *St. Petersburg Nights*, based on two Dostoevski stories, in 1934. In 1965 she made *We, The Russian People*, which has not been shown in the United States. She is thus the senior active female director in the world. But what American film buff knows this?

The best of the youngest female Russian film-makers is Larisa Shepitko, born in 1940. Her *Wings* is a modern tragedy of a woman flier, a hero of World War II, who becomes widowed, hardened, and loses contact with the generation of the 1960s. Shepitko was twenty-seven when the picture was made.

I personally am not fond of the work of Solntseva, whose style, judging from films of hers I have seen, is overblown. Her best film, according to those who have seen it, is *The Enchanted Desna* (1965), made from an autobiographical scenario by her late husband, the world-famous director Dovzhenko. Her *Poem of the Sea* (1958) was also from a script of his. They codirected full-length war documentaries in 1943 and 1944. Thus, two of the four women with the longest directing careers are Soviet. The others are an American and a German who, as a maker of animation films only, is not quite in the same category.

In the U.S.S.R. feature films for children are regarded as a distinct category. The first of importance was by a woman, M. Barskaya. Called *Broken Shoes*, it told of the life of the children of German workers in the years before Hitler. It was made during my family's stay in the Soviet Union in 1931–32, and my kid brother was featured in it.

Knowing that there are female directors in the U.S.S.R., you will not be surprised to find that women have distinguished themselves in other spheres of the filmic art. But it will be news that the classic *Potëmkin*, which appears in all lists of nominations for the greatest film ever made, is identified in an English-language volume of 1935, *Soviet Cinema*, as "by N. Agadjanova-Shutko," a woman. No, Sergei Eisenstein did not steal the credit. In those days the film writer was regarded in that country as more important than the director, and the scenario was hers. Because that movie is beyond argument the best ever done on a revolutionary theme, it is highly pertinent to this book that Nina Agadjanova, born in 1889 and still living in 1969, the date of my last information on her, was not a film person at all but first a fabulous revolutionary and then an early Soviet diplomat. From a merchant family and educated as a teacher, she joined the Communists at eighteen, did underground work in six cities, served five terms in prison and two of exile before she was twenty-eight, and in 1914 was managing editor of the famous magazine *The Woman Worker*. She was personally a leader both in the overthrow of the Tsar in early 1917 and in the Communist Revolution late that year, for she was a member of the St. Petersburg city committee of Lenin's party and was elected a delegate to the city soviet from its most revolutionary industrial quarter, the legendary Vyborg District. Next she was sent to do underground work in a leadership capacity in the industrial heart of the area held by the anti-Communist forces, the Donets coal-and-steel country. She served as executive secretary of the *Military* Revolutionary Committee on the westernmost front of the civil war. Agadjanova became one of the earliest Soviet diplomats, in Czechoslovakia in 1921–22 and Latvia in 1934–38, when those countries had anti-Communist governments. Finally, she taught for seven years in Moscow's famed Institute of Cinematography. So no one need ever wonder again whether *Potëmkin*, about a sailors' mutiny on a cruiser in 1905, was written with authenticity. What I want to know is when they'll make a film about Agadjanova's incredible life.

Another film universally regarded as a classic, *Fragment of an Empire* (1929), was also written by a woman, Katerina Vinogradskaya. This showed the changes that had occurred in Russia during the first dozen years after the Revolution through the eyes of a soldier who lost his memory to shell

shock in World War I and recovered it in the 1920s. Vinogradskaya also wrote the marvelous *The Great Beginning,* the
women's liberation film starring Vera Maretskaya that I describe in another chapter.

A third leading female scenarist is M. N. Smirnova, whose
best film, *The Village Teacher,* was also on a female theme
and starred Maretskaya, whom I admire not only for her acting skill but for her unwillingness to accept scripts she regards
as not worthy of her abilities.

The most remarkable puppet film ever made was the full-
length *The New Gulliver.* In 1934 the jury at the first Soviet
Cinema Festival issued a special award to Sarah Mokil for
her creation of its masks and puppets. She has descendants
in spirit in the thirty-eight children, chiefly girls, who comprise
the Florichika "company" of makers of cartoon films in the
Soviet republic of Moldavia. It made three dozen films in five
years up to 1973, which have been shown in France, Japan,
and Finland as well as in communist lands. The sole adult
is the manager, Victoria Barbe. The most talented director
is Galina Robu. She was still in high school in 1973. Florichika is one of four thousand amateur film-making groups
in the U.S.S.R. It is financed by the Ministry of Education
of the Moldavian republic.

A. N. Pakhmutova is one of the leading writers of songs
for films in the Soviet Union. Which brings us to music.

Veronika Dudarova is probably the only woman in the
world conducting a major professional symphony orchestra,
the Moscow State Symphony. She is of a small nationality,
the Ossetians, native to the Caucasus Mountains, and was
born in the oil city of Baku, where that mountain range meets
the Caspian Sea. Her people's language resembles Iranian and
that of the city in which she was born is like Turkish, so
she is in a sense a female counterpart to symphony conductor
Seiji Ozawa: a person of non-European cultural heritage who
has attained the highest level of success in an art form of
European origin. Ozawa was still a young child when Dudarova became assistant conductor of her orchestra in 1946. She
has been chief conductor since 1960.

Her biography is that of a person of the Soviet generation.
She started learning the piano at four and began attending

one of the system of free children's music schools at eight. There she won a scholarship to Leningrad Conservatory, where she still intended to become a pianist. But one day when two young composers were doing a bad job of four-hand performance at two pianos, she started conducting them, with results so good that they themselves urged her to enroll in the conducting class. Later, when one of her teachers was rehearsing the opera class in *La Bohême,* he laid down his baton and said to her, "You try it."

Her style is reported to be bravura, so much so that even in Cuba, a country of high temperament, she was described as "fiery." In private life she is married to a biologist of Jewish origin. Like every prominent Soviet woman I know, she has one child, a young man in college at this writing.

Another female conductor, Dilbar Abdurakhmanova, an Uzbek, directs the orchestra of the year-round Tashkent Theater of Opera and Ballet.

Our limited space here must go chiefly to women already professionally accomplished in music, but I would like to mention the Nakipbekova Trio, a violinist, a pianist, and cellist who are sisters aged twenty-one, twenty, and nineteen at this writing, still students at the Moscow Conservatory. The head of that extraordinarily demanding institution has already called them "a unique phenomenon, a rare talent, great industry and modesty."

If I choose them for description here it is because they, like Dudarova, are non-Europeans, being of the Mongolian race, Kazakhs by nationality, from a coal-mining town which is only forty years old. In their grandparents' generation, Kazakhs were uniformly nomads, and therefore most comparable to native Americans in our ethnic mix. They, like Dudarova, had attended one of the free music schools that are part of the standard structure of Soviet education for children everywhere. From that point on it was "only" a matter of winning the competitive entrance exams to what is certainly one of the most prestigious conservatories anywhere.

If the Nakipbekovas make it as a trio after graduation, they will not be the first Soviet female group to reach the front rank in chamber music. The Prokofiev Quartet of youthful women string players performed in New York in 1970. Three were Russian and one Jewish.

Non-Russians are a high percentage of leading Soviet female instrumental musicians. Liana Isakadze, violinist, a Georgian (Stalin's nationality, from the Caucasus), won first place in the international Sibelius Competition in Finland in 1970. Soviet and Canadian men placed second and third. Tatiana Grindenko, Ukrainian, is another outstanding young violinist. Victoria Postnikova, ethnically Russian, a pianist, recently won second prize in Britain's Leeds Piano contest, and has concertized in England.

If directing is the peak of the movie-making art, composing holds that place in music. As of 1968, two hundred Soviet women earned their livelihoods as writers of music, as indicated by their membership in the union of professional composers. There were fifteen hundred men. Obviously, most of them work in lesser forms and perhaps half are not known beyond the confines of the various ethnic musics of the Soviet peoples. In the West women have been composing serious music since the middle of the nineteenth century: Clara Wieck-Schumann, Cécile Chaminade, Agathe Backer-Grondahl. The first female composer in Russia, Julia Weisberg, although trained before the Revolution, did her most successful work afterward. She is best known for her tone poem, *The Twelve,* written in 1923 to the words of Alexander Blok's very long poem of that name, regarded as the first great verse on the theme of the Revolution. She is also known for her music to a fairy tale, *The Geese-Swans.* In style she was very much influenced by Glazunoff. Leonid Sabaneyeff wrote of her in 1927: "Weisberg is a master in the full sense of the word," but said "a certain dryness is peculiar to this creative art, a certain 'rationality' is felt back of these fine and confident strokes of her pen."

Other women have also become noted particularly for music in large forms designed to appeal to children: a vocal suite by Z. A. Levina, for example, written about 1950. E. N. Tilicheyeva is another with this interest.

When and where a truly great composer will emerge, no one can predict. But being female, and of an ethnic minority, does not stand in the way, as is clear from the case of Dilorom

Saidaminova. Born in 1944, she is just at the beginning of her career, having been admitted to the Union of Uzbek Composers in 1971. She is of the first truly modern generation of this ancient Asian people. Although her mother had already been a music student, and as a child Dilorom heard Chopin, Tchaikovsky, and Shostakovich performed at home, the family was traditional. The stringed *dutar* of the Uzbeks was always being played, the music improvised in the traditional fashion. Islamic grace is still said in her parents' home, and she, an atheist, participates out of respect.

Her first musical training was both at home, where her mother taught her, and at the Young Pioneer Palace (elaborate city-wide children's activity center) of the Uzbek capital, Tashkent, where she studied ballet. Then, as with the performers we have described, came music school, followed by the conservatory, where she studied piano and composition.

Saidaminova writes both serious and popular music, none of it identifiably Uzbek. By the time she was twenty-eight, the Philharmonic Orchestra of Uzbekistan had played her first symphony and first piano concerto. A quartet of hers was performed on radio. Her songs are in the repertoire of a popular singer. An Uzbek-language theater company has incorporated music of hers into a play for children. She has a commission from the Tashkent Opera and Ballet for a one-act ballet and is a professor at the Tashkent Conservatory. She is married—her husband is a viola player, Armenian by nationality—and they have a child.

"Good music is free of language barriers," she says. "I love the imagery of Dmitri Shostakovich, Benjamin Britten, Gustav Mahler, George Gershwin." Whatever her works may ultimately prove to be worth, the performances they have been given and the encouragement and recognition she has received can only be the envy of any young composer, of either sex, in any society.

One Russian female composer has had an opera performed: Nina Makarova, whose work, *Zoya,* was on the subject of Zoya Kosmodemyanskaya, the young woman partisan of World War II at whose statue on the Moscow-Leningrad road I saw truck drivers stop, bare their heads, and lay wild flowers as late as 1970.

There are many books in English on ballet and ballerinas
and a couple on Soviet theater. I have tried to emphasize female artists in fields rarely mentioned in our literature on the
arts. However, there is one that is constantly called to our
attention by the mass media, which cannot go unmentioned:
literature itself.

Everyone who has gone to school knows the name of Leo
Tolstoi; everyone who reads a paper knows of Solzhenitsyn.
But that's the problem: Tolstoi is pre-Soviet, Solzhenitsyn
anti-Soviet. American television and the press simply do not
publicize those Russians who find their society acceptable.
One result is that we are unaware that female novelists, short-
story writers, and playwrights exist there. Do they? The following is a partial list of those whose work is deemed worthy
of discussion in four books by American scholars—Vera Alex-
androva's *A History of Soviet Literature*, Xenia Gasiorowska's
Women in Soviet Fiction, Joshua Kunitz' *Russian Literature
Since the Revolution*, and Marc Slonim's *Soviet Russian Lit-
erature*. Those who have had books published in English are
italicized. Chiefly publication has been in England or Moscow,
so only major public and college libraries would have them:
Antonovskaya, Chertova, Davydova, *Emelyanova,* Forsh,
Gauzner, Georgievskaya, Gerasimova, Iroshnikova, Karalina,
Karavayeva, *Ketlinskaya, Kollontai* (she was a novelist, too),
Koptiayeva, Korevanova, Leonova, Levakovskaya, Lvova,
Nikolayeva, Panova, Pavlova, Rudskaya, Serebriakova,
Seyfullina, Shaginyan, Sheremeteva, Uspenskaya, Vinogradskaya, *Voinova,* Voronkova, Yakhontova, Zernova. These are
only the best-known prose writers (Soviet people would in-
dignantly make substitutions and additions to that list) of the
seven hundred female professional writers of prose, poetry,
and drama. There are also four thousand female journalists.

The circulation of books in the U.S.S.R. is unbelievable.
Passing through the ancient town of Novgorod in 1970, I
bought at the hotel newsstand a fifty-page booklet of the work
of an utterly unknown young local poet, well printed on good
paper with an attractive cover. Her name is Irina Savinova.
Publishing information on the back page, required there by
law, gave the printing as ten thousand copies, the price as

the equivalent of fifteen cents. Such publishing support for a beginning American female poet would be rare indeed.

The lives of many of the writers listed above have been truly stranger than fiction because of the history of their country. Galina Serebriakova was born to an underground revolutionist couple (her mother had given up a career as pianist) in the middle of the unsuccessful revolution of 1905. At fourteen she ran away to fight on the Communist side in the civil war and joined the party, to which she has belonged ever since. Her literary interests were shaped by this background. She is a historical novelist, her first being *Women of the French Revolution.* She has devoted most of her life to novels about Karl Marx. It is quite possibly because of her interpretation of political matters in those books that she served eighteen years in jail and exile under Stalin. But while a similar personal experience turned Solzhenitsyn against the Soviet regime, she apparently regards that injustice to herself and so many others as an aberration, and is a staunch defender of her society. It is interesting to read in succession Professor Gasiorowska's *Women in Soviet Fiction* and Serebriakova's fierce criticism of it entitled "What Mme. Gasiorowska Kept Silent About," in the American translation journal *Soviet Studies in Literature* (Summer 1972). Other women writers may also be found in the journal, notably Vera Panova, with an article, "What Prompted Me to Write *The Train*" (her most influential novel), in the Winter 1966–67 issue.

The only continuous source of English translations of creative works by Soviet female (and male) writers is a Moscow monthly, *Soviet Literature,* also in leading libraries and available inexpensively by subscription. Brief lyrical verse by female poets is widely available in translated anthologies, in my opinion because such works do not challenge the societies existing in English-speaking countries as do many of the virtually book-length poems that some of the same poets have written. Names to look for are, chronologically, Hippius (Gippius), Akhmatova, Parnok, Tsvetaeva, Odoyevtseva, Chervinskaya, Prismanova, Shkapskaya, Habias, Inber, Aliger, Bergholz, Akhmadulina, Matveyeva, Kazakova.

My first memory of the Soviet Union, when I was taken there for a year as a young boy in 1931, was standing on the Moscow River bridge near St. Basil's Cathedral and watching in amazement as eight-oared shells, four-oared, pairs, and single sculls went by beneath me in a massive parade, with *women* at the oars. Female rowing as a sport only appeared in the West in the 1950s. My 1955 set of the Britannica has not one word on women in its long article, "Rowing." But a comparable article in my earliest Soviet encyclopedia, 1952, devotes two of its four photographs illustrating techniques to women: a four and a single scull. The *World Almanac* still lists only male champions, individuals and crews, in reporting American results in its edition of *1974!* The editors seemed to find no contradiction between that and the fact that it carries a special over-all article "Women 1973: The Struggle Goes On," which they chose to place right before the sports section.

Nor did the Soviets have any hang-ups about trying out Western women's sports for men or mixed participation. During that same first visit over forty years ago, I had my only experience in what used to be called (is it still?) a Vassar canoe, which holds sixteen, I believe. In this country it was used by women only. Groups of either sex or both could paddle one on the Moscow River. As we passed the beaches for nude bathing, the American adolescents in the canoe—children of the small English-speaking colony—stood up for a better view. It capsized and the next thing I knew I was diving for my life to avoid the enormous prow coming down on me in the water.

At this writing, the first issues of the American magazine *womenSports* have appeared, and the subscription coupon reads: "Dear Editors: Sounds fantastic! Especially the part about 'couple sports' and 'Olga Korbut.'" So a tiny Soviet gymnast who was the darling of the 1972 Olympics at age seventeen has become *the* symbol of women in sports even in a magazine published by Billie Jean King. Korbut has been immortalized for a full generation of Russians by getting a paragraph of her own in the Large Soviet Encyclopedia—new editions appear only every twenty years.

These things are truly remarkable when you consider that

sports didn't exist for women in Russia until the Revolution. The U.S.S.R. has won three of the six Olympics in which it has participated and four of the five winter Olympics, and it is women who have given it the margin of victory. They have done it even though the summer Olympics have female competitions in only six sports as against twenty-four for men.

Toiling in the fields and factories does not make one an athlete. If it did, the United States would never have stood a chance, because labor is more physical in every other country than here. Yet the United States won all but one of the twelve Olympics held before the Soviet Union was admitted to competition. We won partly because of sports-mindedness, but chiefly because we had the largest system of higher education, and in the West amateur sports were initially primarily a college activity later extended to high school. We also have private athletic clubs participated in by men (specifically men) with the time and money to do this after finishing college. The military was also a reservoir to some degree, but entirely for men and primarily for officers until very recently.

In a word, the United States won because it had the most democratic access to participation in athletics and training. The Soviet Union has caught up and surpassed us (it has won three of the last five summer Olympics) despite our tremendous long-accumulated reservoir of experience and coaching skill, because it has now become even more democratic by opening access to facilities and training to young working-women and men through clubs and stadiums associated with their places of work, in which membership costs less than a dollar a year. The government, the place of employment, and the trade union cover all costs.

The New York *Times,* in a full-page study of Soviet sports, November 2, 1967, put it thus: "Before the Revolution, sports was an upper-class activity. Aristocrats hunted, rowed, raced horses and sailed at the Imperial Yacht Club. Merchants' sons skated and worked out in athletic clubs inspired by German traders. . . . In 50 years, from nearly a standing start, the Soviet Union has increased sports participation from 50,000 to 50 million. . . . There are no professional teams in the Soviet Union to skim the athletic cream, no factions struggling for control of amateur sports."

But things did not move smoothly upward in the thirty-five years between the time I had seen the female rowers and that article. World War II had intervened. The *Times* survey closed by quoting the Soviet national track-and-field coach: "'We had many problems. We didn't have enough food and tens of millions were living in holes in the ground. Houses come before swimming pools and potato fields before tennis courts. Now we are building those tennis courts and those swimming pools. It's as simple as that. And someday we might build a golf course. Why not?'"

Yet by the date of that quote they had won two Olympics. And with their background of war devastation in mind, there can be only one explanation for the pre-eminence of Soviet women among female athletes worldwide: it reflects a degree of equality for women that none of the noncommunist countries has yet attained. In 1972 there were 15,700,000 Soviet women participating regularly in athletic activities, or a little over one third of the total for both sexes. Of this number, 37,800 women were professionally concerned with sports as physical education teachers or coaches and trainers. Girls have equal access with boys to the thousands of free after-hours sports schools at which they begin their training. There have been no breakdowns of Soviet athletic expenditures by sex because there is no sense of the discrimination against women that has been the cause of such studies being made here. Billie Jean King's complaint to a U. S. Senate hearing that "women's sports programs in the public schools receive only about 1 per cent of what men's programs receive" would be greeted with shock by Soviet athletes. As a matter of fact, they'd probably wonder how American women do as well as they do in international competition when they must emerge from such underfinanced preparation.

Official intersex competition is not widespread in Soviet sports, but where it exists there are no hidden bars. None of the three dozen female jockeys in the United States has yet ridden in the Kentucky Derby, much less won it. The equivalent of that race in interest and prestige in the U.S.S.R. is the Trotting Derby. The first woman to win it was Maria Burda, in 1964. Her career record was over five hundred victories, the competition being primarily male. Moreover, she struck a direct blow for women in that sport internationally by competing in Copenhagen, after which the Danish trotting society finally admitted women to competition. In 1972 the U.S.S.R. Derby was again won by a woman, Alla Polzunova. On International Women's Day in 1973 women riders celebrated by a race for themselves at the Moscow track.

When Helena Novikova, 1968 Olympic fencing champion, chose to enter a men's tournament in the Soviet Union in 1970, no issue was made of it—but she won only half her matches.

Women wrestle in the Soviet Union, but only in its version of judo, called sambo—appropriately a condensation of the Russian words for self-defense—in which lightning speed, agility, and precision of movement are the determining factors.

Soccer, on the other hand, is barred to women as being "too rough," although about a million women in the rest of the world, including East European countries, play it. Yet when the International Gymnastics Federation ruled in 1973 that Olga Korbut's double backward somersault on the balance beam was "too dangerous" and henceforth barred, she was backed by the Soviet authorities. They also support women's basketball, in which the Russians are the world champions, although there is a good deal of body contact there if only in fouls. The soccer decision would seem to me to represent a remnant or resurgence of the "it's unladylike" attitude and spoils an otherwise excellent record. For example, a Soviet sports pamphlet of 1965, not devoted to women, points out in passing that their Olympic sprint and swimming times and high-jump heights already surpass those of men recorded at the first modern Olympics at the end of the last century, although no one claims that genetic changes have occurred in either sex during that period.

On an international scale, the Soviet emphasis on female sports has helped women elsewhere, not only by enabling them to point to the Soviet example (as with the Danish jockeys) and by playing upon national pride in urging that their countries be given a chance to do as well, but also by direct Soviet demands of the International Olympic Committee, starting in 1957, for inclusion of more women's sports in the program.

The best aspect of the Soviet attitude toward sports is its emphasis on mass participation for the sake of health. In the large city of Gorky, for example, a winter family "Olympics" was held over a three-month period, with mother, father, and primary school children participating in cross-country skiing, each against members of their own age group and sex, for the title "most sports-minded family in town."

In the late 1950s the Communist party itself launched a drive to enlist people over forty in physical-culture groups. Obviously no Olympic champions were expected from among them. By 1961, over four million in that age category were engaged in sport. Moscow's Central Stadium had a hundred groups of women—housewives, workers, and pensioners between the ages of forty-five and seventy—meeting twice weekly under guided supervision for appropriate gymnastics, swimming, and other sports.

From the standpoint of women's equality, perhaps the single most satisfying aspect of the Soviet attitude toward sports is that its press, whether reporting internal or international competitions, gives absolutely equal billing to female and male events. If the best performance at a meet relative to previous records is achieved by a woman, that quite naturally gets the headline and the lead. It is unheard-of in Russia to omit detailed listing of female event results when listing male, or to put the latter in bold type and the former in ordinary, as often happens in American reportage.

As this book went to press 13,000 people packed San Francisco's Cow Palace for an exhibition sold out a month in advance by the Soviet gymnastics team, led by Olga Korbut.

Chapter VIII
Down on the Farm

> And so now the war has ended,
> I alone remain alive.
> I'm the horse, the ox, the housewife,
> And the man around the farm.
> —Popular Russian Women's Folk Jingle, 1950s.

In a Soviet film of the 1970s, *The Right Person for the Job*, a young, college-educated man who rides a motorbike is a newly elected collective-farm chairman. He goes to a team loading grain sacks and orders its one woman member away with the words: "Don't let me ever catch you around here again!" because he feels the work is too heavy.

I saw the film in the company of a number of Moscow University faculty members, specialists in the teaching of Russian. Virtually all were female. Some were of rural birth. Many had worked on farms as students or during World War II. I told them American women's liberationists would be horrified by that scene, and I shared that feeling. The Russians could not understand that at all. To them, the collective-farm chairman was applying the recent policy of relieving women of heavy physical labor. They heartily approved; women had worked too hard for too long. They took for granted that she would be given other work. As a member of a co-operative, she had to be. They shrugged off his manner as secondary.

In a wonderful Russian film of the same period, *The Stepmother,* the wife of a farm-machinery operator has to shove toys into the hands of her husband and tell him, *"You* give them to her." She is desperately seeking ways for both of them to win the confidence of his withdrawn daughter-out-of-wedlock whose mother had just died in a remote part of the country. To him, his responsibility was fulfilled by his unilateral decision to take the child for upbringing by the woman he married after he fathered that girl. That was just as "natural" to him as that his wife should raise their own son. His job, as he saw it, was to provide the children with nothing more than a roof, food, and clothing as best he could.

In the same film the wife's mother, an old-time peasant type, constantly berates her daughter for accepting the child. The mother-in-law moves out, although her presence and help in the household had previously been taken for granted by all, including herself. Her objection is not at all based on her son-in-law's attitude toward child-rearing. She is against an "outsider" being taken into the family, and she knows the traditional village attitude that a stepmother is evil to a stepchild as a matter of course. Her daughter is now seen in that role. Even the young schoolteacher coming to visit the home of her new pupil (concern for home conditions is a job responsibility of the Soviet teacher) glares balefully at the stepmother and utters some remark about her working the girl too hard around the house. Yet the facts are exactly the opposite, and not even the silent child herself has made such a charge. The mother-in-law's views of right and wrong are so hidebound that she actually threatens to go to the local head of the Communist party over the injustice, in her eyes, of her daughter being burdened by a child not hers and being put in the position of stepmother. No one takes that threat seriously, but it's too bad we are not shown how the local leader would have dealt with that problem.

A film cannot be taken as representing universal sociological truth in the society it depicts, but neither would it have gained wide audience acceptance, as this one did, if it did not represent a reality general enough for the audience to relate to. Moreover, if regarded as giving an unfair picture of

Soviet life, the government review board would have forbidden its showing.

In old Russia a country woman with a job was a contradiction in terms. That situation was described exactly in the 1960s by anthropologist Raphael Patai, of the Herzl Institute, New York, writing about other countries today: "If a girl in an old-fashioned Indian or Japanese village does not want to live out her life as determined by the age-old local mores, what can she do? In the village, there is no alternative way of life which she could adopt. . . . When the position of women in all Afro-Asia will be one of equality with the men, in the sense, at least, in which this has been achieved in several countries of the modern Western world, it will signify a transformation of human life unparalleled in magnitude in all history." (Raphael Patai, ed., *Women in the Modern World* [New York: Free Press, 1967], p. 17.)

That transformation has occurred in the U.S.S.R., and a hitchhiker we picked up in 1970 exemplified it. Before this woman of about thirty-five got into the car she asked if we minded what she was carrying with her, opened a huge shopping bag, and showed us a baby pig. It was sick, and she was taking it to the veterinarian. It turned out that she was the director of the village community center, which had nightly movies, offered lectures twice a month, and did group work with children.

In the U.S.S.R. a woman can stay in the village and be other than a peasant wife, "long on hair and short on brains" as a Russian folk saying put it. That phrase was accurate, not because women's intelligence was inferior but because, in the words of Pankratova, a female Soviet family sociologist, "It is not surprising that the attitude toward women—limited in their legal rights, never having traveled anywhere, never having seen anything, in most cases unable even to sign their names—was one of contempt."

She wrote this by way of contrast to what she found in a study of six thousand Soviet rural women in the late 1960s in four provinces of Central Russia, one on the north slope of the Caucasus Mountains, and one ethnic minority area, the Tatar Republic on the Volga River. A famous Soviet study of the 1920s, known to sociologists throughout the world, had found that in a village fairly privileged because it was near a railroad, only 1 of 144 women had a nonmanual occupation: the schoolmarm. There was also a seamstress, a maker of the birchbark sandals peasants then wore, and two who worked for the railroad. All the rest were peasant wives who, in the words of Professor Xenia Gasiorowska of the University of Wisconsin, "proved exceedingly difficult to liberate." They were angry when one of their own would find value in cleanliness or take part in politics, never mind having an illegitimate and unbaptized baby. As Pankratova put it, women over thirty-five resisted attending classes to eliminate illiteracy, and the younger were "too shy to."

Yet in that typical area today Pankratova found that 40 per cent—two in five—of the younger rural women live by nonmanual work, generally requiring at least high school education. The rapidity of progress is phenomenal, for *no* woman over twenty-seven years old had a mother with a high school diploma. The mothers of the youngest group of working age, sixteen to twenty-seven, averaged less than four years' schooling. Yet those mothers are generally under fifty, and many are under forty. So the revolution in rural women's real, as distinct from legal, status came in the very recent past, contrary to statements by Germaine Greer and others that Soviet women have been shoved back down after some mythical utopia in the early post revolutionary years.

A sociological volume written by another Soviet woman, Zinaida Monich, reveals an extraordinary achievement in the light of Patai's statement above that nontraditional life for a peasant woman would be "a transformation . . . unparalleled . . . in all history." Females are 30 per cent of professionals and paraprofessionals having to do with the production of tangibles (farm products) in the countryside: crop agriculturists, animal husbandry experts, economists and accountants, engineers at lumber mills. They are a third of all rural administrators, who include local government officials, co-op store managers, heads of post and telegraph offices, leaders of community centers, school principals, hospital directors. But they are three quarters of the physicians and teachers. What is most important in view of the tremendous gap that once existed, and still does in many aspects, between rural and urban life

Down on the Farm 163

in Russia is that these figures are not much lower than those in town. Also, they are reasonably typical of the U.S.S.R. as a whole.

Monich is not satisfied with these achievements. She points out that rural professional and paraprofessional women are *better* educated than men at all levels: more are college graduates or have some college education, more are graduates from paraprofessional schools, more are high school graduates. In terms of the very recent past of the peasant woman, illiterate till well after the Revolution, that is mind-blowing. But Monich is concerned with the present and the future. She writes: "It would be logical to presume that the greater number of women among the rural professional and paraprofessional population, and the fact that they have a higher level of education than men, would make for a numerical dominance of women among the managerial group." Then she points out that in fact men in such posts outnumber women two to one. (Another source says that women head 15 per cent of rural local branches of the Communist party, and 20 per cent of rural governments.) Monich concludes:

> On the one hand, there is evident a clear underestimation of the capacities and potentials of women as executive personnel. This is manifested in the fact that when candidates are advanced for posts of leadership, men are a majority although there are no adequate grounds for this. On the other hand, the fact that women are burdened with two jobs (the other being their work in the home) creates certain difficulties in their performance of functions of management . . . [which deprive people of much of their free time]. Therefore it often happens that women themselves do not agree to being promoted to posts of leadership.
>
> The way out must be sought primarily in easing women's work in the home, in abolishing the residues of their inequality in life off the job, and in creating conditions enabling them to reveal all their creative capacities and leadership talents.

But a good sign for the future is that the high figures for women in prestige occupations in the countryside are accounted for chiefly by the very youngest women, under thirty years of age, who vastly outnumber men in such jobs. Middle-aged rural women are chiefly uneducated and do unskilled work on the farms to which they belong (private farms are almost nonexistent). So the revolution in women's occupational status in the countryside *has actually taken place in the past ten years.* If these younger women find husbands who meet their cultural standards, they remain in the villages. There they can be expected to increase in percentage in posts of higher rural authority as they gain experience and no longer feel that their children need all their spare time. Sociological studies have found that such women tend to marry equipment operators, whom these same studies show to be the most progressive and open-minded social category of rural people in all respects. The equipment operator represents modernity in the village, while the male farm-office employee tends to be as routinized in his mentality as in his work, even though better educated than the man on the harvester combine, truck, or tractor.

I remember asking to see the interior of a home on a collective farm in Soviet Estonia. My guide knocked on a door. The wife ran the farm's testing laboratory, and the husband was a truck driver. Incidentally, that home would have met the standards of an American farm or working-class home-owning family today in all respects except that there was no car. But Estonia is the richest republic of the U.S.S.R. Most farm homes elsewhere in the Soviet Union are like those in the United States forty years ago, except that American homes even then were much larger and the families almost universally had an automobile. On the other hand, Soviet rural people live in villages, and for the most part have always done so, so many things can be done on foot. They go out to the land to work in trucks provided by the farm, if lucky. Otherwise, there is an hour's walk each way, on the average, in planting and harvest time. That's one reason why women work chiefly in the dairy barns (very highly paid), pig pens, and offices, or right in the village, and men run the farm machines. The women want to be close to their children, and that they will do the cooking is taken for granted by both sexes.

The most important improvement in the country home is that every cottage now has electricity (the last ones, in the most remote places, received it only in the past five years); every village has a general store and a food store (the old village had absolutely nothing but a saloon and perhaps a church); there are seasonal day-care centers for five million rural children during the planting and harvesting months, including nearly three million of school age; there are *year-round* child-care centers for two million preschool children in the countryside alone; and there are schools for all, a library in every rural community, and a community center having at least movies and dances and often offering a variety of activities, in all but the smallest hamlets.

The results were most neatly summed up by a farm woman in her thirties hitchhiking home from the county seat who told us, "Now I can relax in the evening and watch television with my husband." She no longer has to bake bread. She doesn't have to depend entirely upon her own canning and preserving for out-of-season foods, although she still does a great deal of that, partly to save money to buy things like TV. She isn't forced to keep a cow for milk, although most still do, for the same reason (every rural family is given a large lot behind its home for a household garden, and it is the woman who does most of the work raising its vegetables and fruits, caring for the chickens, a pig and its litter, and the cow). It is chiefly the professional and paraprofessional women who dispense with the cow and pig, although chickens and a garden are pretty universal; but it is also *their* husbands, whether of the same occupational category or equipment operators, who are most enlightened and help in other than the traditional male functions of home repair and firewood hauling and chopping.

Yet even older women have developed new values. In a two-week driving tour taken deliberately to pick up hitchhikers and get material for this book, one of our passengers was a peasant grandmother. (Young people, proud to have a ruble in their pockets, generally wait for the infrequent country buses; older ones, with smaller incomes or memories of hard times, hitchhike!) She told us that her son lives in the newly opened farmlands of Asian Kazakhstan, two thousand miles to the east. He has a brick house with conveniences, while she lives in the usual peasant log cabin with all facilities outside. But she doesn't approve of the life out there. There are no fruit trees on that open prairie. More important, her son's small community has only a four-year primary school, so her grandchild, who is beyond that level, has to live in a boarding school miles away, as the unpaved roads don't permit busing. She herself could hardly have had over four years of schooling, but she had lived to a time when junior high school education is available in long-populated country areas close enough so children can live at home, and the notion that an eleven-year-old had to be in a boarding school didn't appeal to her.

But washing clothes still means pounding them with a board while bent over the bank of a lake or stream in summer, or hauling water home in buckets over a yoke for boiling and scrubbing in the old washtub in winter. Carrying the water is still chiefly women's work, although I have seen many young boys now doing it, and at least enough men, from youthful to elderly, to be noticeable.

When I was first in the Soviet Union over forty years ago, the peasant woman made all the family's clothes from the skin out, except for birchbark sandals that were bought or leather boots for those rare individuals who could afford them. It was all done by hand, and she often spun the flax. Today at most she sews dresses, on a sewing machine and from purchased cloth, using patterns in magazines. But sewing machine sales are steadily dropping because of general availability of ready-to-wear clothing. She may also knit if she chooses. Her husband repairs the leather footwear; there are no rural shoemakers and, again, no car to go to the county seat to get it done, although bus service is spreading.

Yet another of our hitchhikers said, "Our children wear store-bought clothes and are as well dressed as in Moscow."

Having a high school education and holding a job outside the peasant cottage are not all that liberation requires, as Western women know only too well, despite the "unparalleled transformation" these changes signify. What do these women earn *relative to men*? What about the earnings of those who continue to do physical rather than mental work? Are they still tied down by large broods of children? Are their opinions respected, in the family and outside? Do they hold jobs just for bread and butter—and TVs—or for higher values? Do their husbands deign to do "women's work" in the home and on the farm?

Pankratova's cited survey of six thousand women in Central Russia, the Tatar Republic, and the North Caucasus, at the close of the 1960s, found answers so positive as to have no parallel on earth, but in almost every case the situation was far from perfect. In a word, the Soviet solution to the problem of women's inequality has proved itself, but complete equality has not yet come. Here are the figures:

In terms of earnings, among married rural Tatar women, from an Islamic culture that held them in the most severe bondage, one in five is now the major earner in her family! And this includes the older semiliterate age groups. Among women of Russian nationality, from one-quarter to *one-half* are the major earners in their families depending upon province! The latter are in the dairy-farming areas, where older, undereducated women are able to earn as much as or more than a skilled worker in town of either sex, more than office workers and even low-paid professionals. This is similar to the American pattern of the construction worker of low education earning more than the female college graduate, but there the sex pattern is reversed.

In a sense, men are paying the penalty of unwillingness to do "women's work." This is illustrated in Vasilii Belov's *An Ordinary Occurrence,* a very moving novel published in 1966 and describing life only a decade earlier. The wife of a good-hearted peasant who loves her works herself to death by going back to her dairy-barn job too soon after she has borne their ninth daughter. The reason she does this is that they need extra money to reimburse the collective farm for damage he did when drunk.

"Ivan had said to her, don't go, rest up some, but no, she hurried over." A Soviet reviewer summarizes what happens: "Katerina wouldn't listen . . . and took on yet another job, caring after calves, and then the idea came into her head that Ivan . . . could take her place, but she immediately realized that a *muzhik* could not work in the barnyard ('the whole village would laugh at him')."

In that case, she paid the price, with her life, of her unwillingness to buck traditional attitudes held by women and men alike. But historically it was at that very time that the government decided that it was now possible to encourage an increase in production of milk and its products, and meat (pork). It raised very high the pay to barnyard and dairy workers. Men wouldn't take the jobs and women did (men remained in their traditional field work).

Katerina, the heroine of the novel, died partly because she had had too many children. She had had them because of another tradition: that it took a male heir to feed aged parents. Although she and Ivan kept trying, only girls were born. A decade later, Pankratova found in her study that that tradition was absolutely gone. Married farm women doing physical jobs averaged just under two children, and those doing nonmanual labor averaged one and a half!

Why do rural women hold jobs outside the family? Asked whether they would quit and confine themselves to homemaking, the children, and the garden plot if they could afford to economically, two thirds said no. Even among the unskilled, one quarter said they work *chiefly* for the respect it brings among people in general and in the family. Most important, male attitudes match female. Asked whether they would want their wives to quit their paid jobs and stay home if the family could afford it, no less than two thirds of men in any social category said no. This contrasts favorably with urban findings.

In the old rural family, the head of the household, who was its oldest male, made all decisions. The woman was not even consulted. Today the majority of wives say that nothing in the family is settled without them. There is still a minority who say husbands *sometimes* act on their own, but after joint discussion, and only among unskilled women is it possible to find *any* who say they are not consulted.

Outside the family, a large minority of women doing physical work believe their opinions influence the decisions taken by their farms. Of those doing office work, from secretaries to physicians, at least three quarters think so. They have not only self-respect but the respect of men. This is measured not only by joint decision-making in the family but by male participation in housework. One can already find households in which men do *most* of the housework: between 5 and 10 per cent, depending upon the province. This is also better than in town. It happens where wives are activists or taking courses or, of course, where they are physically unable to do the housework. Including these, between one fifth and one third of the men do at least their full share. Miraculous, in the light of the attitudes of just two generations ago. But turn the figures around, and one sees the distance that still has to be covered: families in which the wife does the bulk of the homemaking, in addition to holding an outside job, outnumber two to one those in which it is equally shared plus those in which the man does most. Another improvement is that in only one family in twenty does Grandma bear the chief burden of keeping house. The fact that women who have worked a set minimum of years outside the home are entitled to pension at age fifty-five assures that Grandma is not required to earn her keep by carrying a burden beyond her strength: she can walk out. So pensions for farm women and men, introduced in 1964, are also a factor in women's liberation. But the older woman is not turned out: sociologists find that only one rural family in a thousand wishes to institutionalize aged parents.

Perhaps the most remarkable psychological measure of how things have changed comes in answering the question as to who is head of the family. In the past it was "naturally" the householder, who was "naturally" the eldest male. Today only a fifth to a third of women say the man is, but even most of these can't explain why. Only a tiny minority of them accept patriarchal and property-centered values, saying it's because the man is older or because he is the homeowner of record in the given case. The fact that the husband still earns more in most cases doesn't cut much ice. The reason is a fundamental change among rural people in attitude toward education as a value. In the past it was rated low: where would it get you? I know a Soviet woman of thirty-four, a Ph.D. with the rank of senior research associate, which means that she makes her own decisions on what research to do. Her grandparents were peasants. Her mother, manager of a government retail shop in a small city, still doesn't understand why her daughter felt she had to go to college.

In 1970 we gave a ride to a rural mother and her high-school-senior daughter, one of seven children. The mother told us what all the others did and then, with great pride, announced this girl would be the first person in their family to go to college. Education is a value in itself. So farm-equipment operators, who are almost exclusively male, respect wives who earn less than they, Pankratova found, if the wives have more education, and that situation is the *rule* among rural people under thirty-five.

Despite the prestige attached to education in the country-side, it is agreed that division of work by sex helps maintain old attitudes. The remaining stronghold of such division is the operation of farm machinery, in which the percentage of women is negligible. One reason is physical. To change this, the Cabinet issued a detailed order in 1969 both to remove real obstacles and to offer women an incentive. In the latter category, women would get five and a half weeks' paid vacation, or a week more than men. Their output quotas would be 10 per cent less than men's. Starting in 1970, tractors were to be built with spring-mounted seats adjustable for height and weight, cabs enclosed against the weather, shock absorbers, and mufflers.

We take most of that for granted, but in a country whose gross national product is only one half of ours, it was eco-nomically impossible until then. Women were to be given priority in assignment to farm machinery with these facilities, plus power steering, power starting (ever try hand-cranking a car engine?), and other "options." Federal agencies and the cabinets of the republics comprising the U.S.S.R. were ordered to recruit women as drivers for trucks of two and a half tons or less, or those with power steering and automatic transmis-sions. Three-year training schools were to be established. The point is that there are no service stations to speak of, and every truck, tractor, or combine driver is his or her own me-chanic. As a philosopher put it to me in arguing against "un-thinking" equality: should his wife be required to hoist the rear axle out of their car under circumstances in which owners do their own repairs? If those schools have done their jobs, the results should be showing up in farm-equipment job sta-tistics by sex in the years immediately ahead.

Another device, very important in Soviet psychology, has been used to raise the prestige of farm women. Partly because

World War II had such an overwhelming impact upon the country, and partly because the heritage of low education made visual symbolism more important than it is for us, the awarding of medals for outstanding jobs of work is very meaningful there. It is no accident that the design of the highest medal for civilian effort, Hero of Socialist Labor, is identical with the highest for military valor, Hero of the Soviet Union: a gold star. Brezhnev wears two of them. No Soviet male looks down upon a woman with that emblem, and there are now five thousand women wearing them. They have gone chiefly to farm women, mainly to those getting outstanding yields in hard physical work: sugar-beet raising, which has not yet been mechanized much; dairy farming, in which milking, bringing water, and removal of manure still involve much hand labor; tea picking.

When the Third U.S.S.R.-wide Congress of Collective Farmers was held in 1969, 40 per cent of the delegates were women, and twenty-two women were named to the permanent national body established. It can safely be said that agriculture in the U.S.S.R. is a field in which women have most successfully asserted themselves.

Chapter IX
Blacks, Browns, Orientals, and Jews

In 1972 black Congresswoman Shirley Chisholm did the unthinkable: she put herself forward as a nominee for President. But did anyone really believe that she stood a chance, even in that most liberal of Democratic conventions? Or in the November election, if by some miracle she got the nomination?

A woman, Yadgar Nasriddinova, *is* the head of the body corresponding at least in the passing of laws to the U. S. Senate: the Council of Nationalities of the Supreme Soviet ("Congress"). Chisholm's autobiography is an inspiration; Nasriddinova's is the fulfillment of any minority woman's wildest fantasy—a story as remarkable as having a black slave woman such as Sojourner Truth or Harriet Tubman become the presiding officer of the U. S. Senate.

Nasriddinova is an Uzbek from Central Asia, one of the thirty million Soviet people of Islamic heritage. Most of them speak languages like Turkish, which has no resemblance to Russian. Chiefly they look like Chicanos, some like American Indians, and Oriental features are fairly common. There is no hostile racial feeling between those who do and do not look Oriental, but purely tribal bitterness and warfare used to be more the rule than the exception, and this was encouraged by the Russian rulers in prerevolutionary times, much as blacks and Chicanos or Puerto Ricans are played off against each other in the United States today.

Nasriddinova's people rebelled against their colonial bondage to Russia in 1885 and three more times in the next thirteen years. In 1916, during World War I, when the Russian Tsar tried to draft them into labor battalions, the whole area burst into flames. At least seven thousand Russians were killed, but the rebels killed even more native collaborators than Russian officials. Just as Russian women workers demonstrating for bread in the capital city in early 1917 gave the immediate impetus to the overthrow of the Tsar, the immense Central Asian uprising a few months earlier had undermined the monarchy in its outermost reaches.

Within the cultures of Central Asia and the Caucasus, the women were slaves. Perhaps it would not have been quite as bad if they had been slaves of the Russians, for they might then have had respect among the men of their own people, as did the great black women organizers on the Underground Railroad and in the early feminist movement. But an Uzbek "General" Tubman, as she would have been called, is unthinkable. The men of her own people would not have laughed at her, they would have killed her, as they did kill, years *after* the Revolution, hundreds of the first women who wished to share with them its benefits of national and social liberation. The killing was stopped by the overwhelmingly male central government of the U.S.S.R. And whatever one thinks of capital punishment, it was stopped by executing the men who did the killing and educating the rest. This happened well within the memories of people today alive and vigorous: forty-five years ago. The very first Uzbek professional actress, whose amateur predecessor was killed by her own brother for unveiling her face, is still on the stage and only in her sixties. Thus it is preposterous to expect that the attitudes and practices over which this revolutionary struggle raged are entirely nonexistent today. That is what makes Nasriddinova, and the tens of thousands of Soviet Asian women currently elected to village and higher government, so noteworthy.

Once again, before turning to Soviet Asian biographies and history, think of the time factor in American terms. Forty-five years after our Civil War was 1910. A black congresswoman in 1910? A black congress*man* in 1910? Ku Klux Klan terror had driven the last of them out of office a decade earlier. Dr. Du Bois was only just founding the NAACP. Even at this writing, there are three black women in Congress, although in proportion to population there should be seven times as many.

As this is written, two women in the world head elected governments, both in Asia. They are Indira Gandhi of India and Sirimavo Bandaranaike of Sri Lanka (Ceylon). Neither was born a slave or serf either of a higher owning class or of men. Gandhi is of the Brahmin aristocracy and Bandaranaike of the wealthy. And Indira Gandhi was raised by her father, Nehru, India's first Premier, to admiration for the Soviet example with respect to women and to ethnic minorities, in letters he wrote her from jail in the 1930s.

Unlike the people of India and Sri Lanka, the indigenous peoples of Soviet Central Asia are almost solidly Moslem in cultural background. Their branch of Islam provided for probably the worst, most complete, and most degrading oppression of women existing in any large population in modern times. Today, no Arab country permits women to vote. Many rural girls get no schooling at all, and the proportion going beyond the primary grades is small. Only in Algeria and the Sudan is any significant proportion of women employed outside the home, where they are directly under the thumbs of their husbands and of mothers-in-law steeped in traditions of women's inferiority and blind obedience on the part of the young wife. The veil and a shroudlike caftan is still the rule in Morocco and elsewhere for all but a tiny handful of wives and daughters of wealthy European-educated types. Divorce is still reserved to the male, who need only say "I divorce you" thrice. There is no alimony, and few if any ways in which a divorced woman can earn a livelihood. The double standard prevails: chastity is an absolute requirement for women, while recourse to prostitutes is taken for granted among men. Unmarried women who have sex relations are still killed by their own brothers for the "shame" brought upon the family; married women are murdered by their husbands for "adultery."

All this was true of Soviet Central Asia at the time of the Revolution, except that there was no significant education for women other than rote learning of religion, no exceptions to the wearing of the veil except among certain nomadic and seminomadic peoples who had never practiced it, and not even prostitution as economic recourse for an Islamic woman not part of a family. The prostitutes were Russian!

Now consider the life of Yadgar Nasriddinova, Uzbek head of the "Senate" of the U.S.S.R. Her father was a farmhand and died shortly after her birth in 1920. Her mother, then still in her teens, was sold in marriage (all marriages were sales in the literal sense) to a man who insisted that the little girl be abandoned. In pre-Soviet times she would simply have died. The death rate even among children in families was horrifying. But by the mid-1920s the government had at least been able to found orphanages in Uzbekistan, and they were one of the few levers then available to it to demonstrate what life for women could be like.

Although at that time primary schools could take only one twelfth of the rural children in Uzbekistan, and virtually no Central Asian peasant father would send a daughter to school, for her, as a ward of the government, education came as a matter of course. Although the government had forbidden the marrying-off of underage girls, this was still going on quietly in the villages of Central Asia on a significant scale. Yadgar, protected by *not* being a member of a family in that culture, was fed, clothed, and housed by a government that wanted children, particularly girls, to continue their educations as a deliberate step toward equality for women in the society. She did so, and then went on to high school, although just a few years earlier, when she had entered primary school, there had been only *nine* country children in high school, out of a school-age population of a million in rural Uzbekistan. The nine were all boys.

Yadgar Nasriddinova was graduated from high school in 1937. She entered college that year, to study civil engineering. All higher education is and was then free in the U.S.S.R., and students are supported by the government. Two years later, while she was still an undergraduate, a two-hundred-mile trunk canal, virtually a river, was being dug for irrigation by the pick-and-shovel efforts of 160,000 people in Central Asia. It is standard procedure for Soviet students to be assigned to field practice, and the Young Communist League, of which she was a member, plays a leading role in recruiting volunteers for summer construction projects, and in their organization.

Nasriddinova's executive abilities first had a chance to manifest themselves on this canal project. Upon graduation as the first Uzbek woman ever to become a civil engineer, she played a leading role in the development of new coalfields in Uzbekistan. She also became the head of the youth organization, with hundreds of thousands of members.

In the postwar years she held subcabinet-level posts in the ministries of construction and transportation of her republic. In 1953 she became Minister for Construction Materials, then Vice-Premier, and in 1959 became its president. And in 1970 the House of Nationalities of the U.S.S.R. Supreme Soviet elected Yadgar Nasriddinova its presiding officer.* She is married and has grandchildren.

With Nasriddinova gone up to Moscow, there are now eighteen Uzbek women of cabinet or immediate subcabinet rank in the government of that republic of thirteen million people. (The Uzbeks are one of the fifteen major nations in the Union of Soviet Socialist Republics. Each is organized as a republic in its native territory.) One hundred and sixteen Uzbek women are the heads or assistant heads of major industrial enterprises. One thousand seven hundred and twenty-seven have Ph.D.s, which is six times as high as black female Ph.D.s in the United States in proportion to population, and sixty-three have the exalted title of *doktor*. The Ph.D. and *doktor* figures represent increases of 50 per cent in just five years! Among them are specialists in women's studies, like Khadycha Suleimanova, a member of the Uzbek Academy of Sciences, who read a paper on changing family relationships in Central Asia at the Third International Sociological Congress. Or the granddaughter of the very first Uzbek woman lawyer (just retired), herself a legal scholar, whose presentation at the International Congress of Women Lawyers in France, in 1972, was devoted to legislation to protect women against the forced marriages, marriages of children, bride-

* She retired as this book went to press.

purchase, and polygamy that were the rule under Islamic law and established tradition.

Eighteen per cent of the judges in Uzbekistan are women, as against three per cent in the United States. Yet this is a measure of the continuing *backwardness*, by Soviet standards, of the status of women in the areas of Islamic tradition, inasmuch as, for the U.S.S.R. as a whole, women are one third of the judges. There is no doubt that that gap will close rapidly, reflecting the recent closing of the gap between female and male educational levels. In 1955 girls were still only one quarter of Uzbek high school enrollment, but by 1970 they were already 49 per cent, i.e., exactly their proper proportion, because boys outnumber girls in the population by a fraction at that age.

This change in female educational attainment is already showing results in types of employment. Not everyone can be a judge, but anyone of normal intelligence and health and the level of education needed to understand machine operation and repair instructions can operate a mechanical cotton-picker, even if it is as big as a truck and a good deal more complex-looking. It was 1954 before the very first Uzbek woman bid for that job, but fifteen years later two thousand of them were "captains," as folk imagination has phrased it, of these new ships of the now-irrigated desert. Among rural Asian women, this was almost as revolutionary a development as when their grandmothers had discarded the veil forty years earlier. In 1972 a correspondent for the monthly *Peasant Woman* asked, "Do you like to work on the combine?" The answer was much more than an indication of personal like or dislike: "They regard us differently now in the village." Another young woman added, "It wasn't the machine that was hard, but something else: convincing parents and relatives. The Young Communist League and the party helped."

So do the women's magazines, whose function is precisely to give such encouragement, although they cover the entire range of female interest. The magazine published in the Uzbek language, *Uzbekiston Khotin-kizlari*, founded in 1926 and with a circulation of 160,000 just ten years ago, now prints 400,000 copies. It encourages women by showing them how far they've come: in Uzbekistan there are 88 female governors, mayors, county managers, and heads of the Communist party at those levels, 50 district attorneys and assistant district attorneys, 4,415 heads of labor unions from the local level up to that of the entire republic (women are under 5 per cent of all union officers in the United States, 56 per cent in the Soviet Union). They are 45 per cent of members of legislative bodies from the village up, in that republic. Neither India nor Ceylon, with women premiers at this writing, has anything remotely comparable in terms of mass participation by women in public affairs.

The women's publications also rally them to deal with the problems that remain, and with new ones. Two decades ago, *seasonal* day nurseries to baby-sit the children of Asian farm women during the planting and particularly harvesting rush were a great boon. Today these magazines—and the general press, read by men as well—seek to convince rural women that *year-round* preschool centers are good, and to convince men in positions of authority that funds, materials, and personnel must be provided for them. To those there who still argue that because Central Asian rural families have many children, the three-generation family continues to be the usual pattern, and therefore children left at home when Mother works on the farm have Grandmother to care for them and sisters and brothers to play with, a woman replies in *The Woman Worker* magazine:

"Time was when the Tajik woman 'didn't need' the maternity hospital or high school! And she didn't run tractors or harvester combines. And university education was 'not necessary' for her. And she didn't speak from the rostrums of legislatures. . . . When this August [1972], the female professional people of the republic assembled, and one Tajik woman after another ascended to the speaker's platform—physicians, scientists, government and party officials, famous actresses, writers, teachers—would it even pass through anyone's mind that there is anything in the richness and diversity of our lives that is outside the needs of these women, and all their friends not present?" (Contrast this with the fact that 84 per cent of six hundred Chicanas assembled in 1971 for the first-ever conference of Raza women in the United States felt they were *not* motivated to need and seek professional careers, and that higher education was not considered important for them.)

In Tajikistan, which has less than two million rural people altogether, the number of children in the countryside enrolled in year-round preschool institutions has risen from 3,000 to 8,000 in fifteen years, while the money has already been appropriated to provide for 25,000 more in the next five years.

If Nasriddinova's Uzbeks are the Egyptians of the U.S.S.R. —oasis farmers—the Tajiks are its Tibetans, because they live in its highest mountains, at the west end of the same range whose other end terminates in Tibet. Many Tajiks dwell in isolated hanging valleys where earth to build terraced fields was carried load by load on human backs. They share with the Uzbeks the same tradition of an extraordinary level of oppression of women. It used to involve not only the wearing in public of a black horsehair veil lacking even eye slits, but prohibited a woman, once married, from being seen unveiled by another woman outside her immediate family, for the other might describe her face to the outsider's husband!

Dealing with the residues of such attitudes is one of the duties of Ibodat Rahimova, who is a topmost official of the Communist party of Tajikistan. She has a very pleasant, round, dimpled face and looks like a Chicana worker. Her face was covered with the horsehair veil when she reached the age of seven, as tradition demanded. She wore it for a decade in the years immediately after the Revolution. However, her father was very much more progressive than most. When he had learned to read and write in a class to end illiteracy in the 1920s, he performed an act of great daring: he sent his two daughters to school. Ibodat was then sixteen. Within four years she had joined the Communist party, quite an extraordinary act for a Tajik woman at that time. By the outbreak of World War II she had graduated from teachers' college, and found herself working double shifts because the male teachers, who were a high percentage in Central Asia, were drafted.

What brought her into politics as a career was her willingness to read letters from soldiers to illiterate womenfolk, and to write replies. The Communist party sent her to Moscow for a three-year course in its own graduate school in Moscow, from 1957 to 1959. It was the popularity she won among women that led to her election to the City Council (Soviet), and for more than twenty years she has been a member of Congress (the Supreme Soviet) in Tajikistan. In her present post, second secretary of the party, she is responsible for science, education, cultural activities, the press, radio, and television. In that country of less than three million there are more than three thousand scholars doing research under its Academy of Sciences, and they come to her to use her influence in Moscow for funding, for assistance in getting priority in acquiring unusual instruments, for convincing figures of national reputation to take posts in this remote place, and so forth.

Unlike the situation in India, just nine miles south of the Tajik border, where there are virtually no females between Indira Gandhi and a sprinkling of rank-and-file professional women, Rahimova does not sit in solitary grandeur in terms of representation of her sex. The Vice-President of Tajikistan is female, as is a Vice-Premier who, typically, is a peasant's daughter and ex-teacher. The mayors of four towns are women, and, most important of all, women elected to the grass-roots level of public office, village and city councils, are virtually half the total: 45 per cent. Two major female industrial executives have risen to be the assistant heads of the meat-and-dairy and the consumer-goods manufacturing industries. Three of the very largest clothing factories, one of which employs thousands, have women managers. These are all Tajiks by nationality, although to me the fact that there are now four thousand employed college-educated Tajik women is far more impressive than the achievements of outstanding individuals.

There are Tajik women like Professor Hakimova, who is a corresponding member of the U.S.S.R.-wide Academy of Medical Sciences. She is a researcher in hormonal regulation of the reproductive function, reached the super-Ph.D. level of *doktor* at age thirty-three (forty is about average), is the author of some fifty scientific papers, has herself trained fourteen Ph.D.s and two other *doktors,* and has spoken at learned meetings in Austria and elsewhere. A current photo of her lecturing to her class shows a person not much past forty, with a substantial number of men among those busily taking notes. In Central Asia that is phenomenal. Among women there are recognized Tajik poets and architects. Before the Revolution the latter profession didn't exist and the former was exclusively male.

In a country where these changes are so exceedingly recent, the problem of overcoming archaic attitudes still exists. In 1971 Rahimova told a Soviet reporter, "I still wouldn't say everything is 'normal' in our republic." She told a story of a teen-ager not in some mountain fastness but in the capital city of Dushanbe, with 350,000 people in the 1960s. The parents wanted to marry her off in the old way; she hadn't even seen the bridegroom they had chosen. In the past, a young woman in this position would simply have accepted her parents' choice and begun preparing for her wedding. Now, as she did not wish to marry the man, she went to the borough party committee with her problem.

Law forbids forced marriage, but it was more important to convince the family rather than antagonize it. "We had literally dozens of talks with her parents before we could convince them that if their daughter went through school and college and got a good job she'd be a far greater help, and then she could marry for love; but we did in the end, and now she has a lovely family."

Nasriddinova's and Rahimova's biographies are less exciting than those of many other women of the Soviet ethnic minorities because they did not have to contend with traditional family backgrounds. The former became a ward of the government, which became her "family," and the latter had a father who sent her to school.

Bibi Palvanova did not have such good fortune. She, too, was born in 1920. While Nasriddinova is Uzbek, a nationality with a long-established tradition of irrigated agriculture, Palvanova is of the Turkmen, who were Bedouin-like nomads at that time, wandering the deserts with their horses, camels, and sheep west of the Uzbeks' cotton-growing oases. When Bibi was ten, her father was told that his daughter would have to go to school. Even though the Soviet government had established separate schools for girls and boys in Islamic regions to meet the rock-hard prejudices to which older women were actually attached even more than men, Bibi's father was not satisfied. He moved to the largest town in Turkmenia specifically to avoid sending her to school: he thought no one would know of their existence. That boomeranged tragically because 1930–31 was a year of extreme hardship in the U.S.S.R. due to the bitter struggle over collectivization. Even I, enjoying the privilege of special rations because my father was an American engineer under contract to the Soviet government, had no sugar in any form for months, and our tea was made from carrots (we arrived in 1931). People not known to the authorities had no ration cards and were out of luck. Bibi's father and a brother died of starvation.

Neighbors sent the children to school not for education but because it would entitle them to rations of bread and clothing received by all Soviet trade school and college students who need it. But in her mother's opinion, a young woman's destiny was to be married. And the mother needed the bride-price. So when Bibi reached fourteen, her mother falsified her age as sixteen—the legal minimum for marriage in Turkmenia at the time—and sold her to a man as his third wife under Islamic law, although Soviet law forbids bigamy.

Bibi's school principal went to her mother and mother-in-law and threatened them with the courts if they did not at least permit her to complete her education. The principal was practical: no threat of exposure of the illegal bigamy was apparently made. Bibi Palvanova's husband was killed in World War II.

After graduating from the carpet-weaving industrial high school, she stayed on there as a teacher. During the war, she was one of the women who replaced drafted men in government jobs. She continued her education, majored in history, and became the first woman in Turkmenia, a country of two million, to win the degree of *doktor*. She was also the first woman in Turkmenia of any nationality (there is a large Russian minority) to become a member of its Academy of Sciences, which had been founded in 1951 in a country practically totally illiterate at the time of the Revolution about thirty years earlier. In 1958 she became the first woman in the Soviet Union to head a university. There are female *college* presidents, as we know from a previous chapter.

After nine years in that post, she was appointed in 1967, and remains, Minister of Education of Turkmenia. Not quite of retirement age, her life spans the gap from the time when only one in twenty thousand Turkmenian women could even read and write. Today several thousand are college graduates and consequently professional people, for in the U.S.S.R. a college-educated woman who is not employed is most uncommon. It is significant that Palvanova's own academic specialty is the history of women in Turkmenia, on which she has written three books. When a friend of mine of long ago, an American woman resident in the U.S.S.R., interviewed her in 1971, Palvanova pointed to an illustration in one of her books showing a young woman whose mouth was covered with a yashmak veil, and said, "It was the symbol of our silence."

Precisely the same type of statistics and individual stories of women's achievement and participation can be quoted for Turkmenia as for Tajikistan. Our newspapers, when they do run anything about women in Soviet Asia, choose reports of Communist party resolutions that reveal instances of bride-purchase, underage marriage, and bigamy in order to push efforts to eliminate these archaic relics. I'm not ignorant of inequities in the American South, but I gasped at a report in the San Francisco *Chronicle* by physicians, male and white, of a town below the Mason-Dixon line where "a nurse in the white wards of the hospital routinely washes a newborn baby, but the Negro mother must get out of bed and walk three floors down to the basement to wash her own newborn child." That kind of savagery is long forgotten in the Soviet Union, and, frankly, its people, who generally have a high opinion of us, would be appalled if they read it.

Our world of high culture takes pride in what it regards as its openness to "visible minorities" and is very free with its criticisms of government controls in Soviet culture. But as a dance buff, I have yet to see a black prima ballerina or male lead in classical ballet in a racially mixed company in the United States, despite the acknowledged primacy of blacks in dance.

Malika Sabirova, Tajik, was born in 1943. At the age of eight, when girls a generation earlier were sold in marriage, this stubborn child, whose talent in dance had been discovered in kindergarten, broke down her mother's resistance (nothing is said of a father) to an offer to send her to the school of choreography in far-off Leningrad. Education and maintenance in such schools, entirely government-financed, are completely free, and a regular academic curriculum is given.

At fourteen she was the star of the graduation ballet put on in the Kirov Theater. At eighteen, back home, she was prima ballerina of the Tajik Theater of Opera and Ballet—both being art forms unknown in the Pamir Mountains till very shortly before her birth. She danced many of the classical prima ballerina roles, as well as the lead in the first ballet by a Soviet composer of a people of Islamic heritage: the Tatar Yarullin's *Shurale*.

When she was twenty, a Moscow jury chose her and her partner to be among the Soviet representatives at the First International Ballet Competition, and they took second prize. By now she had already been sculpted by an artist of her own people. After this triumph, the great Ulanova took over her training, and she became part of the touring company of the Moscow Bolshoi Theater, dancing in India, Burma, Japan, and England. Since then she has performed in Rome and Montreal as well. Finally, when a hundred of the finest dancers from twenty countries competed in Moscow in 1969, she won first prize.

Women listening to my radio broadcasts ask me whether the Soviet Union has female poets and other creators—rather than performers—of recognized distinction. There are many. I did not deal with that in the chapter "Cosmonaut and Milkmaid" because I wanted to focus attention on occupations thus far unattainable in the West, and we certainly do have female poets of wide fame. In the Soviet Union the percentage of women poets who have attained real distinction is far higher: Akhmatova, Inber, Aliger, Bergholz, Akhmadulina, Matveyeva, Kazakova, to include only those whose talent is sufficiently recognized in the West that their work can be found in English anthologies. These names include Jews and a Tatar, but all are culturally Russian: they use that language to write in. In the United States blacks write in English, of course, but in the U.S.S.R. it is language much more than race that is the mark of ethnic differentiation.

Poetry is written and published in more than sixty languages of the Soviet peoples, and translated into or out of Russian and others when it has any merit at all. Before the Revolution there had been women poets writing in Russian who had won recognition, but among the nationalities that regarded teaching a woman to read as unthinkable, there obviously were none.

To'ushan Esenova has published ten volumes of poetry. She looks like an American Indian. She is Turkmen, and if I earlier compared that people to Bedouins because of their Islamic heritage and geographic location, comparison to semi-nomadic Indians in the United States would otherwise be equally apt. Her childhood followed a pattern with which we are already familiar. Born in 1915, one of nine children, she was six years old when her father took her to a prospective suitor as a child bride. Although it was before the Revolution had won in Turkmenia, the father's conscience was troubled: "I'm not the only one who has had to do it." Her nine-year-old sister was sold, but To'ushan escaped that fate because her head had had to be shaved due to illness, and she was therefore not "marketable." The father apparently was sincere, because when the first school opened in their village after the Revolution, she was sent to it at once. When a girls' boarding school was opened in the capital, Ashkhabad, in the 1920s, the government offered parents the bait not only of free maintenance for the children but also exemption from agricultural taxation, and To'ushan was enrolled. From there she went on to the Central Asian University in Tashkent, Uzbekistan.

Having graduated in 1933, Esenova's life might have been relatively uneventful if she had gone into teaching or even medicine—in a clinic for women, that is. Today female Central Asian physicians treat men, too, but forty years ago that was inconceivable. But she chose journalism, a profession that did not limit her contacts to children and women. Colleagues were sarcastic, some flatly hostile. She was sent for stories to remote parts of her desert country, where even male reporters were not always welcome.

At that time it was unheard-of for a woman to drive a vehicle in Turkmenia. But Esenova disdained a mere truck or even passenger car. She applied to flying school and she was accepted for the two-year course.

By this time, 1936, she was getting verse published in periodicals. These lines tell us what it was that moved her, particularly in her first volume in 1938, to be "entirely devoted to the theme of emancipation of Oriental women." I found them in English translation.

> O women! Tear the yashmak from your face!
> Submit no more in silence to disgrace!
> Lift up your voice: you will not speak alone!
> Millions now make their aspirations known:
>   To work for peace and happiness of all,
>   No longer abject, no more serfdom's thrall!

When this volume appeared, she was already editor of the paper whose staffers had made life difficult for her five years earlier. Soviet newspapers are not private property. They function to carry out the government's and the party's policy. That policy called not only for liberating women to do whatever they were individually capable of, but for undermining male attitudes of superiority by deliberately placing women in highly visible situations previously regarded as only within the male province. This policy got her an education at a time when the number of Turkmen women attending universities was infinitesimal; it also got her her job as a reporter and her admission to flying school. Under Central Asian circumstances, this certainly had to be a factor when a new editor for her paper was needed, and she was chosen. Otherwise, a man would have gotten the post as a matter of course. Incidentally, she did not join the party until eleven years later; membership was not a condition for the editorship.

That she is also a member of the city council of Ashkhabad, present population a quarter million, will not be surprising. Although she was not the very first Turkmenian playwright, a comedy she wrote in 1939 was the first there to deal with life on a collective farm. Her most recent work is a novel based on material about Turkmen women collected by herself and sent in by readers of her newspaper.

She is a woman's writer in the fullest sense. The form of

poetry regarded as most difficult and most honored in the Soviet Union is the very long poem: a novel in verse that may run from a couple of dozen to two hundred printed pages. In 1955 she published such a full-volume poem, and its subject was the life of Turkmen women in prerevolutionary and Soviet times. She is not ethnocentric. During the Spanish Civil War of 1936–39, when she had just begun to write, this young woman of the Asian desert wrote two shorter long poems, "Lena Odena," about a real-life hero of that struggle, and "To a Girl of Spain." In 1951 she published an entire collection entitled *To the Women of the East.* The Stalin era had faults and worse than faults, but it instilled in peoples who had only just learned that there was a world beyond their own villages a sense of oneness and support for the rebellious oppressed throughout the world that simply had no precedent in human history.

Esenova was married twice. She has a daughter who majored in English at Turkmenia's own university, and two grandchildren. She says of them, "They take advantage of me, but I love it!"

In the 1974 International Women's Day issue of Moscow's important *Literary Gazette,* she had a poem celebrating the hands of the female cotton-picker in Central Asia today—hands so small that they can be enclosed entirely in a man's but that can also write laws, that in the war gripped guns as firmly as did men's. "But it is better to pick cotton in the sun's blaze, to bathe a child, to carry flowers in May. I am a woman, and understand that. I am a woman, and have all of this in me."

The Soviet equivalent of the nightclub is the *restoran.* If you come in and no table is free, you go to one that has empty seats, and say to the people there, "May we?" The answer is "please," unless they are really waiting for others.

One evening in Alma-Ata, capital of Kazakhstan, 180 miles from China, my wife and I were dining in the hotel *restoran,* when a charming couple in their very early twenties seated themselves at our table in the manner described above. They were obviously Kazakhs. After a while I introduced myself. She, it turned out, was in her senior year at the local university, majoring in mathematics. He was an engineering student at a college in another city, so they didn't get to see each other very often. But he was the Soviet boxing champion in his weight class and was flying to Cuba for bouts. So they were celebrating.

When I explained to her the women's liberation movement that had recently gotten under way in the United States, she said, "Oh, but you must talk to my mother!" I asked why. "Because she raised five children, and then graduated from the Higher Party School, and is now a top executive in radio broadcasting."

It occurred to me afterward that in my very considerable association with women's liberationists here and in reading their literature, I had never encountered one who thought of her mother as a model of the liberation of women.

The other youthful Central Asian woman with whom I have shared an evening is a Tajik, and the head of the Young Communist League of that mountain republic. Our meeting was in Berkeley, in the home of a friend who teaches in a junior college, and who had invited a number of her students, several of them Third World. For hours Guljikhon ("Flower of Peace") answered questions, many displaying an uninformed hostility. She never lost patience or command, and I still cannot picture how a person of her intelligence and force of character would have functioned in the horsehair-veiled secluded women's quarters of her grandmother's day. Perhaps she would have been broken in the clash with the mother-in-law who ruled all younger women in the household. Very probably, had she survived to reach that station, her caged energies would have made her a particular tyrant over the younger women.

She was one of a delegation of three from the Women's Committee. I drove them home afterward. After a grueling day of receptions, interviews, and quizzes, the three began laughing lightly about something, and broke into gentle, timeless songs, in harmony, of Russian peasant mood.

There is another Central Asian woman my wife and I became acquainted with. One day in Moscow's Red Square in 1970 we saw a Soviet Asian couple of about forty. I introduced myself. They proved to be Kazakhs, she an obstetrician-gynecologist, he a historian. They urged us to visit them in Alma-Ata, which we did.

On the evening we spent at their home she was delayed at the hospital by a difficult confinement. When she arrived, he set the table and participated in serving dinner in a manner indicating that he did so frequently. He did not draw me aside from the women for discussion, nor was there any feeling that this was a family dominated by the wife due to individual force of character. Because he does much of his work at home, he seemed to have possibly more of the responsibility for their two children than she. This was all the more remarkable because he, at least, was a practicing Moslem. And he was not the rare case of a Kazakh born in an intellectual background: he carried with him at all times his late father's identification card, bearing the only words his father had ever learned to write—his own name. In Kazakhstan there are three women cabinet members and nine women vice-ministers. There are 170 women among the 482 members of its Congress.

A few days earlier we had been in "Academic City," the world-famous Siberian center of Soviet science, where a team of scholars delivered a private lecture for my wife and myself on their studies of a small Siberian tribe. The three women in the group, which was about evenly divided by sex, included one who looked like a cross between an Eskimo and an American Indian. She was an Altai tribeswoman, and for one of that nationality to be a Ph.D. and curator of anthropology in the museum of an institute of the U.S.S.R. Academy of Sciences is more astounding than cabinet membership, university presidency, or factory management for a Central Asian oasis farmer.

While the depressed status of Central Asian women is associated with Islam, which is modern as the history of religions go, the Altais were shamanists except for some tribes that had been converted to Christianity. There have been few cultures in which the exploitation of the women of the poor was more overwhelming than among the Altai. In one of her works, Dr. Toshchakova, Altai anthropologist, has written: "The Altai woman bore the main burden of labor in herding and agriculture, played an exceptionally large role in household industry, performed the difficult daily work of keeping house, and cared for the children. But this is not all."

In the study just quoted, published in 1958, Toshchakova reports the recollections of a seventy-year-old woman of her life before the Revolution. At dawn she would milk ten cows, then boil the milk, pour it into leather bags she had sewn, make fermented-milk liquor, drive the cattle to pasture, tie the calves not far from the wigwam, then make breakfast. Her husband meanwhile drank his *arak* (60 per cent alcohol), rode off to look over the livestock, maybe went hunting, or else visited with friends. Having fed the children, the woman went to cut hay for the young animals, and then stored it herself. If there was no field work to do, she would make cheese for the winter, or clothes or footwear. In winter she brought in hay and firewood. They lived in a bark wigwam.

Another woman, who at the time of the interview chaired the village Soviet, had been given in marriage at age eight to a rich cattle-owning tribal nobleman, and spent fifteen years in that family. She was paid nothing and did all the house-work. The mistress only gave orders, sat at the fireplace, smoked, poured *arak* for guests, or went visiting.

When a child was born, a ritual question would be asked: "Is it a needed one, or not?" A boy was "needed," a girl was not. The visible symbol of women's inferiority was a sleeve-less gown of enormous weight, interfering with work and movement: the hem consisted of nine layers of cloth glued together with dough. When a boy reached seven, a maternal uncle would give him his best horse; a girl got nothing. The exceptional poverty of most of the Altais led to slow matura-tion: a girl was regarded as adult at sixteen or seventeen. In the earlier years of marriage she was simply a slavey. And the complete lack of sanitation, plus hunger, led to an extraor-dinary death rate. Dr. Toshchakova insists this was socio-economic: children of the poor went entirely naked to age ten in summer, although average July temperature was only 55°. In January, when the average was below zero and tem-peratures to −60° were recorded, a child of the poor had a secondhand sheepskin coat over its nakedness and patched hand-me-down footwear. Illiteracy was universal, of course.

Perhaps the space I have given to the work of this one

Inessa Armand.

Sofia Kovalevskaya,
mathematician.

Sofia Perovskaia.

Monument to Nadezhda Krupskaya. It identifies her as a
personality in her own right, with no mention of the fact that
she was Lenin's wife. It is at a building where she taught
workers' classes in prerevolutionary times and recruited them
for revolutionary activity.

The best workers of a Siberian steel mill. Women operate
cranes and other heavy equipment.

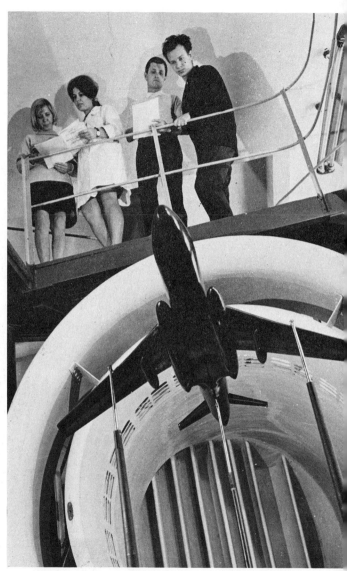
Aircraft engineering students at the Aircraft College.

Watching a factory performance by a major repertory theater.

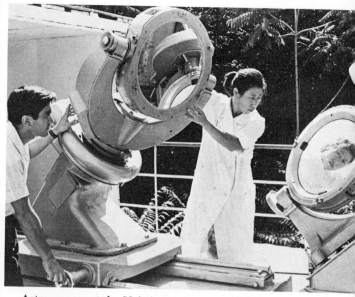

Astronomers at the Uzbek Academy of Sciences, Central Asia, preparing a spectrograph for observations.

High school seniors build electric power generator for rural school.

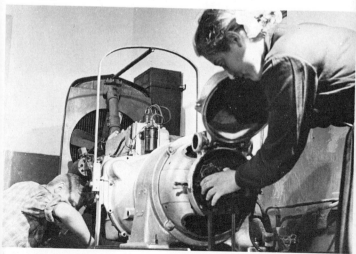

Compatability, U.S.S.R.

Chief physician at bedside consultation with nurses, doctors.

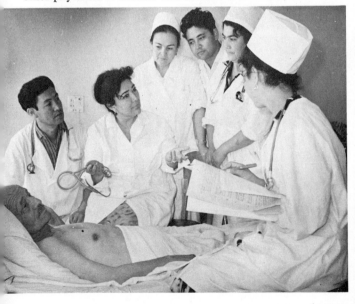

Village mayor performs a wedding.

Kindergarten railroaders in a former palace of the nobility.
Note girls playing with train.

Typical Russian family togetherness.

Valentina Tereshkova, spacewoman.

Leningrad subway system traffic controllers.

She operates a cotton-picker.

Villagers watching a touring fashion show.

This gynecologist, a Ph.D. (center), being honored on her retirement, was one of the first Uzbek physicians of either sex. Today there are 10,000 female Uzbek doctors, 60 per cent of the profession in that Soviet republic.

Hon. Yadgar Nasriddinova (center), Central Asian Uzbek chairwoman of the Soviet equivalent of the U.S. Senate, the House of Nationalities. She is an engineer by profession.

Country general store. Today fewer yard goods are being sold and more ready-to-wear: sewing eats into women's free time.

In Central Asian Tashkent, where women were murdered for exposing their faces forty-five years ago, public exhibition of a painting of a nude in the art museum is as revolutionary as was the opening of San Francisco's Museum of Erotic Art in the 1970s. The viewer is Uzbek ballerina Bernara Kariyeva.

A flying doctor (center) arrives by helicopter to treat a pipeline builder. The pilot is carrying her bag.

The teacher receives universal respect. The gold star medal identifies M. Gogleva as holder of the title Hero of Socialist Labor, the highest award whatever for achievement of any kind.

Satellite-tracking system operator. The entire network is commanded by a woman, was largely designed by female engineers, and is often operated by them in the field.

woman, of one very small people, is disproportionate. But the notion of a woman of this background and of an age indicating she had to be very much part of this life, becoming, by 1958, editor of the *Learned Papers of the Mountain Altai Institute of History, Language, and Literature,* overwhelms me. Incidentally, by the time I met her, a second Altai woman had also won a Ph.D., and a third, only twenty-four years old, was one of the five representatives in the House of Nationalities of the Supreme Soviet of the 170,000 people of the Mountain Altai Autonomous Region.

Despite all the oppression of the Central Asian peoples and the extraordinary backwardness of those like the Altai, it was the Jews whom Lenin, before the Revolution, rightly called "the Negroes of Russia." Just as, among all the minorities in the United States, a special stigma is borne by blacks, so was that true of the Russian Jew. The depressed place of the woman in Orthodox Judaism itself does not help. For a Jewish female to aspire to governmental recognition in tsarist Russia would have been regarded as ludicrous. A distinguished Soviet scholar tells a story from his childhood in which a Jewish mother who wanted her child admitted to high school crawled on her knees from the principal's office door to his desk. This was in the twentieth century. But there were some Jewish female physicians.

In 1972 a Jewish woman, Natalia Satz, won the Soviet equivalent of a Pulitzer Prize, not a private but an official national honor. In 1918, immediately after the Revolution and with civil war raging, she entered the Moscow Soviet at the age of fifteen, applied for permission to found a children's theater, and asked that a building be given her. Asked who the director would be, she replied, "I, of course." An official of vision supported her. By the mid-1930s she had put on 4,500 performances of forty-three plays, dances, dramas, operettas, marionette shows, and concerts to audiences totaling 3,500,000.

But in 1970 *alone,* the 144 permanent professional children's theaters now existing put on 95,000 performances for 30,000,000 children and teen-agers. They employ an average of seventy-five persons each! Every ethnic republic has at least one such theater, and the largest has nineteen.

Maya Plisetskaya, also Jewish, is today the prima ballerina of the Bolshoi Theater, and since 1959 has held the highest honor a Soviet performer can be given: the title People's Artist of the U.S.S.R. Lina Solomonovna Stern, a physiologist, was elected to the Academy of Sciences in 1939 and was awarded a Stalin Prize in 1943 for her studies of the barrier between brain and bloodstream, regulating the cerebrospinal fluid.

Several of the leading women poets are Jewish, as is the best children's writer, Agnia Barto, who has had a total printing of twenty million copies of her works.

A professional theater ensemble performing in the Yiddish language is headed by Anna Guzik, its lead performer. A Jewish woman is among the five members of the U.S.S.R. Supreme Soviet from the Jewish Autonomous Region, Birobidzhan.

Grunie Melamud, who escaped from under a pile of corpses in the Nazi massacre at Babi Yar in 1941, fought in the Red Army, winning eleven decorations for heroism. Her feats were recalled in print in 1972 in a Yiddish publication of limited circulation, but a booklet on the heroism of a nurse, Leah Kantorovich, was publicized in 1970 by the most respected, very widely read Russian-language magazine of literature and social criticism, *Novy Mir*.

In the U.S.S.R. formal honors are awarded not only by the central government but by the affiliated republics. The Ukraine, for example, issued an award in 1969 to Dr. Esther Minuhin, medical director of a tuberculosis sanatorium, and Roza Slomnitzka was decorated the previous year for her services as a revolutionary in pre-Soviet times. Another Jewish physician, Dr. Evgenia Izrailovna, is also the mother of one of the Soviet cosmonauts, Boris Volynov, whom she raised after divorce. In music, there is the woman composer Rivka Boyarska, whose volume, *Music to the Songs of Yiddish Poets*, was published in 1967.

For Jewish women to be in medicine and even physiology is not surprising, but an engineer, Sophia Belkin, was a 1964 winner of the Lenin Prize, equivalent within the U.S.S.R. to a Nobel Prize. In painting there is Nina Lieb among others. The list of full professors in various fields and at the best universities would be too long to print, and some one learns of purely by accident: the mother-in-law of a friend of mine recently retired from that rank in the economics department at Moscow University, for example. Jewish women were among the founders of field anthropology in the U.S.S.R., spending years and traveling thousands of miles by horse and dogsled in easternmost Siberia and the Arctic. In psychology an entire issue of the translation journal *Soviet Psychology,* Winter 1972–73, was devoted to excerpts from the monograph *Personality and the Psychology of Activity,* representing the culmination of the forty-year career of Professor Bluma Zeigarnik, and published by Moscow University Press in 1971.

In all, there are now 200,000 *college*-trained Jewish women *employed in their professions* in the U.S.S.R. *This is nearly half the total Jewish female population of working age.* There is nothing remotely like that anywhere in the world, including Israel, which has the same number of Jews, or the United States, with twice as many. Nor does it exist among any other nationality—majority or minority—in any country on earth. In the United States only one eighth of even white women have finished college, and a great proportion of these make no use of their education in paid employment, or are unable to do so.

The Jews, however, along with Gypsies, Germans, and Poles, are distinct from other nationalities living in the U.S.S.R. in that they do not originate there. Whatever the complaints of nationalist Russians or Uzbeks, they do not seek solution of that particular problem by seeking to leave the Soviet Union: it, or their ancestral region within it, is their native land. But the nationalist fraction among Jews or ethnic Germans seeks to meet that psychological problem by moving to the land they associate with the origin of their people: Israel or Germany. Through 1973, a couple of thousand Germans and eighty thousand Jews had done so. This is little more than 4 per cent of Soviet Jews. That is well below the figure for nationalist-minded persons known to exist among all Soviet nationalities. However, free emigration is not permitted, and Jewish women have been among those demonstrating, and in some cases suffering for, their desire to leave. Emilia Trachtenberg, Lilia Ontman, and others have been jailed.

Ruth Gruber describes others in *Ms.* (April 1974). On the other hand, Julia Finkelstein left her émigré husband in London and returned to the Soviet Union with their son. R. N. Baliasnaya, a writer, joined with a male writer and other Jews of both sexes in statements supporting Moscow's policies with respect to their ethnic group. To remove an obstacle to détente, Moscow permits vastly more emigration by Jews than by members of any other ethnic group, including Russians. Armenians from abroad have moved to their traditional homeland, which is in the U.S.S.R., in numbers three times as large as the Soviet Jews who have left for Israel.

Ethnic prejudice and mistrust is something we in the United States are all too familiar with. Its decline in the Soviet Union has been spectacular, as measured by both sociological surveys and such persuasive data as intermarriage. True, intermarriage often represents marrying up: a male seeks a wife of an ethnic group with higher status. In our society the higher one goes in the power structure, the rarer is interracial and even interreligious marriage. I am not talking of people in the highly visible world of entertainment, but of those in positions of control. In the U.S.S.R. the picture is sensationally different, and has been for many years. Stalin's Foreign Minister, Molotov, and Defense Minister, Voroshilov, were married to Jews. Today, in the Tatar Autonomous Republic on the Volga (Tatars are of Islamic heritage and speak a Turkic language), the higher one goes in the very large Russian population, the *greater* the percentage of Tatar spouses: 3 per cent among skilled workers, 6.6 per cent among professionals, and 14.7 per cent among heads of enterprises and institutions.

As top executives are almost exclusively members of the Communist party, what emerges is that the Communists practice the internationalism they preach. This is confirmed by data for Latvia. Among politically unaffiliated Latvians, 10 per cent have married across ethnic lines; among Communist party members 15 per cent, and among members of the Young Communist League, the generation among whom pre-Soviet traditions of ethnic insularity are lowest, fully 29 per cent are intermarried. Latvia is a Soviet Baltic republic.

With respect to Tatars and to Central Asia, it must be remembered that Islam absolutely prohibits marriage of its women to infidels. Orthodox Judaism and Christianity are little, if at all, better. Law itself, under the Russian Empire, prohibited interreligious "miscegenation"! In Tashkent, the largest Central Asian city, only 2 per cent of marriages were transnational in the first Soviet years, 1921–25. But by 1971 the figure was 30 per cent. In most Soviet Central Asian cities, women of the local nationalities now intermarry as freely as men, although we know that two generations earlier the only marriage was by a sale arranged by the father and invariably to a Moslem.

Even more striking is a study of intermarriage involving Jews in Soviet Daghestan, a high mountain area at the Caspian Sea end of the Caucasus, whose people are chiefly of Islamic heritage. Jews—I am Jewish—never intermarry where they feel themselves oppressed: it is regarded as betrayal. Think of Tevye's horror in *Fiddler on the Roof* when one of his daughters fell in love with a Russian.

In 1940, a full generation after the Revolution, the number of Jewish-Daghestani marriages in the capital city of that area was *zero*. But between 1959 and 1968 there were already 366 marriages of ethnic Jews to non-Jews in that city, as against 512 in which both parties were Jewish.

Wherever one looks in the Soviet Union, the data do *not* show the Jews to fall into a category of their own, which certainly was the case before the Revolution. For example, in Latvia, Jews intermarry more than do Latvians or Russians, but less than Belorussians, Poles, Ukrainians, or Lithuanians, the other major nationalities there.

The purpose of the research I drew upon was to determine, among other things, the levels of nationalism among Soviet nationalities, measured by intermarriage and interethnic friendships on the positive side, and objections to working with or under persons of another nationality, as well as to intermarriage, among the criteria on the negative side. Marked levels of nationalism were found among 5 to 10 per cent of each ethnic group: an exceedingly low figure. A higher level was found only among older rural women—the most isolated, least educated, and most religious element in the population. A University of California study in 1966 showed that only one fourth of church-going American Christians were entirely free of anti-Semitic prejudices. That is exactly the opposite of the *worst* Soviet figures, in which 25 per cent was the highest figure in *any* social stratum of *any* nationality showing other than positive attitudes (negative plus decline-to-state). Of all nationalities in the U.S.S.R., interestingly, the Russians and the Jews showed the lowest levels of nationalist feelings directed against others, including each other.

All in all, the status of Jewish women in their individual relations with men, as well as in education and occupation, is undoubtedly the best of that of any nationality in the U.S.S.R., including the Russians. This is because the Jews are the most urban people, and it is in the countryside that tradition hangs on longest despite law, education, persuasion, propaganda, or whatever. In the cities it is in the families with the most recent or continuing ties to the countryside that residues of the patriarchal family are strongest. In 1959 a Jewish woman of little education, married to a Russian plumber, told me that their neighbors in a Leningrad apartment house didn't associate with them much because her husband adhered to what she thought of as Jewish norms: their idea of an evening with neighbors was not getting drunk, and he didn't beat her.

In the past, women of the Islamic peoples would take any kind of treatment. On the one hand, religious law gave them no recourse whatever. On the other, they took their own oppression for granted. Today this is changing rapidly. One study in the Caucasus concludes: "The rather substantial percentage of divorces in mixed marriages initiated by Daghestani women is indicative of their rising initiative." In one Central Asian city, 70 per cent of divorces in 1969 were on grounds of the husbands' habitual drinking. Obviously, the women initiated them.

In our country visible-minority women suffer higher unemployment, drug addiction, the bane of the ghetto, and prostitution. In the U.S.S.R. there simply is no measurable unemployment, prostitution, or drug addiction. So ethnic origin makes no difference.

Ethnic minority women there do not live in ghettos, although prerevolutionary Russia was the classic land of the ghetto half a century ago. It cannot be too strongly emphasized that *there are no ghettos.* The women do not sally out in the morning to jobs as housemaids or hotel or hospital service workers in a foreign world, returning at night to a totally different culture. Neither by visible physical differences, language, or religion is there any association between unskilled, physically exhausting, unpleasant, or simply low-status jobs and ethnic origin, although in prerevolutionary times there was, and observers still reported it twenty years later. When the first Chicano group ever to visit the Soviet Union (staff and students of the ethnic studies program at the University of California, Berkeley) did so in 1972, they told me that their first and strongest impression was the contrast between London Airport, where black and brown people were doing the dirty work, "just like at home," and Moscow, where whites were doing it. They visited Central Asia, and saw that there is no lack of visible-minority people in the U.S.S.R.

Where do ethnic women go from here? Those whose native language is not Russian constitute half the women of the Soviet Union. Most of them cannot in any way be compared to immigrant nationalities in the United States, because they live, and usually comprise majorities in, the territories their forebears inhabited for a thousand years or more. They are no more a single cultural group than blacks, Chicanos, Orientals, and American Indians here.

Some female ethnic populations, chiefly Slavic and Baltic, and the Jews, are equally or even more advanced in status relative to men than are Russian women: percentage of college students, of employed college graduates, members of major professions, judges, high school principals. Others, chiefly in the Caucasus and Central Asia, have to combat more deeply rooted traditions, both in themselves and particularly in men, than in the rest of the country. For example, the Armenians, one of the world's most sophisticated peoples, seem to have the most firmly rooted divisions by sex roles of any indigenous Soviet nationality of significant size. Among them, the percentage of judges who are women is little more than one third the U.S.S.R.-wide average, but *four times as high as in the United States.* Only 9 per cent of high school principals in Armenia are women, while in Russia, by far the largest republic, it is 31 per cent, and in Latvia, another small one, it is 41 per cent! A Kazakh woman with a key post in chemicals technology reports that a reason for her entering such work, as recently as 1964, was men's prejudiced belief that women "weren't much good at such work. I'd show them." Clearly, the Soviet Union is not a country but virtually a world, whose components are at different stages of cultural development in different spheres of existence.

What of the future? Among some in the United States it is now fashionable to put down female predominance in the teaching profession on the grounds that it represents channeling of women into a nurturing role. A century ago it was not looked upon that way: men had been the schoolteachers, and female entry into the profession on a large scale was regarded as a triumph. In Soviet Estonia, for example, women have virtually taken over the teaching profession: 91 per cent. Does that mean they are in a depressed status in that culture? On the contrary, they are over half the judges there, making it one of only two Soviet republics in which that is true.

So it is not good that women are only 39 per cent of teachers in mountainous Tajikistan and 44 per cent in desert Turkmenia, although by comparison to the past that is splendid. In this area of Islamic background, any figure less than half means they haven't yet reached equality. Many of the women teachers may be of other nationalities, because only a quarter of the ethnically Tajik and Turkmen college students are female, although women are half of the U.S.S.R.-wide student body. Gauged very roughly by percentage of the labor force consisting of women, the situation in Central Asia and the Caucasus today is what it was in Russia on the eve of World War II.

Steps to correct this situation are taken at two levels: by the central Communist party in Moscow, and by party and government in each republic. In addition, indigenous ethnic women of achievement, who number in the thousands by now even in these places, take measures of their own, as emerges in the following pages.

In 1970 the Congress of the Communist party of Uzbekistan heard a special report and adopted a resolution with regard to women. The speaker was male, which I think is good because, unfortunately, the overwhelming majority of the delegates were male. He was unsparing. There was no sustained concern, he said, for training female executives and upgrading their qualifications, or for mechanizing hard-labor jobs. Some local committees underestimated the need to activate women. Government departments were not giving the attention they should to promoting women. Agriculture was particularly bad. In some places women were promoted in response to pressures from above but not given help in learning their new responsibilities, more complex than they had ever had. There was not much concern in Uzbekistan for creating conditions enabling women to hold jobs: shopping facilities and service industries, public eating places.

The resolution was most specific. Admissions of women to the Higher Party School, and to undergraduate and graduate levels of colleges and universities, were to be increased by preferential selection over men, all other things (grades, exam scores) being equal. In the most backward categories—rural women and urban housewives—they were to be drawn out of a completely household-centered existence via amateur performing groups, organized trips to movies, concerts, and the theater, persuasion to visit and use libraries, conferences of readers of their favorite magazines, evenings of questions and answers, and even such elementary steps as dressmaking and home-economics clubs to appeal to those with entirely traditional views of their roles. An "atmosphere of harsh condemnation" was to be created with respect to "manifestations of an incorrect attitude toward women . . . shameful instances of offenses to women's honor and dignity. . . . Many party organizations and government agencies are guilty of a lenient attitude in dealing with persons who violate Soviet laws on marriage and the family."

Nationwide membership organizations of women ceased to exist in Russia proper forty years ago. At that time, women had gained the confidence to stand up for themselves in mixed organizations and to function in them, and had in practice attained essential equality in employment and education, that is, outside the home. In Turkmenia and Tajikistan, male supremacist attitudes on the one hand and the traditional timidity of women on the other are still pronounced and extensive. As a consequence, various kinds of women-only gatherings continue. In Turkmenia there are nationwide women's congresses every few years. In Tajikistan there is a republic-wide "girls' council." There the Young Communist League introduced an annual Bibi Zainab Prize in 1968, named for the first Tajik woman ever to head a local Soviet. She was killed by counterrevolutionaries in the 1920s. The first award went to a woman farm-equipment operator, for success in pioneering a new field for women in that republic.

There are "girls' clubs" on Turkmen collective farms. At Turkmenia's university, in Ashkhabad, the Poppy Club, an all-women's club, was founded as recently as 1966. (To Americans, who take sex-segregated institutions as normal, it is necessary to explain that there is no such thing as a men-only club in the U.S.S.R.) There are 1,200 female students in the day-session enrollment of 5,200. The club has not only debates, discussions, lectures, literary and sports activities, but also domestic science and needlework groups, the latter famous for their carpets and embroidery. Males are permitted to attend its functions by invitation only.

While women's magazines exist everywhere in the U.S.S.R., there are no special women's sections in newspapers, where it is assumed that matters of concern to women are of concern to men as well, and that women will write to the papers as freely as men. But in the national newspaper in Turkmenia there is still a special department, "Women Speak," devoted to criticisms and exposures of male supremacist behavior. Female students appear on TV to describe how they settled difficulties with their parents about going to college, so as to help others still having similar problems. The city-wide women's council in Ashkhabad conducts an "oral magazine," essentially consisting of meetings at which women of achievement in all fields speak to encourage others.

Separate women's teachers' colleges had to be established in Central Asia, one of them as late as 1944, and they still exist in those areas because most rural parents would not consider permitting their daughters to attend mixed schools away from their home villages with adult males. One hundred per cent attendance of girls through high school graduation was to be sought. Actually this was a measure to improve a situation that was already far advanced. In not one of the Soviet republics of Islamic heritage by 1944 were girls less than 48 per cent of enrollment in the high school grades. But in Russia at large they were 58 per cent, reflecting a universal tendency of some boys to drop out and take physical jobs. Finally, the Communist party was instructed to step up the work of women's councils (not part of that party) at every level from the collective farm up.

Women throughout the U.S.S.R. were for many years promoted to positions of topmost authority over men of comparable merit as a matter of conscious policy, in order to encourage other women and to compel a proper awareness in male colleagues. In Russia proper, this is no longer done. Personally I believe that it is still very much needed. But in Central Asia the party itself recognizes that this continues to be necessary. For example, in 1971, a twenty-six-year-old Turkmen woman historian was named Vice-Premier of Turkmenia (2¼ million population). She had completed graduate work at the party's Academy of Social Sciences in Moscow, which trains its top leadership, and had written her thesis on the elimination of illiteracy in Central Asia. At the time of promotion to this post, she was the head of the Young Communist League in Turkmenia (co-ed, of course) and assistant head of the Turkmenian Communist party's Department of Science and Higher Education.

The same thing is done at lower levels. In Azerbaijan, subsequent to a criticism by the Communist party in Moscow published in the major Soviet newspapers, twenty-one female farmers were promoted to positions of leadership in the collective farms in a single county in 1970.

Asian women are now still fighting for such public criticisms and changes as did Russian women forty years ago. For example, a joint letter by a group of women in a Turkmenian paper reads: "One still hears talk to the effect that administrative posts and responsible jobs are man's and not woman's work, and that a woman is 'better suited to' ordinary work. . . . It must be said outright that party and government organizations do not always help such comrades to break with their 'granddaddy' habits."

A woman heading a department of a teachers' college in the capital of Tajikistan wrote that many collective farms had no bathhouses or even bakeries to ease women's work in the family. Her use of the word "even" meant that bakeries were already regarded as normal, a phenomenal change from the situation only a decade ago, when a farm woman there with an average of five or six children had to bake her own bread in addition to the work on the farm.

Perhaps the status achieved by the women of the Soviet peoples of Islamic heritage can best be summarized by comparing a single statistic to the figures in other countries in various categories. In 1970 there were 211,000 women college students among Islamic peoples in the U.S.S.R., whose combined populations are 34,000,000. Long-civilized France, with 50 per cent more people, had only the same number of women students as these Soviet areas where the veil, the harem, and illiteracy were universal half a century ago. Yet France has the largest student body of any West European country and the highest percentage of women in it. Japan, the most advanced capitalist country in Asia, had a slightly larger number of women students (216,000) than the combined Soviet areas of Islamic heritage, but a population exactly three times as large; that is, only one third as many women in proportion. India, under a woman Prime Minister, had a few more women students (250,000), but sixteen times as many people, so it is entirely out of the running. Egypt, with which the comparison is fairest because it has exactly the same population as the combined Soviet peoples of Islamic heritage, has less than one sixth as many women students despite remarkable progress. Finally, Sweden, with the highest percentage of students to population of any Western country but the United States, and with what is regarded as the all-round best status of women in the capitalist world, had 10 per cent less women students in proportion to its population than these Soviet nationalities.

If the same comparison were made for the professions of medicine, engineering, and law, and for the percentage of women sitting as judges or running high schools, the lead of the Soviet women of Islamic nationalities would be incomparably larger.

Except for teachers and social workers, the comparable figures for black professional women in the United States are so low that to cite them would be to reinforce the racism of the American mind. If one lumps together the schoolteachers at one end and the migratory berry pickers still moving between Florida and New York State at the other, it is possible that the average living standard of black women in the United States may still be higher, in the purely material sense, than that of the average in the Soviet Union, because this country is so much more economically developed. But no Soviet woman, and specifically none of an ethnic minority, need fear the experience of twelve- and fourteen-year-old black sisters in Montgomery, Alabama, who were sterilized by a federally financed agency in 1973 because, the United Press reported, "boys were hanging around the girls" and the agency felt that sterilization was "the most convenient method . . . to prevent pregnancy." It had ordered eleven sterilizations that year, and they came to light only because of a suit on behalf of the sisters. In the U.S.S.R. women and minorities are both treated and respected as human beings.

Chapter X
Women Speak Out

Contrary to the picture of unsmiling gray uniformity and brainwashing created by the American press and electronic media, the Soviet people do not all think alike. There is a great variety of opinions among women as well as men.

Therefore no one should accept any story that follows as expressing the opinion of *the* Soviet woman. There is no such person. There are young, middle-aged, and old, urban and rural, highly and poorly educated, Russians and members of numerous different *kinds* of nationalities, atheists and those influenced to a greater or lesser degree by several varieties of Christianity, Islam, Judaism, and other religions. Beyond all that they are individual human beings. Two young, urban, atheist, ethnically Russian, college-educated women, married and with one child each (a very large category has all these characteristics combined) may well have very different opinions about how many children one should have, what it is that a husband should contribute to the work of the home, whether the schools should provide sex education, and just about anything else. For example, opinion as to family size differs sharply between Minsk, a large city of a million, and Moscow, a great one of seven million, because 90 per cent of the population of Minsk has come there since it was devastated in World War II, and therefore consists of the country-born and their daughters.

As in every other country where public opinion matters—

and it very definitely does in the U.S.S.R.—spokeswomen have emerged for female views. There is the Soviet Women's Committee, which is rather official but has come up with ideas very much its own, including some that might be shocking to some feminists in the West. For example, in a country where women's access to occupations has come to be taken for granted, that committee, in speeches and publications, states with great pride that it has convinced the government in recent years to bar women from coal-mining. In its literature the Women's Committee explains that women have worked too physically hard under worsening conditions for too long, and with all sorts of other work always available, why permit some to go on endangering and dulling themselves? Upholders of untrammeled individualism may be outraged, but that is how that group feels.

Then there are sociologists, whose findings and views are being listened to more and more carefully. Some of the most prominent, particularly in this field, are female. They are not unanimous in their convictions and recommendations. Dr. Zoya Yankova is the most outstanding. As we will see, she is not terribly radical: her views on some subjects are closer to those of the average American woman as revealed by polls than to others here who regard themselves as in the vanguard. For example, the *Psychology Today* poll in 1972 found only 15 per cent of U.S. women in favor of ending marriage in its present form, no more than 37 per cent in favor of equality in housekeeping, and 42 per cent in favor of child-rearing without sex-role stereotyping.

While there is no Gloria Steinem in the Soviet Union, there are female journalists of great prominence who devote themselves chiefly to furthering women's interests as they variously see them. Larisa Kuznetsova is one, Ada Baskina another. They do not necessarily agree either with each other or with other categories of spokeswomen.

The role played in American life by the actress as a voice for women is, because the history of Russian culture is different, filled there by the female novelist and "serious writer." Marietta Shaginyan is one. Vera Panova, who died recently and whose ideas are influential because her books continue to be read, is another.

Finally there are writers of letters to the editors. The Soviet press consists very much more of reader-written material than does our own, and there is an abundance of diverse opinion constantly being expressed by women about women and men.

I have met many Soviet women, from semiliterate elderly peasant hitchhikers to Ph.D.s, workers, film writers, botanists, teachers and doctors, Communist party officials, diplomats, and individuals in any number of other occupations. I have also learned the views of those women who won't talk freely to a man, through my wife and other foreign female visitors to and residents in the Soviet Union, exchange scholars, wives of Soviet citizens, and so on.

This provides a rich basis for judgment. Yet my knowledge of what Soviet women think ranges from firm data gathered with the most sophisticated techniques by their social scientists, to areas of vagueness because great numbers of women still won't talk freely even to other women about problems regarded as intimate, for reasons we discussed earlier, much as was the situation here a generation, and certainly two generations ago. But some did talk to me about these things.

It is reasonable to assume that a really popular journalist or novelist must represent a widespread segment of female opinion, particularly if her views correspond to measurable behavior, such as buying habits, and to social survey findings.

One article by Larisa Kuznetsova is quite unusual, not because it was a response to a letter to Moscow's *Literary Gazette* from an American woman, but because it was an angry, annoyed response. Usually, except on matters of foreign policy, Soviet people are so extremely courteous in discussions with foreigners that it's hard to get a productive argument going, as they consider it bad manners to argue with visitors.

But when Mrs. Elizabeth Pollock, of Norfolk, Connecticut —prompted by an article in Moscow's *Literary Gazette* which was reprinted in translation in many American papers—wrote the paper some perfectly sincere advice about how to hold and get men, Kuznetsova went through the ceiling. She wrote:

> In the past half century we Russian women have become objects of close examination by everybody. . . . Sometimes we are looked at as though we are utterly out of the ordinary and not

entirely beings of this world. . . . I'll make so bold as to say that there is no other woman, not even Brigitte Bardot herself, about whom as much nonsense has been written as about the ordinary Russian woman. She doesn't know how to use eyeshadow, powder and lipstick, and eats dumplings and omelettes fried in lard without the slightest thought to her weight. It is such women who nearly always find their way into the lenses of "objectively" aimed cameras.

Neither I nor my colleagues would undertake to judge the appearance and morals of American women by certain illustrations in certain magazines in which women who are more undressed than dressed look as though they are advertising themselves in a particularly demeaning manner.

Let's speak frankly. The meaning of all the talk about female beauty and cosmetics is a great deal deeper than might seem to be the case at first glance. It isn't about powder at all but about woman's social role.

Yes, for entirely too long the eyes of our women were penciled with the dark blue of fatigue and their lashes powdered with the dust of construction sites and the smoke of cities burning in the war. Time passed, our country recovered, and Russian women gained the time and desire to be concerned about their appearance. But the manner in which we use the contents of various jars, boxes, flasks, and tubes brought home from beauty aid counters will hardly determine the resolution of any significant problems of life.

Let me return to the basic notion in that letter from America: that woman's major destiny is to win the love of a man. Be it noted that *to that truly sacred destiny* [my emphasis] there had been added another. I refer to women's work at a job. You may organize a worldwide lament over that or, on the other hand, dances of joy, but that won't change the historically progressive essence of that development. The truly modern woman is no longer capable of gazing into the eyes of her husband with devoted submissiveness, and of belonging wholly to that world of family and homemaking in which Mrs. Pollock feels so comfortable.

As far as our country is concerned, the task of liberating women from slavery to the family cell was one of the serious problems we had to solve. Never and nowhere in all human history has women's level of education, culture, and occupational status been as high, and her role in economic and social life as great as in our country. I'm not going to repeat truths known to all that our women often exceed their men in level of education and for all practical purposes have "occupied" a number of professions. Today it is already clear that modern woman has acquired an "ego" of her own [Mrs. Pollock had advised that one must never, never offend the male ego] and demands understanding and respect for that fact from the man who loves her.

Here Kuznetsova makes a profound comment basic to our understanding of where Soviet women are today:

The appearance of that great self-awareness on the part of women, their sense that their *own* personalities have worth, doesn't exactly make it easier to get along with men. *Rather the contrary*. It introduces new complications into our love because it demands of us the solution of additional problems that our great-grandmothers didn't have to deal with. There are lots of such problems, and their real essence is not competition between the woman's job and family roles but the fact that they comprise a unity of opposites. What is she to do both in the one and the other, because thus far, society, having involved women in work outside the home, does not always provide her insurance in the form of the needed support.

And it would clearly be an untruth to say that the life of a woman with a job is very easy and pleasant and that she makes no sacrifices for the sake of her standing as an independent human being. She makes them. . . . It was not for nothing that a certain great man said that the level of freedom of a society is measured by the position woman occupies in it.

Do I hear a chorus of "right on"? Count me in. Kuznetsova also wrote that she regretted that Betty Friedan's *The Feminine Mystique* had not been published in the Soviet Union. She clearly felt that its demystifications were needed by Soviet women and very much by Soviet men.

Kuznetsova's qualified notion about winning the love of a man is the preponderant view of Soviet women today. But not of all. Liubov' Iunina (an *-a* ending denotes a woman in ethnically Russian names) ripped into an article by a man worried about the declining birth rate. He wrote about all the unmarried men around, in which Iunina saw something very different:

"But I respect bachelors!" They are men "who cook, who mend, who take their suits to the cleaners themselves, who sew on buttons, and who (how magnificent!) wipe the dust from windowsills all by themselves." But since the census shows that there are as many women as men in the population up to age forty-three, then "there has got to be an equal number of single women or, by the old classification, old maids. Both, depending upon character and inclinations, either suffer from loneliness or take pleasure in it. I can swear that the latter are a minority."

She went on to say that married men want the benefits of having a wife without the restraints. Using the very words of the man who wrote reprovingly of the carefree life of the bachelor, she responds: "Among the married, too, there are plenty who are lovers of life, bon vivants, and sociable fellas with bantering glances. Just try and tell who's married and who's not by that."

But the core of her article was a discussion of the problems and attitudes of the *new* Soviet woman:

In the old days the "right to propose marriage," to coin a phrase, was possessed by men, while a woman could only wait in trepidation until she was chosen, and as a rule did not dare to refuse, for what if no one else came along? And her only destiny was to take care of a family. There was no more pitiable lot than that of the old maid.

Today a woman makes her own choice of a companion in life, and is perhaps more choosy even than a man. . . . Whereas in the past a woman, *as a rule,* married without love, today the concepts "love," "marriage," "family" are interwoven. And for two people capable of loving each other to meet in life isn't all that easy.

She puts a very interesting interpretation (others don't agree) on the fact that, starting at age twenty-five, the percentage of Soviet women getting married drops twice as fast as that of men. "Are they too old for marrying? By no means. . . . Men are marrying women older than themselves quite willingly [I was also told this personally by women]—life is more interesting with such. The reason lies elsewhere. At twenty-five a woman generally attains her fullest economic in-

dependence. She has an occupation, satisfactory pay, and
housing." The thoughts that follow have the ring of Malvina
Reynolds' *We Don't Need the Men.* Iunina writes:

A woman who is independent economically in our society
has no need for someone simply to be a husband. She wants a
companion equal in everything: in rights and in duties as well.
. . . She doesn't want to exchange clear advantages for dubious
ones. And she reasons just like the bachelor: "Marriage is extra
bother, and if somebody wants it, let him take it on: but count
me out." . . .

The reader doubtless thinks that I am outraged by such a
woman. *On the contrary, I rejoice in her* [my emphasis]. *I rejoice in her high ethical standards for marriage. That she will
not compromise.* What is marriage today for the majority of
women? It is a working day as long as her husband's on the job
and then another working day at home. The woman often bears
this entire burden alone. Some husbands do help their wives
to some degree."

And she quotes the man she's debating:

"Married men feel the condescending hand of bachelor friends
on their shoulders: well, brother, you're groaning? It's your own
fault—what did you take on that load for? And it hurts most if,
when this happens, your hands are loaded with shopping and
you've still got to rush to pick up your kid at the kindergarten.
I'll bet that at such a moment the worm of doubt begins to gnaw
even at happily married men."

And here again Iunina uses language Gloria Steinem would
rejoice in: "So that's the root of it, that cursed 'worm' of
male psychology: that housework is for women to do. And
if you, a man, share it with her, it means you've been dealt
short in personal happiness." (A Soviet exchange scholar I
knew fell right into this category: he really shared fully, including cooking, but was bitter about it when pressed. The
husband of a rising natural scientist is the same, but I know
two other full-sharers who have no psychological hang-ups
about that at all.) Now Iunina makes a point that would win
her hugs from everyone from De Beauvoir on. Bachelors are
not free of that burden. They make at least breakfast at home,

shop for food, take their shoes to the repair shop alone: *"So it turns out that when a man does housework himself because he has no wife he can shift it to, there is nothing shameful about it; it even brings honor to some degree."* She drives this home with a striking story:

> There's a bachelor I knew in three periods of his life. First when he was married and, by his own words, didn't know how to put a teapot on to boil, never mind eggs. And it took an argument for his wife to get him to go down for bread. Then he got divorced. A miracle followed. He could have been a professor of homemaking. His room wasn't simply clean, it was downright sterile, and the dinners he made for friends were beyond praise. He could bake cakes, and pickle, and put up jams. And he laughed at the helplessness of his married friends in this regard. During this period I often ran into him with bags of food in his arms. Then he remarried. And immediately stopped cooking dinners, making pickles, and it took an argument for his wife to get him to go down for bread.

(One Soviet social psychologist calls this the traditional "parasitism" of men on women, and actually says men are "hopeless" in this regard.)

"So really, bachelors, why should you fuss in the kitchen and run to the laundry? Get married! All your problems will disappear." Satire having done its work, she becomes straightforward: "Marriage is a union of hearts, minds, characters . . . that helps people live, fills life with meaning, and the principal essence of which is perpetuating yourselves in children." But she is bitter about men who marry for another reason: "It's a rare man who proposes by saying: 'I want someone to wait on me!' He says: 'I love you.'"

Iunina doesn't oversimplify, however. Going back to the rising number of women of twenty-five and older who stay single, she writes:

> Before heading for the marriage bureau, a woman (of that age) takes a good look at the man she has chosen. And often she finds that he *does* love her, he *does* respect her, but alas *does not have a full understanding that everything in their future lives must be on a basis of equality*. And she doesn't want this, she

sets her face against it, *because she is a woman of a new mold* [my emphasis].

It would not be the truth if I were to say that single women are happy, that for them loneliness is joy. Of course not. *But they prefer loneliness alone to loneliness in the presence of another.*

Finally, she turns to the mother living alone. "A woman with a child is even less eager to marry again than a single one" over twenty-five. "She already has a family for all practical purposes and her personal life, too, has rich meaning. Some women find a solution to the problem in having children out of wedlock." (I know an anthropologist in Leningrad who did that in her late twenties. She was a competition skier and a splendid partner on the ballroom floor: tall, graceful, slender. Simply finding a man to marry would have been no problem. The child was not by a lover but a friend—she just wanted a baby. The head of a Moscow obstetrics-gynecology center told me of a similar case among the thirty women physicians of whom she was in charge, of a female school principal, and others.) "Today a child is rarely born out of wedlock unless the mother deeply desires it and decides to give birth to a child knowing beforehand that it will have no father. That, I would say, is a kind of feat of moral valor."

I was very careful, in opening this chapter, to make clear that Soviet women are not unanimous in their opinions. Both Kuznetsova and, particularly, Iunina state as facts attitudes of Soviet women that are not borne out entirely by Soviet sociological research, much of it conducted by women. But when people writing in a million-circulation national weekly, which is where both these articles appeared, believe things to be true because their personal observations and conceptions combine to form such conclusions, that in itself gives them a certain truth. It becomes a self-fulfilling prophecy: if enough people believe something to be true and conduct themselves in accordance with that belief, that will help to make it come true, wholly or in part, if it is a phenomenon that can be affected by belief. You can't will the sun to stand still, but if you haven't met a man you wish to marry, yet deeply desire to have a child, an article like Iunina's may cause you to decide that you're not going to tie your life to Ivan Ivanov's just for the sake of having a child, but will bear one anyhow. And undoubtedly a much more common and socially significant result of both these articles is the effect upon women married to spouses not entirely unredeemable where male chauvinism is concerned. It gives such wives better organized and phrased and more extensive arguments in the battle to change that old devil, male psychology. And it also gives them material to show each other and reinforce their morale.

One effect of such articles, quite naturally, was to advance the argument and make it heavier. In the two years after those quoted above appeared in 1971, the burden of discussion shifted to that of sex roles. While Soviet male sociologists, in several books and numerous research papers I have, unanimously supported the view that male psychology must be changed as Kuznetsova and Iunina desire, and particularly that men must be taught and persuaded to share in homemaking, occasional male writers, some with advanced degrees in fields giving them no expertise in this regard, have fallen back on the old argument of differences in the genes.

A very popular female journalist in the field, Ada Baskina, has also done this. She wrote in a 1973 article that lots of family arguments could be headed off or more easily resolved if each partner were more aware of the psychological traits of the other sex. She stated her case, to which another woman, E. Svetlanova, responded: "The reasons are rather to be sought in general individual psychology independent of sex, and in the person's culture of intellect and spirit." In a manner that obviously had to set readers thinking about the validity of the marriage institution, she referred back to the Russian, Alexander Gertsen, who over a century ago played the role in stimulating thought about women in that country that John Stuart Mill did a decade later in the West. Gertsen is quoted: "Cohabitation under a single roof is of itself a terrifying thing on which half of marriages break down. Living intimately together, people get too close to each other entirely, see each other in entirely too much detail, with it all hanging out." (Modern slang rescues me here from an otherwise untranslatable situation.)

Svetlanova says we have to think about that again from

the standpoint of present-day knowledge of society and of human beings. The family's evolution is being accompanied in all countries by a rising divorce rate, chiefly in urban areas, and the duration of marriage at the time of divorce is increasing: "More and more often it is mature people made wiser by life who are not held back by the firmness of family ties. *Perhaps this is a 'sickness of growth' of the new family, today built not on economic foundations but on those of the spirit?* Such ties are complex, many-faceted, and do not arise out of simple addition, a bilateral contribution of material capital. Here it is capital of the spirit that has to merge.

"Soviet society is not at all indifferent to the state of the family. . . . How can we increase the 'yield' of human happiness?" And she tells us that this is not a matter to be left to amateur efforts, but neither can it be entrusted to the experts alone: "The degree to which this depends upon our efforts, what they should be and in what form they can best manifest themselves, is a serious subject for concern and thought by sociologists, writers, physicians, psychologists, economists, philosophers. *Each of us.*"

Then Svetlanova goes to her own point. Many books had stated flatly that personality traits were defined permanently by sex. "Science has refuted these categorical assertions. The judgment of history is different: it is not the *physical* nature of the individual but one's *social* characteristics that define the essence of a person." Ada Baskina had cited *A Man and a Woman* and another French film in which men and women drew different conclusions from the same circumstances, to support her view about inborn psychological differences. Svetlanova responded that they simply showed the results of the different sex-role acculturation to which women and men are subjected in the capitalist world. Baskina had asserted that women's feelings are all sharper than men's, to which Svetlanova responded: "What about Romeo?" She also referred to Othello's reaction to the whereabouts of Desdemona's handkerchief. "Trial statistics for murders out of jealousy would probably confirm that it is precisely men who are a majority of evildoers out of emotion."

While Romeo and Othello are familiar in the arguments of women's liberationists in the West, Svetlanova piles it on out of the European and Russian intellectual and cultural traditions: Goethe's Werther, Pushkin's Lensky. She quotes the classic rationalist philosopher Leibniz: "We need feelings in order to be able to think. If we had no feelings, we would not be able to think." From this Svetlanova deduces: "So to yield mechanistic thought and logic to the orbit of male psychology, and feelings, emotion, and intuition to the female is hardly fair to the truth."

Regarding intuition, which journalist Baskina classed as exclusively female, Svetlanova, who clearly is vastly better educated, responds:

Without intuition, many of the greatest discoveries of male thinkers would never have been made. More than once have they found solutions without being able to explain the logical processes that got them there. . . . Let us note, however, that there are researchers who conceive of intuition as a process of logic! (Is that yet another compliment to women?)

We know that people are all different—deeper or shallower, kinder or more evil, keener or more complacent, more or less vain or egotistical, firmer or more inclined to give in, more inclined to display confidence or more suspicious. Just try to fit any of these traits of character into the psychological profile of a man or woman. . . . And can one really take seriously the classification of subjects in conversation [by Baskina]: "primarily female—children, clothes, men" and "purely male—soccer, hunting, fishing, and jokes of a kind that women really shouldn't be compelled to hear"? . . . Each of us has met women, even virgins and even little girls, who quite complacently not only listen to but make generous use of obscenities in conversation. And tell jokes—the very same ones that Baskina puts in the "not for ladies" column. . . . So what happens to the psychology of sex?

So we know that the same differences of opinion exist among Soviet women on these matters as among American, with the very important exception that the "it's not ladylike" attitude, although dominant in this country in reality, has lost the battle in print. The thought that equality with men means being like them is not present today in the U.S.S.R. The best statement to the contrary in the Soviet Union, and certainly that which has been seen by more people than any other, is the treatment of a platoon of women antiaircraft gunners in World War II, of whom five are killed in a scouting patrol, in the enormously popular 1972 film *The Dawns Are Quiet Here*. As they are pictured first in their quarters and then in the ordeal in a swamp, they are very, very womanly, but this in no way affects their ability to be effective and heroic soldiers. Sisterhood (as distinct from comradeship) comes through loud and clear in many scenes, such as one in a bathhouse where the whole squad, women of perfectly normal physique, gasp and call out their admiration when they see a new member, particularly shapely and with extraordinary hair, for the first time in the nude. While the director was male (there was a female assistant director), no one who knows Soviet people would challenge the fact that the film accurately describes the prevalent self-image of women there as *different but equal*.

Svetlanova knows this but she doesn't accept it as immutable beyond the fact that only women can bear and nurse children and that they are at a disadvantage, for example, in a hand-to-hand fight with a man of equal skill but the average difference in reach and muscular strength. She writes: "We know from the experience of society and the practice of medicine how deeply, how seriously individual psychology can be reorganized. . . . All in all, there can be far more psychological incompatibility, division, inability to establish contact among members of the same sex but of social groups or occupations or levels of knowledge markedly different in development than between two spouses. . . . And if two individuals belonging to two such different categories happen to be man and wife, it is easy to see how those differences can be misread as differences in the psychology of gender."

She goes on to point out the sharp differences in psychology as life roles change: from new bride to wife to mother-in-law. While until now the discussion has been very little different from one between, say, Betty Friedan and Ann Landers, Svetlanova, with no reference to the non-Soviet world at all, turns in her argument to realities of their life that make clear that the proportions, emphases, and directions in women's psychology there today are of another order than here. She

states: "We know, for example, that women are becoming
the chief force in the economy of most of our collective farms.
. . . Can this 'economic' circumstance fail to be reflected in
the 'psychology of gender'? . . . In practice, the behavior of
women is becoming quite different. And her traits of character
are also different."

I am reminded of a recent Soviet film on farm life, *The
Right One for the Job*. A middle-aged woman is forced to
retire as milkmaid because of an occupational disease: arthritis
in her fingers (only in 1970 did the use of milking machines
begin to account for as much as one half the milk produced
on collective farms). The farm chairman creates the
job of assistant chairman for her and firmly insists that she
perform as an executive. You see her on the phone telling
department heads to make their own decisions instead of
bucking them up to the head office. This is not the traditionally
submissive Russian peasant woman of the past. Nor is
she only somebody's secretary. By making the decision as to
the level at which something should be settled, she *is* functioning
as an executive.

Svetlanova says: "A woman who spends days on end busy
with the house, the garden outside, and her children has one
psychology. While she who, for whatever reason, knows neither
family nor children, but spends her entire days—and
whole life—working on a job or perhaps always on the road
if, say, she is *a geologist or builder* [my emphasis], has an
entirely different psychology."

Speaking directly to Baskina's subject of family arguments,
she says that the behavior of men and women toward each
other is largely determined by the thoughtfulness of their upbringing,
"the more so as many scientists assert that, the lower
the general level of personality development, the more dominant
in it is that old 'psychology of gender,' the shadow of
our hoary instincts." To the other woman's advice that a
couple should not spend all its free time together, Svetlanova
says that generalized pat answers are no good. One marriage
might be saved by that, another destroyed, while to a third
it would make no difference either way, because its problems
lie elsewhere.

We know that the more complex and subtle an individual and the more significant as a personality, the more difficult it is to find personal happiness. Both the level of such a person's demands and the abundance of points of contact complicate this. The more powerful and all-embracing a feeling is, the harder it is to expect complete understanding of it by another. *But the male and female character are equally capable of this kind of difficult and powerful emotion* [emphasis mine]. As far as the essence of family arguments is concerned, Pavlov's classification by types of higher nervous activity is far more important than consideration of features of a sex as such.

Perhaps I should repeat with regard to Svetlanova my comment on the Kuznetsova and Iunina articles. Her views, however erudite, are not indisputable, but their presentation encourages those who are inclined to think similarly, helps shape their behavior, and gives them documentation for discussion and argument. If Baskina is the relative "conservative" in speaking for Soviet women, Iunina and Svetlanova are the "radicals." But a rereading of their views makes clear that the basis in reality for the entire discussion is the shift that has occurred in the U.S.S.R. away from the household orientation of the Western woman and her relegation to low-status work. When a male population specialist, worried by the drop in birth rate in the U.S.S.R., proposed that women be paid salaries during the years they stay home raising children, female professionals spoke out against this in extraordinarily sharp terms. Lydia Litvinenko, Ph.D. in economics and a senior researcher with the labor resources agency under the Cabinet of the Russian Republic, a mother of two, said in an interview with the magazine *Zhurnalist* reprinted in *Soviet Life,* March 1972: "What happens to a woman who leaves her work and goes back to it ten, fifteen, or twenty years later? By that time she's lost her professional skill. Her knowledge is obsolete and a good deal of her energy is gone. She has to begin from scratch again, practically as an apprentice."

While Soviet debate is usually remarkably free of attacks on opponents' ethics, the proposal Litvinenko opposed was so threatening to women's gains in her view that she ignored that practice:

Some people will say, "since the family is the primary and most important social unit, woman's greatest duty to society is raising her children." This may sound logical, but it's really quite dishonest.

First, a division of responsibilities on the basis of sex shouldn't be tolerated, regardless of the results (I'm not talking about hard physical labor, of course). Second, it's obvious that a woman excluded from the work collective, which is a major area of life, *is being cheated* [my emphasis throughout]. This is particularly true when she has been prepared for such work from childhood and *encouraged by public opinion. . . .* Third, *many people* forget that *financial dependence is as oppressive to a woman as it is to a man.* However much she loves her husband, she dislikes being kept by him.

She is particularly bitter about fellow professionals who supported the opposite view:

The press has been featuring letters from women who maintain that child-rearing and housekeeping are women's prime social function. Most of these women seem to be working at intellectual-type jobs. I suspect some of them aren't being very honest. They seem to say: "I'm clever and competent, and that's why I'm holding down this job. But since others aren't capable of anything but housework, that's what they should do."

In dealing with this "woman problem," *the only right and humane solution is to find out why the idea of genuine emancipation hasn't taken hold yet.* What we have to settle is not how women can find more time for their families, but how they can be emancipated in every way: economic, social, psychological, etc.

When the interviewer, not identified by sex, rejoined: "It's a fact that many women have too little time for their homes," and asked "what reserves of time are available," Dr. Litvinenko immediately made clear that the questioner was looking in the wrong direction: "For women, spare time is almost nonexistent. . . . On the other hand, many men have time available for household tasks. . . . We women spend two or three times as many hours as the men on home and family. *In other words, a woman works for her husband too.*"

As often happens with people who are firmly persuaded

they are speaking for others—and who frequently get to do so just because they have that conviction—she slipped into the editorial "we": "We cannot agree with the phrasing of the question 'How can society make housework easier for women?' The accent should be not on women's but on family housework. *The husband should do as much as his wife.*"

Baskina, lending her much greater authority to Litvinenko's criticisms in her comment a year later, said, "If man and wife both work, they ought to share the household chores"; but true to her belief in psychological sex roles, she added, "But equality is not identity. The differences remain and should be considered when the chores are parceled out."

Litvinenko lashed out at certain phrasings used by the highest Soviet leaders: "It's not right to call, say, home delivery of groceries a benefit for women; it's a benefit for the whole family." Taking advantage of the fact that she was being interviewed in the magazine of the journalism profession, she challenged that craft directly: "In some articles we read, it's obvious that the author equates housework with women's work. It makes things worse when the author is a woman. . . . That's an outdated philosophy, and it should be seriously criticized in the press. Such confusion of relations and condescension do a lot of harm; they prevent both men and women from learning the meaning of genuine equality."

In closing, she gives fair warning that those whom she believes to be trying to turn the clock back are going to face a stone wall: "Equal participation by women in the country's economic and cultural affairs is an indisputable virtue of our social system, a big step forward in the *ethical development of humanity.* . . . And no amount of propagandizing or poeticizing about the family hearth will make us change our minds." When I quoted to Soviet women the statement of a space-agency general that no more female cosmonauts were being trained, they were neither angry nor pleased, but quietly confident: "There will be. Nothing can stop us." Perhaps nothing speaks better for what their society has done than the tone of that reply, offered by a seventy-year-old retired professor of literature at Moscow University. She had seen the change during her own lifetime, and as part of her own life. If she could make it, and raise a child, under the conditions of poverty, incredible overcrowding, and lack of not only appliances but even hot water in the prewar and war years, no idiot general could make a significant difference today.

The proposal to pay women for raising their own children (hundreds of thousands of women are paid for helping raise *others'*, of course, in child-care centers and after-school programs, and women with very large families have for many years been given support payments regardless of husbands' earnings) was dropped, but the issue of what goes on in men's heads remains. The most influential of today's Soviet film directors, who made the remarkable tribute to female soldiers in World War II described earlier, said to me in 1973, "I am against the emancipation of women." I was so shocked that I couldn't find the right way to deal with that until we met again the next day. I asked what he meant, and he said, "They work too hard, in construction, in industry. And now we have this problem of only one child per family. I, too, have only one child. Of course, my wife is an actress." I asked what his solutions were. He replied: "I don't have any. But you've seen my pictures. Am I against women?" I saw the war film seated next to a nationally known figure in the American women's movement who is exquisitely sensitive to the slightest nuance of chauvinism and is also a film buff from way back. She approved his picture entirely. But it's obvious from his remarks to me that he does not understand that the solution lies in men's fully sharing the homemaking role. And since his first phrase, taken alone, could be misused, I should add that I heard it, and worse, from a Soviet woman painter of prominence and connections: "I've had emancipation up to here. I'd rather be in a harem." She comes from a nationality originating in a part of the U.S.S.R. where harems used to exist. But she meant exactly what the film director did. She explained that she, like many other women, had borne the total burden of her home in spite of her career, yet she now bears some of the responsibility for her grandchildren because neither her husband nor son-in-law shared these tasks equally with their wives.

Another woman, Valeria Peruanskaya, has dealt with this

directly in an article titled, "Take Care of the Grandmothers." This, too, was in response to another male demographer worried about too few children, who in his thrashing around for solutions, wanted to load the burden of child-rearing even more completely onto grandmothers. Her article is illustrated with a wonderful photo of a sturdy elderly woman in a "babushka" (which is Russian for "grandmother" and which they do *not* use for "headkerchief") carrying home a large wooden hobbyhorse she had bought for a grandchild.

Like Dr. Litvinenko, Peruanskaya, a writer, is quite acid. She begins by describing a street scene she had witnessed. A middle-aged woman, in tears, was telling a woman ice-cream vendor that her married daughter had simply brought her young grandchild to her place, said "Take care of her," and walked out. On which she comments: "An extreme case, of course. But like all extremes, it reflects a certain trend, echoes of which come through clearly in the article by the respected professor."

In responding to his proposal that it be made easier for mothers-in-law to be housed with a married child and grandchildren, she says fine if they want it, but that he's ignoring the virtual disappearance of the family consisting of three generations under one roof. Essentially, she says, the professor wants to compel people to live together who won't get along because they come from different backgrounds. To his idea that because, for historical reasons, there will be a sudden rise in the number of grandmothers around 1980, those women in late middle age should be called upon to solve the baby-sitter and after-school-care problem, she responds that "it's hard to take it seriously and even harder to support it."

We must also not forget that the grandmothers born 1924–29, upon whom all these hopes are placed, aren't at all the same kind of grandmothers there used to be. These grandmothers will leave their jobs after having lived their lives in a work force and with pensions on which they can live without despair. These will be grandmothers who were members of the Young Pioneers [the Communist children's organization] and the Young Communist League. Their horizons, as a rule, are not confined to the family hearth and cannot suddenly be reduced to that.

This is not only obviously what the artist-grandmother meant, but it applies to every woman of that age, or even older, that I have met there.

Peruanskaya, too, emphasized that many of the latest crop of grandmothers are in no hurry to retire at fifty-five, when women are entitled to. And as far as wanting to undertake housework is concerned: "The grandmothers born in the 1920s were young during the war and postwar years. For decades on end they rose at cockcrow to hasten to work and then rushed back to take care of their families. How many man-hours they spent at the washboard when there were as yet no laundries, washing machines, and detergents! How many tons of food did they haul in their shopping bags so all would be fed? *Is the society that owes so much to these women* not under obligation to ease their lives in their declining years? Society is doing that. . . ." But there are those who are wondering if "these grandmothers can't be harnessed up again."

Peruanskaya can't imagine that anyone who had dealt with the problem personally could make the proposal she opposes: "Caring for a child under age three seems easy only to someone who has had neither children nor grandchildren. It's easier to stand up for a day at a machine. It's no accident that young mothers hasten to go back to their jobs as soon as they can. And if a young woman falls off her feet at the end of her day as a mother, what can one say about an elderly one?"

As she writes on, she gets angrier and angrier. Young people naturally have to be free to take courses after work, read books, go out and off on vacations. Grandfathers, she says, quoting the general opinion, ought to be allowed to enjoy their earned rest when pensioned off, go fishing, and play dominoes, while grandmothers "have to fulfill a critical so-called demographic assignment. But if there are things young people need to do and grandfathers are permitted to do, then grandmothers too need to and should have something in life over and above the grandchildren they love. Grandmothers, too, if you will forgive me, need books and theaters and the movies and friends."

Chapter XI
The Layer-Cake Family

A Russian couple I know, let's call them Maria and Ivan, are youthful, vigorous grandparents. They are urban and very highly educated. Her grandmother was a peasant and had sixteen children. Her mother lived in town and had four children. Maria has two. Her daughter has one, seven years of age. Maria and Ivan's views on family and roles are very typical. That is why I am going to tell you about them and our conversation at some length.

Ivan's mother was a commissar in the Revolution, and lived that way to the end of her days, not long ago. "Why buy a blanket? I've got my leather coat to throw over me. Furnishings? Who cares?" She didn't bother cooking; she ate a chunk of black bread, a thick slice of bologna, tea sucked through lump sugar held in the teeth, and perhaps boiled potatoes. One could always buy a bowl of soup or a snack somewhere on the run. She didn't clean house or mend. Meetings, organizing, discussions, were her life. Ivan was raised in a Soviet orphanage. His mother was too busy. "You didn't turn out badly," I said, referring to his personality, not his successful career. Neither Maria nor he disagreed.

But I wonder what his commissar mother would think of his manners. He is, like most Soviet intellectuals over forty, a courtly European gentleman. He is always there to open a car door for you (female or male) and to close it behind, despite a leg in braces caused by a wound in World War II. My wife had made a bulky purchase; though he carries a cane, he picked up the package before I saw what had happened, and I almost had to fight to prevent him from carrying it. At a snack counter, when they were our guests, he tried to pay the check.

Their two children—the daughter an engineer, the boy then a sixteen-year-old volunteer summer helper on an epidemiological expedition to Siberia—were not raised as he was, and certainly not like Maria's grandmother's sixteen children. Of her mother, aunts, and uncles, Maria said, "They grew like the grass. If there was a pair of shoes, it was handed down from one to the next as long as it lasted. If there was a coat, the same, and it was patched when there were holes. Today raising a child is more complicated. There are winter boots and summer shoes to be bought, a light coat for spring and a heavy one for the cold weather. My daughter and her husband [also an engineer] want my granddaughter to learn to play an instrument and to know more English than is taught in school, and the little girl herself wants to learn figure skating. At seven, someone has to take her to these activities."

Who does? "Until now it was easy. She was in nursery, then kindergarten. We have enough of them for all, in Moscow, in Leningrad, everywhere except a few towns in pioneering areas where the population is very young and there are lots more children in proportion. Anyone can afford it. Twelve rubles [seventeen dollars] a month! Fathers help, and take the children to and from. If necessary, you can leave them all week and take them home only on Sunday." (A taxi driver told me that he and his currently nonemployed wife put their seventeen-month-old infant into a nursery on his days off if they feel like a picnic in the woods.)

My wife said, "I hear there are Soviet women who feel the child-care institutions aren't good enough and would rather raise their children at home, and some are taking them out. Personally, I think it is very good for children to learn to live in a group."

Maria agreed strongly. "But our nursery teachers need a higher level of training. Our standards are rising. We demand more." This, not the rise in feminism internationally, is the reason for increasing Soviet attention to matters of concern to women in the past decade.

I wanted to know why things were harder now that her grandchild was of school age. "We've solved the problem of care for preschool children, but not that of the after-school time of the school-age group. Virtually all our mothers have jobs. We now have extended-day schools [providing for five and a half million] but not enough, and the trouble is that that's just what they are. They use the school buildings. There is a school atmosphere, like supervision over doing homework. It's as though the children had to go to school for eight hours. That's too much. Something else has to be done."

How does that affect them personally? "Our grandchild has to be taken from school to her other activities in the middle of the working day. My son-in-law—he *says* he believes in women's equality—wants our daughter to quit working for a couple of years because of this. We said that if she quits we would not help them, as we did when she was going to college." (Because the government provides living expenses to 80 per cent of students, these grants have to be small, and are not calculated to support a child as well.) "If a woman quits work to care for her children, she forgets what she has learned. Technical knowledge advances very rapidly nowadays. She falls behind." Maria was not worried that her daughter would not be able to find work, and the notion that she could not have whatever profession she had chosen was not even part of the thinking of this peasant woman's granddaughter. But she didn't want her to lose standing in her field.

"So how have you solved this?"

"My daughter is trying to arrange part-time work" (difficult, because it's a new notion, while getting a full-time job is no problem whatever) "and meanwhile I will take care of the little girl after school."

"But you have an Ed.D., don't you? What does this do to your work?"

"That's an old story. That's why I work at home, as an editor. When our boy was to be born, I had a very difficult pregnancy, the whole nine months were lost. Then the first year of a child's life a mother really has to take care of it anyhow." (While nurseries take children from the age of three

months, they are placed there at that age only when there is
no other alternative: a single mother whose own mother is
not with her, or can't, or—very rarely—won't take care of the
infant.) "Then my husband worked on his *doktor* dissertation.
You know how that is with us. He had to be kept from all
other bothers."

"So what happens to women's equality?"

"In that sense, it will never be. There are certain things
that are really a woman's to do. Our men help. At least a
third of them help in every way a man can be expected to.
They wash the floors and do the repairs—that of course—and
run the washer and shop for food and take the children to
and from school. They don't cook or mend, and it is for the
mother to keep an eye on the child's schoolwork."

"What if the child is sick, and both parents work: who
stays home to care for it?" my wife wanted to know.

"The mother. Of course. Women are warmer. The child
is used to the mother. There is something in women's nature
causing this."

Mrs. Mandel pressed: "That's just what our young women
object to. They say it's a matter of roles."

Maria said, "But only a woman can give birth to a child.
Only a woman can feed it at the breast."

I asked, "How long can that last?"

"A year. So, all things taken together, women fall behind."

I pushed on: "Your Communist party has solved some very
difficult human problems in its time. Why can't it say to its
men: Okay, comrades, your wives lose two years or more
when a child is born. Afterward, you've got to take on the
larger part of the family burden until they've made up that
lost time."

Maria, a very loyal Communist, changed the subject. Ivan,
both a loyal Communist and a man, looked relieved.

In a population of 135 million women, there is a wide variety of opinion, as you know from the previous chapter. But
Maria's thinking is exactly where the overwhelming majority
of Soviet women is today, as shown by thousands of letters
to their papers and many sociological studies. The legal right
to all the education there is, yes. The right to enter any profession whatever, yes. The right to have the number of chil-

dren you personally wish, yes. The right to make decisions
jointly with your husband, or not to have a husband, or to
get rid of him, yes. Most divorces are now initiated by women
in the U.S.S.R. But if you have a child, or more than one,
rearing is yours, the woman's task. So the relationship is
"equal" in your eyes if the husband does everything but participate in child-rearing and, say, major cooking. And if, as
Maria specifically agreed, this means that a woman spends
twice as much time in connection with the household than
her husband, well, that's what being a woman means. A great
many women, accepting this, believe the solution for them
is part-time jobs. In 1973 the Communist party's daily,
Pravda, carried an article by three sociologists listing the steps
needed for women's emancipation there as being (1) part-
time jobs for those who want them, (2) equitable sharing of
work in the home, and (3) improved consumer-service industries and availability of appliances. That is a step forward
from their long-standing position that consumer-service industries will someday solve everything in this area.

If Maria does not yet believe that traditional sex roles beyond the physiologically inevitable have to be abolished, much
less that women must demand this, she does have very definite ideas on the next practical steps to ease women's lives.
One is further large-scale expansion of home appliance manufacture. The government agrees and is doing this, very rapidly.
Incidentally, less-educated women, those of the blue-collar
class, and particularly their husbands, lag behind the party
and government in that regard. Surveys show that working-
class families, in which not only radios but TVs are a matter
of course, have far less in the way of refrigerators, washing
machines, and vacuum cleaners, even though production and
prices are in the same range as TV sets. There is a deliberate
choice of home entertainment first, and easing the woman's
physical lot a very poor second. As a result, it is educated
families that buy the available supply, although differences in
family earnings between the mass professions and skilled
workers are quite small. But the manufacture and sales statistics curves convince me that it will be no more than another
ten years before appliances will be universal in worker and

peasant homes. That length of time is needed because most rural homes don't yet have running water.

Maria's second area of interest is one in which the U.S.S.R. is in a class by itself. This is child-care. The job of providing urban preschool facilities is essentially done. There are now ten million places in year-round child-care centers, ten times as many as in the United States. The task of convincing *most* women that this is more than a lesser evil has not been fully accomplished. Surveys show that a majority of mothers would rather have their children cared for at home, if not by themselves then by Grandma, a relative, a friend, even a houseworker. They are still oriented overwhelmingly to family upbringing. The conservatism of traditional culture simply does not disappear in two generations. In addition, as their standards rise, they want a higher quality of care for their children. And, most simply, they find a higher incidence of colds and childhood diseases among young children exposed to large numbers of others. That is true, despite excellent medical staffing. A 30 per cent pay raise to preschool teachers in 1972 was designed to attract and keep better-trained personnel, who will complete higher education in this field. It is hoped that the level of care will be so improved that mothers will change their minds. It has long been far above the custodial level, as my wife and I agree after repeated visits to Soviet nurseries and kindergartens, and comparison to our experience with our own children in nurseries here at home. In this sphere the party and government are doing their share. Only time can tell what the outcome will be. A decade ago, an attempt to persuade parents to place school-age children in boarding schools for upbringing failed completely. Parents regard children, even if they have only one, as a chief purpose and joy of marriage.

But it is in the area of after-school care for school-age children that a truly new step has been taken, although much remains to be done. The fact that techniques and methods have not yet been satisfactorily worked out is secondary. The point is that parents want it, and the government has made its commitment to finance and organize it. The "extended-day schools," for all their faults, began as a volunteer parents' movement about a decade ago, when that built-in after-school

child-supervisor, the live-in mother-in-law widowed by World
War II, ceased to be a universal phenomenon. The government's housing program made the nuclear family without a
twenty-four-hour-a-day kibitzer a reality for the majority.
More and more mothers-in-law were people with more than
housewifely skills who did not want to retire to the home and
did not necessarily have the kind of profession that enables
Maria to combine both functions. The government then put
the "extended-day schools" into its own budget. I think it is
safe to say that a dozen years from now the Soviet Union
will have provided universally available after-school-hours
guidance and supervision for school-age children that will be
as distinctly a model for the world as its mass-scale preschool
facilities have been for many years. Likewise, its present provision of a month in camp each summer for twenty million
school-age children is exemplary. But most parents prefer to
take their children with them on vacation or send them to
the close farm relatives that nearly every family still has.

Maria and Ivan demonstrate something else that is to be
seen throughout Soviet society, and that utopian radicals elsewhere completely fail to understand. It is what happens when
a social revolution succeeds, and a small vanguard minority
and the great mass begin to *live* together under new rules:
the woman commissar's son and the brood-hen peasant's
granddaughter. Ivan's mother was absolutely clear on the matter of sex roles. Only she was capable of bearing and suckling
a baby. Everything else a man either could do or could learn
to do. The family was the stronghold of all kinds of conservatism, and a child brought up outside it would presumably be
really the new human being.

The problem is that there were vastly more brood-hen
grandmothers than woman commissars, by a factor of at least
a hundred to one. So either the commissars' children would
isolate themselves from the population as a new caste with
its own life-style and form of interpersonal relations, which
of course would defeat the purpose of the revolution entirely,
or their personal relations would be with the mass of the
population, which had its own traditions in personal life. In
the latter case, either the people would swamp out the new,
which really would have been proof that it was not valid, or

the reality that would emerge would be somewhere between the two, in a constantly shifting ratio.

That is what has happened. Maria is not, like her grandmother, an illiterate baby-factory subject directly to her mother-in-law and indirectly to the oldest male in the house, as we discussed in the chapters on history. However, although highly educated and an independent earner, she still regards her interests as secondary to her husband's and in some ways to her daughter's. Ivan is not the partner insistent on equal sharing that one would imagine a male intellectually committed (as he is) to female equality to be, but he is anything but a patriarch. His family more nearly resembles a fairly enlightened one of similar educational attainment in the West than it does anything corresponding to a new ideal, and this is the penalty paid for the fact that he took the comfortable and easy alternative of accepting his wife's traditional notion that child-rearing and nurturing is her function, with all that implied. Also, perhaps he wanted his children to have a mother's and father's love and care, which he himself did not have. And since the topmost leadership of the Communist party today, which is all male, no longer consists of the idealists of the Revolution but chiefly of people whose personal ancestry is much closer to Maria's than to Ivan's, its policies are much more Maria's than those of Ivan's mother.

The truly emancipated woman of the U.S.S.R. does exist, in the form of large numbers of single mothers and a smaller number of deliberately childless wives. Four hundred thousand women a year now give birth outside marriage, formal or informal, although abortion is available on demand. That is one tenth of all live births. Those with children are not fully equal, because of the demands of nurturing. The most encouraging single figure relates to generational change. A study found that 80 per cent of husbands over fifty years of age contributed less than half as much housework time as their wives, while this figure drops to 50 per cent of husbands whose wives are twenty-five or younger. The other half of the young men spend at least half as much time in housework as their wives. There is a study of rural men in six widely scattered areas, showing one tenth to one twentieth of husbands doing *most* of the housework. In no study did more than one third of the men claim to help sufficiently to satisfy their wives' notion of what is right. In any case, the life-style of true female emancipation in the U.S.S.R. for most would appear to be the fully sharing nuclear family rather than any other form.

The fact that the great majority of men do not share equally in homemaking duties explains why so many educated women —for example, my teachers in a special summer course I attended at Moscow University in 1973 to perfect my Russian —have developed the slogan "We want to be de-emancipated." At first that was a shocker. Do they want to go back to being housewives? I met one woman who actually believed that: "Women who do men's work" (she didn't define it) "lose their femininity. Men who do housework lose their masculinity." I asked how she, very feminine indeed, reconciled those views with her responsible job as a magazine editor (not a women's magazine). She refused to explain.

She was alone in her extreme view. The others, it turned out, wanted to leave neither their jobs nor their professions. They simply wanted the burden on them and on their husbands to be equal, and regarded part-time work for themselves as the solution, since they don't expect or, in most cases, don't even want their husbands to share equally in the home. Soviet family sociologists differ widely as to when, if ever, such sharing will be general. The disagreement is because they, too, represent a variety of convictions as to what is desirable. There are a very few, including the individual of greatest prestige, Dr. Zoya Yankova, who share the opinion of the female magazine editor that such sharing is undesirable. Dr. Yankova's reasoning is very different, however. She said to me, "Why not take advantage of the accumulated experience of each sex in specialized skills (repair versus nurturing)?" I said, "Provided males are taught that the difference is not a sign of superiority, and the time burden is shared equally." She agreed. At the other extreme, there is at least one Soviet family sociologist, V. Shapiro, who expressed in a research paper in 1972 the view that men are "hopeless" in the depth of their desire to maintain a social distance between them and women. Shapiro sought a way out by trying to think through the consequences of parents' being able to decide what sex child they want, which scientists predict will be as available as birth control within a single generation from now. Based on a recent survey of attitudes at Kiev University in the Soviet Union, Shapiro finds that males would then outnumber females three to one, polyandry would replace monogamy as a result, sexual deviance would be a consequence, and society would be revolutionized. That study is the very first sign of willingness to think and talk about alternate forms of sexuality, if only as a possible consequence of probable scientific development.

It is good that financing is available for research and speculation like that, and that the conclusions are now publicly presented. But it is obvious that while science-fiction unknowns must be kept in mind, one cannot build policy on them at this stage. Most Soviet family sociologists take the view that men's heads have got to be changed. Incidentally, more male experts insist on that than female. Perhaps it is because the females are influenced by the reality of their own lives. When a prominent family sociologist and her husband visited me in Moscow, it soon became clear that he, not a specialist in the field, was quite male chauvinist in his views about allegedly genetic psychological differences between the sexes which determined their roles. So his wife tried to equalize the real status of women by inventing and supporting forms of neighbor organizations in housing developments that will reduce the burden on women, with the co-operation and assistance of all sorts of existing government agencies and services.

Essentially her view is not fundamentally different from that of a young woman office employee of Moscow University who responded to my statement that real equality would only come when men share absolutely fifty-fifty: "How are you going to make them?" Scientifically, her opinion is supported by a remarkable survey on what happens to men's opinions when they become fathers. Virtually every *childless* Soviet man—forty-nine out of fifty, married as well as single— has accepted his society's official view that *married* women should not confine themselves to the home or housewifery plus volunteer work, but should hold a job. No sooner do they find themselves with the reality of a child in the house than their views change *very* sharply: now only two fifths of men favor wives working and one half oppose it. The rest have no opinion.

Plain journalistic observation provides the same results. I drew a cabbie, a solid middle-aged type, into conversation. He said, "A married woman with children can't work." I replied, "But a child is the fruit of both the man and the woman, and both should share." He agreed, which his peasant father doubtless would not have, but then the realities took over in his mind, and he said, "For a woman with two children, a job is out of the question."

Very great numbers of women with two children do work, his opinion to the contrary notwithstanding. Yet his attitude finds support in the fact that in the long-urbanized parts of the country, a large minority of women are simply not having a second child. And if that spreads to the new cities and to ethnic areas with large-family traditions, the result will not be zero population growth but an absolute decline. In the Ukraine, a Soviet republic with a population as large as that of France, that is already happening. Abortion-clinic surveys show that if spouses can't agree on whether a pregnancy should go to term and the wife wants an abortion, she goes and gets it. The birth rate in the Soviet Union was almost exactly the same as in the United States in 1971. Ours has since fallen very sharply.

At this moment the Soviet government is trapped by intentions working at cross-purposes. On the one hand, it will not interfere with women's right to decide whether they will go through with or terminate a pregnancy. A middle-aged female head of a very large gynecology clinic in Moscow, Dr. Kazhanova, told me that when she and other women proposed that abortions be forbidden to pregnant *childless* women, the government refused to accept this on the grounds that the result would only be illegal abortions and resulting damage to health, even deaths. (Dr. Kazhanova, as I know from a lengthy tour of her clinic, is very actively prescribing IUDs and the pill. Her objection to abortions is on grounds of health.)

On the other hand, the government wants a larger population in a country that is still very empty by the standards of most of the world, including the United States and most certainly Europe. Right now it seeks to resolve that dilemma by making life easier for all, particularly women. We have already mentioned child-care institutions. The government also hopes that when there are appliances and gas in every home and city apartments are no longer cramped and there is an indoor water supply and sewage facilities where these are still lacking, women will be willing to have a second child, and even a third. But a 1969 survey suggests that it's fighting a losing battle. The *larger* the apartment space per person, the *fewer* women want a second child! The explanation is that those with larger apartments are the better-educated. Their jobs are more interesting, they have wider interests outside work and home, and their notions of child-rearing are more time-consuming. Think back on Maria's daughter, at the beginning of this chapter. Maria recalls that her mother's peasant sisters and brothers just "grew like the grass." Yet the same 1969 survey shows that two thirds of women now want more than one child (generally two), an increase over 1966. (Ninety-seven per cent of U.S. women want more than one.) This was substantiated both by what I was told by a young American woman who has lived in Moscow intermittently since 1966 and by Soviet women public transport workers at their place of employment. Both sources said in 1973 that more women than before were having a second child.

I know no Soviet man over forty-five who fully shares household duties with his wife, and the eldest men (I know scholars and writers in their seventies) don't do anything at home. Under forty-five, those I know personally, with but one exception, share home time responsibilities equally. Two Soviet policies are paying off in greater real equality in the home. One is long-established: preschool institutions. Soviet children in them are taught self-help: serving their meals, clearing the table, drying dishes, putting away toys, straightening their beds (hot meals and midday naps are an absolute rule). There is absolutely no differentiation by sex in these duties. Today's fathers of school-age children were themselves of nursery and kindergarten age when only about one fifth of the children could be accommodated. There is a remarkably close correlation between that figure and the percentage of fathers today who co-operate very substantially, if not entirely equally, in the home. But today surveys find 70 to 80 per cent of pre-school-age children of urban workers and white-collar people in child-care institutions. There is reason to believe that, taken together with all the other factors at work, this will be the percentage of fathers helping significantly in the home when the skills and roles to which they are now being socialized as preschool children become part of their responsibilities as adults. But they play with different toys after the age of three in kindergarten, partly because of home socialization (young women told me they recalled simply going for the dolls when brought to child-care centers), and partly because teachers are trained to instill responsibilities by future sex roles (nurturing versus home repair). So the equally sharing family which I anticipate in most cases a generation hence will be that in terms of time and not of specific duties. Even then, however, the mother would still be the one losing time from work when someone has to stay home to care for a sick child. That will continue to slow women's promotion, even if less than today.

A second factor that has brought a real leap in the practical emancipation of women has been the two-day weekend, established in 1967. Not too long ago only March 8 was "Women's Day," and lots of bitter jokes were made and cartoons published about the rest of the year. (Lots of male chauvinist ones, too.) But now every Saturday is really a day off for many women. For example, on the first Saturday of my 1973 visit I fell into step with two young men in their twenties, clearly working class, pushing baby carriages side by side. I said to provoke discussion, "I guess your wives are home cleaning house." "Why do you say that?" "Well, they're not here." "It's their day off. Aren't they entitled to a day for themselves? Since the baby was born, I've certainly learned a lot about the burden of women." As they strolled along, they fussed over the babies exactly as mothers would. They quieted them, arranged their clothing, covers, and so forth, and exchanged advice with each other. When one cried a lot, the father picked her up and carried her in his arms. When I offered to push, the fathers were equally proud and possessive and as apprehensive about how the baby might react to the stranger as mothers usually are. Being men, they aimed their really long walk at an outdoor beer parlor. But they did not feed any of it to the infants, as I have seen fathers do here. Before the two-day weekend, a woman with children would spend Sunday largely catching up on housework for which there was no time after work on weekdays, and she really had no day off.

There are other signs of increasing male interest in nurturing. I photographed a young couple walking their baby in its carriage. Not only was the father doing the pushing, which I found to be universal, but it was he who would stop and bend over and tuck the cover in around the baby's chin or put the pacifier in its mouth.

At the gynecology clinic, I remarked on a cabinet full of dolls. Dr. Kazhanova said, "We conduct instruction in infant care with them, for both the future mothers and fathers." I asked what percentage of the fathers-to-be participate in those classes. She replied, "Regrettably, only thirty per cent." I commented that in terms of their sex-role traditions, that wasn't a bad figure at all, and reflected that this was just about the percentage of children being socialized into sharing housekeeping when those future fathers were in child-care institutions.

But nothing happens automatically, as so many American students in the turbulent 1960s seemed to expect of revolutionary societies. Dr. Kazhanova said of the fathers, "The way we get them is that they accompany their wives when they visit here." I thought that was a good sign in itself. "And we've adapted the classes in motherhood to keep them coming. We've thrown out all the anatomy, physiology, and we simply give practical advice that is needed not only by mothers but above all by fathers. We consider it important that they know how to diaper a baby, for example."

"Women's consultation" centers like hers—there are twenty thousand blanketing the country—are where all the problems of population policy, abortion, birth control techniques, and the most important of personal-life decisions except marriage itself take on individual human dimensions. Her center, with thirty-two physicians, all female, and forty-two obstetrical nurses, serves one fifth of Moscow, so the statistics of its work pretty clearly represent the situation.

As of 1973, the use of the latest methods of preventing conception was clearly in an early stage. Of about a quarter-million women of childbearing age in her district, only about three thousand were on the pill and five thousand had had intra-uterine devices inserted. The reason there were more of the latter is that women were afraid of the effects of hormones on body chemistry and the physicians agreed. The IUD has been an officially approved technique since 1968, while the pill was still, in 1973, only on the equivalent of the list the United States government calls "New and Unofficial Drugs," although it is legal and sold by prescription in government pharmacies in the Soviet Union. Dr. Kazhanova was very self-critical about having provided her own daughter with Enovid on her marriage when they had received it for testing and the U.S.S.R. was not yet manufacturing its own pills. "The disorders they caused her were so awful that she had to undergo two years of treatment. And she's still taking treatments." Today, pill prescriptions are for a few months' supply, and the woman must come in for an examination in order for a prescription to be renewed.

Results with IUDs have been very good, with minimal side effects, but they are removed and replaced every three years as a precaution. Just as here, the physician's skill and experience makes a difference. I have no reason whatever to doubt Dr. Kazhanova's positive results in her clinic, because she was equally frank in reporting problems with the pill. But I heard horror stories from late teen-age women about their friends' negative experiences with IUDs, and am inclined to think the problem was that the doctor doing the insertion had not yet acquired experience at it. At Dr. Kazhanova's clinic three types of IUDs were being used, one a flat curved zigzag similar to a popular American model, one simply circular, and one, of Soviet design, cross-shaped and opening like umbrella ribs when inserted. All were made of soft plastic, indistinguishable in feel and touch from the American product. The results in preventing conception and in low rate of side effects were essentially equal with all three.

The relatively low rate of use of the latest contraceptives was not merely a matter of recent availability. Dr. Kazhanova said, "You know, women are very complex, psychologically. In one maternity hospital where there is also an outpatient clinic like this one, they put up a big sign: 'Comrade women, whoever wishes to prevent conception by new methods, please come to such-and-such an office.' Only a few individuals came. But in our clinic, we put up no signs, but would say to a patient after an abortion: 'If you want, I'll provide you with a very reliable method.' Before they ever have an abortion, they don't want them. But after, we say: 'We'll send you to a special office for this. We very much want it to be pleasant for you.' Listen, in our clinic they line up at the door for them, because the women feel more confident if we show such a special concern for them—that's psychology for you!"

The point is interesting because of the belief among many women's liberationists here that female physicians are more concerned with women's feelings than male. In both the Soviet clinics, the staffs were female. But at one the individual in charge was more sensitive. Similarly, an American woman of my acquaintance who had a baby in the Soviet Union in the 1960s, with female physicians in charge, says they were verbally very rough with patients in the labor room: "Your mother had you without making such a fuss," they would say. "Keep control of yourself." A female instructor at Moscow University had only the highest praise for the gentleness of male specialists who treated her own extremely painful complications after childbirth. She prefers male doctors.

Today the vacuum method is used in abortions. They are much simpler, given under anesthesia, and with much less subsequent pain. Yet Dr. Kazhanova told me that the ratio has gone down from three abortions per live birth "previously, when we did not have contraceptives" (she meant pills and IUDs) to one-to-one at present. The eight thousand women equipped with modern preventive measures by her clinic are only 3 or 4 per cent of those in the fertile ages in her area. (Tying off the male ducts is simply unknown to average Soviet people, and the rhythm method is regarded as an advanced technique used by a few who are well informed, and concerned!)

WHY MARRY? WHY—AND HOW—DIVORCE?

In sixteen years of conducting a radio program, with phone-ins, on the Soviet Union, I have never had a more poignant question than one from a young man, clearly of poor education and by accent probably Chicano: "Can they marry who they want over there?"

In all countries, the overwhelming majority of people want to live in matrimony. Of all proposals to improve women's lot discussed in the American women's liberation movement, the lowest level of support found by *Psychology Today* in a 1971 poll, except for preferential hiring of women, was that for ending marriage in its present form. Although respondents —readers of that magazine—fall into the group among whom conscious feminism is most pronounced, only 28 per cent of those who belonged to a women's organization of any kind and 15 per cent who did not favored an "end to marriage in its *present* form" (my emphasis). So the nuclear family is what they want. Male respondents, not divided by organizational affiliation, fell precisely between those two figures: 23 per cent.

While that question has not been asked in any Soviet poll, marriage and divorce statistics provide an unmistakable answer: 85 per cent of all women aged thirty to thirty-nine were married, according to the 1970 census. What is more, the percentage was higher in *every* five-year age group from twenty to seventy-plus than at the previous census in 1959, and likewise from age twenty-five up relative to the prewar 1939 census. For the youngest groups, it simply means that women are marrying older, because the notion of marrying a man who will support you is now gone even among the peasantry, and women wait until they have acquired a skill equipping them to be economically independent in marriage. The number of divorces, although the highest in Soviet history, is lower than in the United States despite the fact that their population is substantially larger than ours. Therefore their divorce rate is considerably lower, although it is much easier to obtain a divorce there, in terms of both procedure and cost.

Clearly, the answer to my listener's question is that Russians can marry whom they want much more readily than here, where religion continues to be a serious obstacle, as do differences in the economic and social status of the families of people planning marriage. All those factors represent *some* obstacle there, but not much. The figures speak for themselves: larger percentages of people find mates than ever before, and the percentage who decide they've made the wrong choice, which is partly a consequence of having had to choose from a narrower range than you'd prefer (never mind pressures against marrying "whom you want"), is smaller than here.

Do the marriage figures mean that Soviet women have simply resigned themselves to an outmoded relationship? Space doesn't permit a discussion of whether it is really outdated or not, but the fact is that there is nothing to compel them to marry. (I'm speaking of factually living in a monogamous family with a member of the opposite sex, and usually a child or children. There are old-fashioned Victorian rules over there under which unmarried persons of opposite sex cannot rent a hotel room together, or an apartment, but that doesn't force a couple to marry if they don't wish to live with each other. It may cause some to formalize marriages who would not bother otherwise, but that does not affect our discussion of whether they want the family as an institution.)

The essence of the matter is that the family is very different from what it was, although the word remains the same. A monogamous family in which the male dominates in fact and in law, and in which the extended family may be subject to the will of an older patriarch, is very different from one based on an assumption of sexual equality reinforced by full earning power on the part of the wife, child-care facilities, and control by the woman over whether she will bear conceived children or not. A personal experience, and an example from recent Russian creative literature, will illustrate this.

In 1970 my wife and I picked up a hitchhiking woman of about thirty outside Moscow. She was in so desperate a mood that "I'd do anything to get out of this country." Her husband was an alcoholic who sponged off her. She was a conductor on public transportation. They had a child of ten. She had finally gotten sick of the situation. Pregnant again, she had had an abortion, left her husband, and placed her child in a boarding school at government expense. And she was unhappy for another reason. There was a temporary health quarantine on the Black Sea a thousand miles to the south, and she wouldn't be able to spend her vacation there as usual; she'd have to spend the summer in Moscow.

We talked about her when she left the car, and what struck us was how free she was. She could leave her husband whenever she made that decision because she had a job and there would always be one: there's been no unemployment in the Soviet Union for nearly forty-five years. She had wanted an abortion and had had it, legally, on demand. That would not have been legally possible in the United States at that time, or in the large West European countries. She had placed her child in a school and could take him back at any time, at will. A worker of limited skill, her income was sufficient, thanks to government subsidy of vacation resorts, for her to go South every summer. If she wanted a divorce, she would get one. There is *no* list of formal grounds for divorce in Soviet law. If you can't get along, it is issued (at this writing, only Michigan, California, Oregon, and Colorado have approximately that situation, in the United States). And the spouse who does not receive custody of offspring has to pay child support to the other.

The example from creative literature demonstrating the fundamental change in the family is a short novel by Alexander Yashin, *Wedding in Vologda*. The writer, who was actually from the village in north Russia in which the action is set, and knew its life intimately, wrote in the first person. He says to the prospective bride's mother:

" 'What kind of wedding will you have, old-time or modern?'

" 'How can there be an old-time wedding? It won't work.' But then she begins to tell you everything must be in order for it to be good.

" 'And the bride has to cry?'

" 'She has to howl at the top of her voice. Naturally!'

" 'I can't howl,' Galia cut in, in fright . . .

" 'You've got to howl, a little, anyhow,' her mother insisted."

The wedding occurs, seemingly old-style. The piteous folk songs are sung, but the bride's tears just wouldn't come. The traditional mourner and wailer is invited, a woman who still remembers all the laments. The author goes on: "It turned out that hardly a single one of the girls knew these bitter olden wedding laments," while the bride became utterly distraught, so inappropriate did these songs seem to her. A Soviet critic comments:

"It was not by anyone's evil instigation or edict that the old wedding laments had disappeared from folk memory, if one is speaking of the younger generation of peasants. Something has changed in life if the bride of today, whether in village or town, does not wish bitterly to sing a lament about being married off. What had changed was above all the economic, the social status of that bride, as well as her sense of the ethical and aesthetic." She had been working away from home for three years, and had made her own choice of the boy she wished to marry.

The time of the novel is twenty years ago. Had it been set in the first decade after the Revolution, a time pictured by some as a near-utopia in feminist terms, the bride would have had no trouble howling. All the young women would have known the laments, and no one would have regarded them as inappropriate. The rural family of that day had changed little from that in which a wedding was an occasion for mourning for the bride going to serve a strange family in the capacity of wife and brood hen.

There are three aspects of getting married in the Soviet Union: the legal, the ceremonial or ritual, and possibly the religious. The legal is simple. It is a matter of going to a government office where both parties sign a notice of intent to marry, waiting a month (a measure instituted to avoid hasty marriages and quick divorces), going back to the same office and being married. That used to be dull and routine. But the fact that the people, women in particular, very much want to remember a wedding, has caused a change. Dr. Kazhanova, the obstetrics-gynecology center director, in her other capacity as an elected member of the borough Soviet, chairs its Committee on New Rituals.

The civil wedding, she told me, now takes place in a banquet hall decorated with flowers. Representatives of civic organizations and of the local government get up, one by one, to congratulate the newlyweds. They, in turn, generally rent a Chaika (the Soviet luxury car), and decorate it with a doll, symbolizing offspring, on the radiator, and with ribbons, in an updating of village ritual. They then drive to the Tomb of the Unknown Soldier at the Kremlin wall and place flowers there. Then family and friends take off for a private celebration. Dr. Kazhanova said her committee now also sponsors silver weddings and, recently, a golden wedding "very ceremonially."

I've seen a wedding celebration in a hotel in town. Much food, ample vodka, lots of dancing, altogether rather like a New Year's Eve party back home. But when it is in a private home, or particularly in a village, many ancient formalities are observed, the eating is enormous, the drinking gargantuan, with toasts, wonderful singing, dancing. In people's minds a country wedding is an amazing mixture of tradition and their notion of utopia. In 1973 a young man in Moscow who had been raised in the country said of one: "Something else! Three days' running. Communism for real!"

Church weddings, involving a priest in gorgeous vestments, magnificent musical chants, and the literal crowning of both spouses, have today declined almost to rarity, although they are still entirely legal and not interfered with in any way. The ritualized new civil ceremony is part of the reason, and is intended as such. Dr. Kazhanova said, "So we try to *win* them away from the Church. Prohibiting things accomplished nothing."

Soviet divorces do not require going to court at all if there are no minor children and no one contests. The spouses go to the same office that registers marriages, and sign papers. If a case is contested, a court decides. If there are minor children, the government holds that their interests are a matter of public concern, and therefore a court hearing is required, with a decision as to which parent gets custody (usually the wife), which party shall pay child support (normally the one that does not get custody), and how much (the basic schedule is fixed by law, as a percentage of earnings, modified if and when the individual has a new family to help support; it is 25 per cent of income for one child, 33 for two, and 50 for three or more).

There are many provisions for special situations. One is of interest to us. A husband may not file for divorce if his wife is pregnant or has an infant less than a year old, even if it is not by him. I know personally of a case in which a father of two, the second child born after he and his wife had separated, filed for divorce. The wife came to court and demonstrated that the husband had failed in his duty to the family, specifically by not seeking to find housing for them (a serious problem in Moscow) after he had, in the wife's absence from the city, sold their joint co-operative apartment and himself gone to live elsewhere. The wife made no secret of the fact that she had no desire to live with him, but made it clear that granting the divorce would free him of responsibilities he had deliberately sought to dodge. The judge, a woman, did not conceal her outrage at his behavior, and took advantage of the fact that he had filed two weeks before the infant's first birthday to deny the divorce ("What's two weeks?" he asked when caught in this). There are distinct advantages to women in the fact that nearly one third of judges are female. A court consists of a professional judge and two citizen juror-judges, and a majority vote decides. In this case, one of the juror-judges was female (nationwide women are 50 per cent), and she was as upset as the presiding judge. The male member of the court said not a word.

There is plenty of need for the courts, particularly to protect women. A Soviet Justice Department study of a town of 120,000 showed 1,200 men's wages being garnished for child-support payments. There are 2,500,000 children in the U.S.S.R. under eighteen whose parents are divorced or whose mothers are single and have claimed and won support, by voluntary admission or court action, from their fathers. (There are 85,000,000 under-eighteens in the U.S.S.R.) But since nearly three quarters of the women who bear children out of wedlock make no attempt to have the father's identity established, it may be calculated that there are about

7,000,000 children of incomplete families, minus those whose mothers subsequently marry or remarry. This also tells us, by subtraction, that over 90 per cent of children are in families with fathers. (I have used the word "incomplete family" because it is an established term. Actually, there are Soviet women who have protested inclusion of the question "Head of family?" in the census, declaring in published letters: "A mother and a child *is* a family.")

The confusing changes in marriage and divorce laws to which we are subject when we move from one state to another do not exist in the U.S.S.R. Everywhere in that country, a woman may take her husband's name, keep her own, or use both. Most *do* take their husbands'. There is equal ownership, use and disposal of all property (house, car, piano, furniture) except for that which is clearly sex-associated in the culture: brooches, earrings, etc. Everything bought after marriage is community property. The surviving spouse is the sole heir as a general rule (usually this is the wife, since women there live nine years longer on the average), although minor children and parents lacking means of support may petition a court for a share. The point is that it is taken for granted that minor children will be supported by the surviving parent and that aged parents will normally have either pensions or support from other surviving children. Upon divorce, community property is divided equally. If a divorced wife is not eligible for a pension (this applies to the 8 per cent of women who are housewives), the former husband must maintain her after long married life, if she is above working age or incapable of working. The court decides what constitutes long married life. Beyond these basic principles, valid throughout the Soviet Union, the marriage codes of each of the fifteen republics have provisions resting upon their ethnic cultures.

Parents, or a single parent, may be deprived of a child or children by courts only as a last resort requiring clear proof of (1) failure to care for the child or (2) abuse of it. If parents are conscientious in their efforts, delinquency on the part of the child is no basis for deprivation of parental rights. The children's interests are always overriding, but Soviet authorities believe experience has demonstrated that children raised in a family environment, with personal warmth and concern, turn out better than those brought up in the best of institutions. Therefore they provide a middle ground: a trustee or guardian for a child, without depriving parents of rights to it. If a child is given over to another person or couple as though the latter were parents, then legal duties run both ways: the surrogate parents are responsible for the child's welfare as fully as if they were natural parents, and the child raised by them is responsible for their maintenance in old age, sickness or incapacity (e.g., if a foster mother has been a housewife and therefore has not qualified for pension).

The underlying principle here lies in Karl Marx's principle that "if marriage did not provide the foundation for the family, it would not be a subject for legislation any more than friendship is."

The Soviet Union contributed for the first time in this sphere the view that motherhood is a *social* function distinct from the previous notion that it is a free natural "accident" for which only the mother is responsible. That is why there is an appeal by the state of California to the United States Supreme Court, unsettled as this is written, against a lower court ruling that disability payments must apply to pregnancy as well. It would be unthinkable in the U.S.S.R. There, motherhood is as much a social function as working or defense of the country, and therefore disability due to pregnancy brings public maintenance, preservation of job rights, etc.

At all periods in Soviet history, the mass of women have preferred legal marriage—as protection against runaway husbands, against gossip, and because "a child needs a father." In the 1920s, when common-law marriage had the same standing in law as registered unions, only one twelfth of the people living together did not formalize their union. Obviously, the great majority of men did, and do, want or accept marriage in law.

Divorce in the Soviet Union—I repeat that the rate is lower than in the United States—occurs for much the same reasons as elsewhere. One study there showed nearly 40 per cent for alcoholism, 30 per cent for infidelity, 15 per cent for incompatibility of character, 1 per cent physical incompatibility, etc. Alcoholism is a sex-associated phenomenon. I counted about 150 male drunks and 3 female in a month in Moscow in 1973.

There is a cartoon I saw in one of their publications in which a female lecturer, with a thoroughly soused male slumped in a chair next to her on the platform, points to him indignantly and asks her female audience, "Can one live with such a man?"—to which they respond unanimously: "Yes!" There is a folk belief among Russian women (does it exist elsewhere, too?) that giving a man a home and care will cure him of the habit. But the amount of drinking should not be exaggerated. A survey of the work forces of three factories of different types showed that one third of men and two thirds of women drink only on holidays and at family celebrations. Only one fifth of men drink more than once a week, it claims.

Divorce is also related to reasons for marriage. Marriages for love or liking and respect show a low rate of divorce, while those to avoid loneliness break up more often. Frivolous marriages, chiefly among young people on short acquaintance, break up frequently, but a high percentage of divorces are found among people married for many years. The most stable marriages are found where good education, satisfactory income, and sharing of household duties by the spouses are all present.

Perhaps the changes that have occurred in the family can best be understood if today's Soviet reality is compared to that set forth in two world classics of creative writing, one Russian and one Western. Dostoevski's *Crime and Punishment* is built around conditions of family life nonexistent in the Soviet Union: Sonya takes to the streets to support an alcoholic father, tubercular stepmother, and her little sister and brother. In the U.S.S.R. today, she would have a job at the median industrial wage (she was not stupid, lazy, or unconscientious); her mother would be in a sanatorium or hospital at public expense; the younger children would be fed in school, or aided by a grant from her trade union out of social insurance funds, or placed with foster parents, or institutionalized; and her father could be committed for compulsory free treatment of alcoholism. In the same novel, Raskolnikov's sister's entire decision is whether to marry for money to provide for her impoverished mother and herself, and Svidrigailov, who makes her a cash offer, puts it to her directly that the "more honorable" alternative she has chosen is to marry for money.

Studies in the Soviet Union show that marriages there for material considerations are exceedingly few.

The other classic I should like to look at in terms of Soviet reality is Ibsen's *The Doll's House.* When I saw it in San Francisco in 1973, the audible, sympathetic responses of middle-aged women throughout the audience made clear that they found it very pertinent to their lives. It has about as much relevance to Soviet reality as a play in the United States today advocating abolition of chattel slavery. Nora and her money problems with her husband are unthinkable in the Soviet Union. Only one urban woman there in ten, and one rural woman in six, is economically dependent upon her husband, and that is by free choice.

Consider the motivations for action on which Ibsen builds his plot. Money for a trip to a healthier climate for a very sick person? It's provided out of government funds through one's trade union, in whole or in part, depending upon income. If more is still needed, the union will provide it on personal request. Personal friends there lend money without question, and entirely without interest. It simply goes without saying. Nora's fraud in the play would have no basis in necessity. The need to keep her act of management as a secret weapon against her "loved" husband against the time when she loses her beauty (so she can then demonstrate that she is more than merely a faded doll) is unnecessary for the same reason.

Fru Linde's tragedy is impossible in Soviet society. There is no conceivable situation in the U.S.S.R. in which a woman would have to abandon a lover to marry for money, for the family's sake or any other reason. The tragedy of the nursemaid is also impossible there (but not here!): there is absolutely no need to give up a child for adoption. If it's hard to find a child to adopt here because of the rigid requirements of adoption agencies (except for children of minority racial backgrounds), it's nearly impossible in the Soviet Union because the only real source is totally orphaned children with no close relatives, plus a *very* few women who have had children out of wedlock and don't want to keep them.

Ibsen's question of what will happen to Nora, a housewife emerging from a cocoon, when she undertakes to make her own life, doesn't exist in the U.S.S.R. The whole final speech, so relevant in the United States today that *Ms.* has run it repeatedly, is archaic and quaint in the Soviet Union.

Soviet scholars disagree about much with regard to the family there. But they agree, in varying formulations, about its direction. Pimenova (female) says, "Today's family is in the stage of transition from an autocratic to a democratic structure." But she adds that only 43 per cent of women even say that their husbands are the heads of the family, while close questioning shows that this is the real situation in only one fifth of that percentage, mildly true in half, and not true at all in one third.

A favorite writer of mine, Yuri Riurikov, male, told me that he sees two kinds of families now, the patriarchal, which he defines as one in which the wife is a servant because she carries the burden, and the "ambichate," which he says is prevalent among the higher intelligentsia. The word, which he coined, means a family structure in which both parents are equal heads in partnership.

The very prominent family sociologist Dr. Yankova (female) said to me: "With us, inequality is concentrated at the stage of families with young children. The woman before marriage is really equal" (lots of data supports this) "as is the woman with grown children." (I don't quite agree: think of Maria at the beginning of this chapter.) She went on:

"Equality must not be the same as identity. It seems to me that the error of our literature is that for a very long time, and with great emphasis, it created the impression that men and women are identical, everywhere and in all things, with the result that a great many ridiculous conflicts arose in families. I gave a lecture to farm machinery operators. A man got up and said: 'Last night we had a big argument at home. My wife was washing the floors—she is a factory worker—and when she got halfway through the hallway floor, she put down the pail and broom and said, "Vitya, we have equality: I did half the floor space." I said, "But I just finished chopping the firewood. That's a job for a man. So I can chop the wood; I'll go out now and fetch potatoes. Why should I have to wash the floor?" "Well, but we have equality. You're going to the store? I can go. And for the potatoes too."' Equality," Yankova repeated, "is not identity. Does it mean that I wash the first diaper, and my husband washes the second? In any factory, there is a division of labor."

I interrupted: "On the basis of sex?" "No. But I hold that wherever any small group exists, a division of labor exists. There are differences in people's abilities—she sews well and he doesn't, or the husband is a splendid cook but no good at straightening up the room, or a husband is great at taking care of the baby and the wife is a wonderful cook. Division of work in the family, inasmuch as it is not a formal organization, must in many respects be based upon individual experience, abilities, capacities, and—inasmuch as the family is built on personal relationships—upon love. It also matters to what degree each spouse becomes fatigued on the job, or how well or poorly one feels on a given day. In a formal role—myself as Senior Research Associate, for example—one must learn to play that role and do so unless out sick. At home one can feel a little bad, and drop or exchange roles. . . ."

We moved on to division of work along lines of sex in the family. She said, "Man, because of his *social* experience, cooks better, sews more poorly." I insisted that one has to look at that social experience "as one in which women were always oppressed, in all societies." She agreed. I added, "And as a consequence, man, most men, regard women's work as being something on a lower level." Here she made an interesting point:

"I class home responsibilities in two groups: one from which the doer gains nothing, but merely expends much effort and time. This actually does dull a person. Washing floors adds nothing to a personality. But another category helps in one's own growth. Child-rearing." I noted, "If real rearing." She agreed: "Not mere custodial care."

So the discussion went. Other Soviet scholars lay stress on the new function of the family for "release of workaday tension," a "psychological bomb shelter," and say, rightly I believe, that "the socializing function of the family has even been increasing in recent decades."

I personally am most impressed by the attempt to put the further evolution of the Soviet family in the context of that society's goals for the future, as expressed by Dr. N. G.

Yurkevich (male): "A further increase in the number of marriages based on *complete equality of the parties,* while one of the ideological objectives of socialist society, is simultaneously a most important condition for strengthening the family. If both spouses hold jobs, their obligations with respect to keeping house and raising the children must be *equal in volume.* Implementation of this rule probably should be regarded today as the *major* emphasis to be placed in the struggle to reorganize relations within the family on communist principles."

Chapter XII
The Light at the End of the Bedroom

A nude Russian fifteenth-century peasant woman celebrating the pagan festival of the summer solstice throws her arms around a monk, Andrei Rublev, who, in the fine recent Soviet film about him, has been drawn to watch Russia's greatest ikon painter. She has never seen him before, and he is not portrayed at all as a womanizer—quite the contrary—nor as particularly handsome. She does not try to be seductive or enticing. She is simply passionate, and when he, sincerely religious, resists, she asks why one should not love.

In another excellent Soviet movie, *The Communists,* made in the late 1950s and set in the famine year of 1920, right after the Revolution, a drunken worker wanders unintentionally into a barracks of sleeping peasant and poor working women at a construction site. First they almost kill him for coming in like that. Then he tells them good news that some candy has reached this town and there will be a celebration. They fling him up in the air in a traditional gesture of approval. Then one of them gives him a tremendous hug and long kiss. As in *Andrei Rublev,* he is a complete stranger. She, like the others, is wearing a coarse slip, which is not transparent or clinging or décolleté. As in the other film, the moviemaker was depicting a situation, not trying to titillate the audience.

In Moscow in 1973 I saw a play set in the present. In it

there is a woman forester who arrests men, including a self-important army major and a civilian official she caught hunting in a closed season. At another point in this play, a young woman in love with a man who can't make up his mind flings her arms around him with the same whole-being kiss as in the films.

In the Moscow subway, particularly on its long escalators, I saw any number of couples embracing face to face, oblivious to the world. That was in 1973. Three years earlier I witnessed nothing of the sort, nor had I on earlier visits. On this last trip, I remember seeing in Moscow's Central Park a tall and handsome young man with his back to the river wall looking bored, or trying to, while a girl leaned against and stroked him, in a textbook example of male arrogance and culturally conditioned embarrassment combined with female spontaneity.

But there is also another morality and behavior pattern, one of feminine modesty, and the two sometimes get mixed up in typical human inconsistency. In *The Beginning,* a film of recent years, a textile worker's roommate tells her that she has become engaged. The other asks her, "Have you kissed yet?" She shakes her head, looks down at the floor, and says, "I can't trust myself." The textile worker nods in understanding and approval. Nevertheless, she herself has taken a married man away from his wife with no malice or calculation, but simply because she had fallen in love with him after he approached her at a dance.

Somehow one thinks that where there is such spontaneity in courtship there would also be sexual satisfaction for women. The *only* Soviet study of this, published a dozen years ago, showed that of 295 women being treated for sterility, 12 per cent had never had an orgasm, and one third only rarely. By subtraction, then, even in that group, a majority, 55 per cent, do have orgasms more than rarely. Men are not entirely insensitive. At least they ask: "Have you come?" But very few of them know more than rudimentary sexual techniques. And if they do, it is by hearsay or through openness to the suggestions of women who are psychologically capable of making them.

There is no such thing as a marriage manual in Russia.* The closest thing to it is a fine book by Yuri Riurikov on the history of love all over the world, including its physical aspects. The book does not actually describe them, however, but argues bitterly and brilliantly against the harm done by not treating this subject frankly. Its two printings of 100,000 each were snapped up, and all five copies in the Lenin Library were stolen by readers. Until 1960, no Soviet writer, though he (or she) may have wished to, submitted for publication anything saying his characters were having intercourse, because he knew that it would never see the light of day. In this regard, the situation was better in the first fifteen years after the Revolution, both in literature and on the screen. Movies never showed the act of love, but there was at least minimal reality, from an Eisenstein classic of the 1920s showing peasant boys with their hands naturally in their girls' blouses, to an enormously popular horse opera of the Soviet Civil War produced in the 1930s, *Chapayev,* in which a guerrilla teaching machine-gun maintenance to a woman volunteer puts his hands on her breasts from behind. If the guerrilla treated her as a sex object, her response put him in his place. But then twenty-three years elapsed, in Stalin's dark ages (the earlier films had also been made when he was in power, but not yet dictator), during which the notion that relations between the sexes involved anything physical whatever could not be put on the screen. True, film characters got married and babies appeared, but how that came about was as mysterious as in American films of the same period (we managed to be ignorant without benefit of a dictator to help it along).

While nude bathing, separately by sex, was entirely common during my first visit, in 1931–32, it was suppressed in the years that followed, much more by a change in people's

* One was published when this book was in press. It reported a second study on the female orgasm, which found that only 18 per cent of Soviet women had never experienced one, versus about 40 per cent in France and Britain. Sex is all right, says this book, "anywhere and anytime." If a couple is in love, premarital sex is okay. If not, it can cause "severe psychic disturbances." "Men often overestimate a younger woman's need for sex while they underestimate an older woman's needs." The first printing of 100,-000 copies of the book was sold out overnight.

ideas of what was right than by any edict. I am told that mixed topless bathing has made an appearance on the Black Sea beaches in the 1970s.

Where did the puritanism of the late 1930s, largely present even today, come from? Oddly, that takes us back to Andrei Rublev and the Middle Ages. A Russian prince adopted Christianity a thousand years ago. Over four hundred years later, as the film about Rublev, which is historically accurate, shows, the rulers were still having to use physical force to impose Christianity and its notions of morality upon the people. In the opening scene, soldiers raid a peasant gathering where a folk entertainer has been singing about how women have their beards where they need them, and about a priest who has chased a boy into the woods. The soldiers smash the buffoon-minstrel's harplike instrument, knock him unconscious, and drag him away. When he reappears later in the film, we learn that he was chained ten years in a pit and half his tongue was cut off.

The pagan festival at which the nude woman seeks to embrace Rublev is also raided by troops. She is driven mad by her experiences. Rublev later paints her into one of his ikons. But he himself believes that nakedness is a sin. All the figures in his paintings are fully clothed, in fact magnificently draped.

Anthropologists have found that while the Russian people finally did accept Christianity entirely into their consciousness, many pre-Christian practices and attitudes remained as late as the nineteenth century. In a country so large, this varied widely from place to place. But the general rule in peasant Russia was that peasant girls who had premarital relations were punished severely and their families shamed by neighbors who painted tar on their fence posts. And when the industrialization of the 1930s brought tens of millions of people with these mores into the cities, they swamped out whatever little sexual enlightenment had developed in the tiny prerevolutionary intelligentsia and had spread somewhat among the small urban working class after the revolution. The new city populations and the country at large needed organizers, managers, administrators, to direct and govern a society with unprecedented needs for co-ordination of work, supplies, and products. The required people emerged from that same peasant or, at best, just-urbanized, ex-peasant background. Under the pressures of the times, the education they received was overwhelmingly technical and political in the narrow sense. So they carried the old mores into their positions of authority. The top figures in government today are of exactly that origin.

Writing of the youth of that generation, a bitterly anti-Stalin Moscow writer, Vladimir Kantorovich, who served twenty years in exile under the old dictator, makes clear in a recent book that folk traditions were far more to blame for persistence of old attitudes in relations between sexes than any individual. In fact, what emerges is that cultural policies were progressive as far as women were concerned but were overwhelmed by the weight of established chauvinism and rural custom.

Shipped to Sakhalin, the Pacific island north of Japan, Kantorovich was housed in a room with five young miners, village born. (Exile was not concentration camp: those in exile were required to live in a designated spot far from the mainstream, and could make a living in whatever way was available.) Four of his five roommates were striving to improve themselves, three by attending schools in the evening or by correspondence, and one actually wrote verses printed in the local paper. They were fine fellows in every respect but one: "They were skeptics and cynics with regard to love, and reconciled themselves easily to everything that was coarse and degrading in everyday relations with women."

They talked about the young women they went out with, invariably in obscene language, offered vulgar advice, and bragged about "conquests" real or imagined, always bandying real names about. One evening the "poet" put down with a sigh his copy of Tolstoi's *Anna Karenina,* muttered something about "beautiful feelings," and got ready to go out with some "stupid skirt, who is in love like a cat," adding a few intimate details, to roars of laughter by the others. When one of the others said, "Watch out, you'll wind up married!" he replied, "Don't be stupid. I'll marry a girl from my own village, just like you." Kantorovich asked, "You're engaged to girls in your villages?" "No, they're still growing up." "Is that love?" the writer asked. "To play around here with anyone who comes along, call them tarts, knowing all the while that you'll marry a girl you don't know, *whoever your mother advises you to* [my emphasis], so long as it's someone from back home? You don't have much in the way of feelings. You read good books. You know how Anna Karenina loved and suffered, how Vronsky and Levin loved. You mean you've decided that there's less to you than to a bunch of princes and counts, that you're not capable of deep feelings, that that won't happen in your lives?"

They put their heads together in a huddle, and finally one said, "Do things happen in real life like in novels?"

That was the problem. The government had taught them to read and write, which their fathers did not know. It circulated in enormous editions and very low prices the finest in world literature, not only Russian, and deliberately and successfully suppressed outright pornography treating women as things to be used. Millions of copies of first-rate books were issued and read—books like Sholokhov's *And Quiet Flows the Don,* containing a classical love story about two Russian peasants to whom Kantorovich's roommates could directly relate, and, most remarkable of all, Chernyshevski's mid-nineteenth-century *What Is to Be Done?* which is *the* women's-liberation novel of all times. Its burden is set forth in the author's personal diaries about his own wife: " 'Remember,' he wrote her, 'I love you so that your happiness is more important to me than your love.' " And to himself: "If my wife chooses to live with another, I will say to her only: 'When you choose to return to me, please do, don't hesitate for a moment.' " In explaining this he wrote: "Women must be equal to men. But when a stick has been bent too long in one direction, to straighten it out it has to be bent a great deal in the other. . . . Every decent man must, in my opinion, place his wife above himself—that temporary imbalance is needed so that equality may exist in the future."

And a novel based on that thinking was read by *millions* in the 1930s, whether or not Kantorovich's roommates were among them. But that generation of ex-peasants was simply unable to internalize it, or Tolstoi, or Sholokhov, as more than entertainment. As Kantorovich put it, "The guilt lies most often with the consumerist attitude toward women acquired in youth in 'male company,' and transmitted from generation to generation in the traditions of the barbarous 'love games' played by boys with girls, described with such severe horror by Nikolai Kochin in his novel, *The Girls* [1928, 1935]."

Unfortunately, as *Wedding in Vologda,* described in the last chapter, makes clear, women of those generations in the countryside, which then had most of the population, accepted those mores, and later carried them into city life when they moved to town en masse.

Many a Western woman visiting the Soviet Union in the 1960s was approached by elderly Russian women with the phrase "Aren't you ashamed of yourself?" for wearing minis or micro-minis or *slacks.* In that period I saw young couples upbraided by passersby for simply sitting with their arms around each other on park benches. In 1959 I remember a stern-faced woman worker with a red armband approaching young people in a dance hall in a park in Leningrad, which had been the most sophisticated city in Russia, with the phrase "No dancing 'in style,' " which meant the twist. But by 1970 pants suits were being worn to the theater even in medium-sized industrial towns and skirts were several inches above the knee, although a Soviet paper could still report in horror a case in which a woman was fired by demand of her union committee for coming to work in slacks! Yet in 1973 it was extremely pleasant to see even middle-aged couples, obviously long-married from their general demeanor, walking down the streets holding hands, or leaning their heads against each other when seated in streetcars. Russians are a very warm people and they are now letting it show. And even the middle-aged of today are young enough to have gotten married after the custom of arranged marriages had disappeared almost entirely. In a very impressive percentage of couples, wives and husbands surveyed separately by sociologists describe their marriages as happy. Most of the rest say they are "satisfactory."

It doesn't make sense to believe that none of this has reached back into the bedroom, but if surveyors have advanced to asking questions about that, the results have not yet been published except for the one set of figures I have cited. No Masters and Johnson or even Kinsey studies have yet been made in the U.S.S.R. A scholar, Sergei Golod, did a survey of attitudes on sexual relations in the mid-1960s, but Victorian-minded authorities would not accept his dissertation based on this!

But attitudes are improving. Until my visit of 1973, no one had ever been able to get Soviet women to talk into a tape recorder about intimate matters. An elderly American woman on good terms with her Soviet daughter-in-law, whom she sees fairly often; a young American woman married to a Russian; another who had had Soviet lovers in recent years; others who had been exchange students in the U.S.S.R. living in women's dorms there for a full year: all were willing to help me, but none could provide much information because Russian women still considered these "shameful" subjects for discussion, even with other women.

Thanks to the help of understanding Moscow acquaintances and probably to a very rapid change in attitudes at least among the more sophisticated, I was able to make such tapes. No question was rejected or seemed to cause embarrassment or a request to turn off the recorder, which I offered to do.

Essentially, Soviet women, like many women in the West, think much more about love than about sex until they've actually found themselves pregnant. All current Western studies of the continuing high pregnancy and abortion rates despite the pill agree that that is the reason. If women everywhere are more romantic than men, both sexes in the U.S.S.R. are by now more so than in the West. I remember the amazed manner in which the youthful male president of a college for the co-op movement near Moscow looked at and handled the things for sale in a sex shop in San Francisco, and said to me in a tone of wonderment after we left: "How can people buy such things? The relationship between a man and a woman ought to be the purest and most wonderful thing there is." He is a full generation younger than Kantorovich's roommates of the prewar period.

But the women I interviewed tell me that there's a great deal of plain *macho* and Victorianism in male attitudes. Lots of men won't use condoms because a "real man" shouldn't. Yet they are willing to use coitus interruptus. Pharmacists are invariably women, and a man going in to buy condoms will not utter that naughty word, but will point and then turn his head away as she gives him the product! When an American woman newly married to a Russian told a Russian woman friend that the husband wanted *her* to buy them, the friend replied, "You tell him that if he's not bashful in bed, he can damn well speak up in a store." Even the fact that women were, in 1973, willing to talk to me about sex life is almost without precedent, and an indication that there is now some willingness to talk with their husbands (as one said directly), which is a beginning. Another recent observer reports: "One hears constant complaints from men about Soviet women becoming very choosy, uppity, and demanding in sex relations; and every man who wishes his marriage or affair to last must be very adroit sexually."

But two married women with whom I had a conversation saw things differently. They were both thirty-four. I had noted that American women of my acquaintance who had had sex relations with Soviet men said they are still crude in bed, and I asked them to comment. One of them said, "Yes, of course." The other said, "The men of our generation grew up in times that were entirely different, when there weren't even films in which they could see a naked woman. Even revealing a bare knee was regarded as a leap forward. There was no literature on sex, not to speak of sex education. None whatever. And to this day the majority live by the old laws. A wife is afraid to talk to her own husband. Therefore, when the first night comes, if both have no experience, they think that what happens then is the way it's supposed to be. And they continue that way through their whole lives. And, generally speaking, nobody even tries to improve this, because that's what the mother told her daughter."

I asked what the mother told her daughter. "She didn't tell her anything. Maybe she gave her a dowry of thirty pillows. . . ." The other interrupted: "What she told her was to be a virgin until she gets married: 'Preserve your honor.'" "Yes. That is the principal injunction that is now given in ninety per cent of families. So if a girl permits herself anything, it is kept secret from her mother, who would regard it as a terrible disgrace. Our mothers were raised that way, and no literature, no films or anything else can change them.

They were brought up that way, and that's how they'll be until they die."

"Their daughters would like to live differently. But if she tries to do something—well, she can't, she is still ashamed. We are very constrained. It is only very recently that we have begun to see a few things."

A study published in a Soviet journal for public health personnel says women make their first visit to women's (medical) consultation centers only when they want an abortion. One tenth had been ashamed even to ask *doctors* for advice on contraception, although the obstetrician-gynecologists at these twenty thousand centers, which blanket the country, are *exclusively female.*

One of the women on my tape had married in 1968, three years before the IUD was approved, and since the rhythm method has worked for her and her husband—their one child was desired—she has had no personal incentive to find out about other contraceptive techniques. But obviously that method involves constraint, by the calendar if not by the hour. They had simply never heard of vasectomy.

Using this woman's words on contraception for this book is like trying to take a photo of high-speed motion. I know from experience in many other fields how rapidly innovations are made available to the Soviet public, once its government authorities have decided to make a particular move, and with respect to modern contraceptives that decision has been taken. Even their condom, which used to be thick and often unsafe, is today a good contraceptive, but Soviet physicians write that its bad reputation from the past, both aesthetically and in effectiveness, causes many people to refuse to use it, with the result that the rate of abortion is higher than it should be. While I am convinced that IUDs, and most probably the pill as well, will be in mass-scale use within five years, the bedroom behavior of the current generation of Soviet young people is constrained, as my informant states, by what they *believe* to be true about contraceptives. Perhaps I should add that it was in the very month that I taped that interview, August 1973, that their mass-circulation magazine *Health* (ten million copies a month) first informed its readers about IUDs. Was it feared that an earlier public announcement would cause a mass run that the number of physicians trained in insertion could not yet handle? I don't know, but the first book ever published there for physicians on IUDs and the pill appeared only that year, in an edition exactly the same size as the number of women's obstetrics-gynecology clinics in Russia.

The first Soviet survey of use of family-planning methods based on scientific sampling techniques was taken in 1966, in their pre-pill, pre-IUD era, and published in 1972. It found the following:

Some middle-aged women ignorant of birth control have had as many as eight abortions, but they form a very small minority: only one in twenty-six has had seven or more. Sixty-five per cent have had two abortions or less, which is about the same as in the West, even though abortions are legal in the U.S.S.R. (One in four had had none at all, generally indicating good contraceptive use.) The scholars, a woman and a man both associated with the Demography Laboratory of the Central Statistics Office of the Soviet Union, find that abortion is "a result of ineffective employment of contraceptives and other birth control methods either because they are inaccessible or because the existing and generally employed measures for regulating fertility cause serious physiological, mental, and psychological side effects that disturb not only the natural course of physiological processes but harmony between the spouses."

This team learned that practically everyone uses some means of contraception, which is borne out by the present very small family size. Their figures show that somewhat over half use condoms, and one fifth combined this with coitus interruptus for greater safety. One third used coitus interruptus alone. Fascinatingly, that is exactly the same percentage who used that method, stressful and disappointing for men and a great deal worse for women, in "enlightened" Sweden, where the pill and the IUD were available, according to figures it submitted to the United Nations in 1970. Sweden is not a Catholic country. It has also had compulsory education for a century, compared to forty years for the U.S.S.R. Sweden is also much more urban.

The same Soviet study showed one tenth of the people questioned using other methods of contraception: diaphragms, jellies, etc. Broken down by age groups, the percentage in the twenty-five to twenty-nine category using any form of contraception was identical to that in this country (87.7 per cent in the U.S.S.R. and 86 per cent in the United States). Among older Soviet women the figure was higher than here (92.6 for those thirty to thirty-four and 92.3 for those thirty-five and above, while in the United States it was 84 per cent for the former and 78 to 81 per cent for the latter). In the youngest age group, up to twenty-five, the opposite situation obtained: 74.5 per cent of Soviet women and their partners used means of contraception, as against 85 per cent of American. Young Soviet couples tended to use no means of contraception until they had their child or children, inasmuch as their economic security is not affected by childbirth: a young woman's job waits for her if she returns within one year, another is always available otherwise, and there is free hospitalization and paid maternity leave. Young Americans plan their first child, at least, more carefully, because paid maternity leave and free childbirth hospitalization are enjoyed by few and because of the fact that the husband's economic position is also uncertain. On the other hand, the pill was already available in the United States, so that one could have contraception without interference with sexual pleasure. One quarter of Americans seeking to control childbirth already used that technique, chiefly in the youngest age group.

Finally, the Soviet study gave some notion about the extent of premarital relations at least as reflected in pregnancies. The authors were quite surprised by what they found, saying their figures were "very low by comparison to estimates made in the literature" which were not based on actual surveys. Six per cent of single women had had pregnancies: only one in seventeen.

Once women were married, they had precisely as many children as they wished, thanks to the availability of abortion. Every single unwanted pregnancy among women with three children was aborted, and virtually all among those having one or two. Among those with no children, four fifths of unwanted pregnancies terminated in abortion.

One recent Soviet study has been published on attitudes toward premarital sex. Among five hundred students queried, 85 per cent of the men and 47 per cent of the women reported having had sexual relations. Among the women, only 14.5 per cent were under nineteen the first time, as against 52.5 per cent of the men. Half the women began sexual relations between nineteen and twenty-one years of age, and over a quarter as late as twenty-two to twenty-four.

Unlike the United States, where the student generation has the most open ideas, or did in the 1960s, in the Soviet Union women a little older than student age are more open. A survey by the same scholars of women already employed in research fields found 55 per cent approving premarital intimacy, as against 38 per cent of undergraduate women. Outright condemnation of sex before marriage was voiced by 27 per cent of the female undergraduates but only 7 per cent of the researchers. People are willing to permit themselves things they oppose as a general standard. One hundred twenty-six white-collar workers (neither students nor researchers but office personnel, engineers, etc.) were asked: "Is premarital sex permissible for you personally?" Affirmative answers were very high, differences between the sexes small: 91 per cent of the men and 81 per cent of the women said yes, if the experience were with a loved one. But when the distinction was made between love and sexual release, an extremely sharp difference showed up: 60 per cent of the men thought relations with a casual acquaintance permissible for themselves personally, but only 14 per cent of the women held that view. For women, clearly, sex and love are inseparable in the overwhelming majority of cases. That it is also true of two men in five is encouraging. This is the generation of the children of Kantorovich's Siberian roommates thirty-five years ago, whose sexist attitudes so shocked him. (He is now seventy-three.)

Finally, the surveyors inquired into the area of the double standard, asking whether one's sex partner should be free to have other sex relations. From the statistics of the replies, the author concluded, not surprisingly: "The double standard is in process of withering away. But at the same time it is also demonstrated that vestiges of it remain; men are more liberal toward their own sex behavior than toward that of women, and women are more liberal toward male behavior than toward their own."

Enough of statistics. Two young women of nineteen, friends, one married and with an infant, the other single, answered my questions on this subject in Moscow in 1973. Both were city-born, of notable intellectual families. The married woman's husband is a blue-collar workingman, both of whose parents are workers. I was interested in their entire self-perception as females, and so began with their earliest memories. When were they first aware of themselves as belonging to a distinct sex? In the child-care centers, they replied, where girls and boys used the same toilets and "looked at each other to see how different people are made." Did boys and girls play doctor? They looked at each other blankly, didn't even know what the game was. When I explained, they said no. As far as sex roles were concerned, it was their parents who first gave them dolls, before they went to nursery. There the kids themselves fell into the standard roles: "I'll be a general; you be a nurse."

In answer to my further questions, they told me that up to the age of puberty, girls and boys played separately—the girls playing Russian games and taking walks, and the boys playing sports. None of their girl friends wanted to play soccer, and there was no clash about girls playing in any games because they just didn't want to play the things boys were interested in. At the Young Pioneer camps (up to age fourteen), all organized activities were for both sexes together, but in their free time boys and girls went their separate ways.

Menstruation began at ages eleven to fourteen. They had learned only six months earlier, that is, in 1973, of the existence of factory-made sanitary napkins available for purchase, but supplies often run out. The cost is thirty for eighty-four cents. (A Soviet medical journal the previous year carried a suggested hygiene lecture to young women which read: "Homemade napkins should be made of gauze that is sterile and has been gone over with a hot iron. . . . Absorbent cotton not covered with fabric [or gauze] should not be used. Napkins should be changed as often as possible.")

One started having boy friends at age fifteen, the other at seventeen. It was the latter who became pregnant and got married. "But now they have boy friends earlier: eleven, twelve, thirteen." Anthropologists would call that a very rapid culture change, but it is consistent with what happened in the United States a few years earlier. It is also borne out by the observation of a young American woman who found the attitudes of nineteen-year-olds working in a Moscow office with her in 1970 sharply different from those of women just a very few years older (she herself was twenty-two at the time and found little in common with the "kids").

The nineteen-year-old who had started dating at fifteen said that she had never kissed on a first date. (Think back to the scene in the film *The Beginning* in which a young woman of about twenty says she has not yet kissed the boy to whom she is already engaged, of their own choice.) Both young women were noncommittal when asked about heavy petting. Of their girl friends, all of whom are unmarried, one said that two or three of six had had sex relations, the other four of eight—because "most were in love." One said that sex relations begin at age seventeen or older, the other at sixteen. If these answers are representative of all women, it would mean a decline in age since the survey reported above, done five years earlier. But that would also be consistent with earlier maturation in terms of menstruation, earlier dating, and medical data showing a remarkably rapid and impressive increase in the height and weight of Soviet adolescents in a very few years as diet and other conditions have improved.

They said that they go "out into the country" to have sex relations. (That means summertime only. Teen-agers don't have cars, and few parents do.) They said that their outlooks regarding sex are very different from those of their parents, to whom premarital relations are a "nightmare."

With respect to contraception, there was clearly a very heavy burden not only upon them but upon their physicians from an earlier period when the quality of all Soviet consumer goods was poor. These young women thought that the pills, about which they knew, "don't work," and their doctors actually advised using them in combination with foam or whatever. I told them of the excellent results at Dr. Kazhanova's clinic with the same pills, and my guess was that their doctors were probably conservative and uninformed, playing safe in light of the previous situation. They said that all three of their friends who had IUDs inserted had had extremely bad experiences, and I told them that success with IUDs had to do with skill of insertion and the amount of practice the physician had had.

The married woman, with problems because her husband won't help at home, had no suggestions on how to make relations between married couples better. Her parents had bought them a co-operative apartment, giving them reasonable space and privacy, but that hadn't solved things. She herself had not gone beyond high school, and was planning to learn a skill when her infant was a little older. I'm not sure about the durability of that marriage. The single woman suggested: "Live separately. Then there are fewer petty things to bug you. When you're together, you'll be in a better mood." I knew that a woman had written that in a paper my informant probably reads, but other letter-writers in it had replied: "Wait till she has a baby!"

One of them asked me how many children there are in a family in the United States? Two or three, I said. She responded, "That's an awful lot." I told them of a Soviet Uzbek scientist I know with four children. "Horrible! What can you *do* with so many children?" I responded, "What do you do with *not* such a large number?" "Raise them, train them." They agreed with my observation that the large number of single or divorced women now having a child out of wedlock is a step forward in women's emancipation.

I told them of the big discussion back home about the future of the family, and said it seemed to me that Soviet women clearly feel a psychological need to get married. "Yes, that's so. Maybe because they're built that way. A woman knows she is a future mother."

There is one problem we have not discussed: extramarital sex. I know of no studies done there, except the one quoted earlier on whether one regards it as permissible. I assume there is some relation between the answers given and how people really behave, but only some. In general, the impression I have from watching Soviet men resident in the United States for periods, and from talking to American women who have lived in the U.S.S.R., is that there is a great deal of extramarital sex. These women tell me it is true of both sexes. They describe it not as promiscuity but as a natural kind of response to attraction and friendship. One such woman says that three out of five couples she knows well have had such episodes.

The one survey on this subject, done among educated white-collar personnel, showed that 30 per cent of the men and 48 per cent of the women accepted the idea of other sex relations on the part of those with whom they are in love, presumably including spouses. What this says by subtraction, of course, is that a majority *don't* want their spouses sleeping around. Summer affairs at vacation resorts are definitely common, partly because spouses, both working, often can't manage to get their vacations at the same time if they are not employed at the same place. On the other hand, the notion that people's morality is other people's business, which is true generally in villages and officially for the millions of members of the Communist party, probably plays a role. It is also true that the number of people who simply don't want to sleep with anyone but their spouses because they're really in love must be distinctly higher than in the past, because marriage for love is now a mass-scale phenomenon. But I just don't know for certain.

I know of a young Soviet woman, nineteen or twenty, who was told absolutely nothing by her own mother even about menstruation. When it began she thought she had a venereal disease, even though she had never had intercourse, about which her spouse was equally ignorant. Later she became pregnant because she had heard that that can happen only if you have intercourse during menstruation, not otherwise!

I spent an evening in Moscow in 1973 with a man who is part of a team of six that is supposed to be working on the subject of sex education. He is worried that men are becoming feminized and women masculinized. When I asked him to explain, he responded: "In the old days, if someone insulted a man, he could challenge the other to a duel. Now you have to think: should I take it up with the trade union committee or the party committee!" It is only fair to add that he is not Russian but of a nationality native to a part of the country where duels are not that far in the past. But for such a person to be engaged in working on sex education? It will be no surprise that his basic answer to all sex problems is "chastity." For women, of course. He doesn't think it's so vital for men.

A certain Soviet psychologist of very high repute, recently deceased, argued for years for the need for nationwide sex education. He finally got the Central Committee of the Communist party to consider the issue, and a couple of years ago it decided favorably.

Thus the need for sex education has been officially recognized. That is a breakthrough. The administrative appointees at present are not people who will do very much. There is a lot of opposition. The reason for opposition was discussed earlier in this chapter in dealing with the rise to power of a peasant-born class full of Victorian and Church-implanted traditional notions—and the politicians' normal way of handling it is to start by appointing personnel to whom their opposition can have the least possible objection. So they named an incredible medievalist like the man I spoke to. The job for those in the U.S.S.R. who want to advance matters is to press for real action that these appointees may just be incapable of carrying out. There is already some sign that things are not standing still. The pro-chastity man I met has already been replaced by a woman as head of the project. Somehow I think that's a step forward. But even that first appointee eagerly took out his notebook and jotted it down when I mentioned to him that there had been sex education, on however small a scale, in the earliest years of the Soviet regime. To bureaucrats precedent is a very important thing.

Frankly, I hesitated about reporting this conversation here. There is so much venom, bile, and bias in the United States with respect to the U.S.S.R., in the feminist movement as everywhere else, that every piece of information of a negative character is taken out of context and broadcast. That is why I have emphasized throughout the nature of the culture from which this society has so recently emerged.

Let's take prostitution, for example. For all practical purposes it doesn't exist in the U.S.S.R. When I visit the Soviet Union, I usually stay in tourist hotels, where people tell me there are prostitutes. True, I spend as little time in or near the hotel as possible. But I have never been approached by a prostitute, much less a pimp, and only twice have seen women who I think were walking the street.

Not many years ago, my father, still very vigorous, was asked by a fellow tourist to help him find a prostitute since he knows Russian and had been to that country repeatedly. Dad, whose curiosity has not dimmed with age, strolled with this man the full length of Leningrad's grand main avenue, Nevsky Prospekt. The tourist, with a lot of experience in this regard all over the world, kept an eye out for likely prospects. At the end of the long walk he was exhausted and disgusted; he had seen no one to ask Dad to talk to.

However, there are some individuals. I know a young Russian who, hailing a cab, found the driver pointing to a young woman in the back seat and saying he'd be happy to keep his eyes straight in front if the fare and she wanted to work out a deal.

To this day, every American study shows that the overwhelming majority of prostitutes are driven to this by outright poverty or by the obstacles facing a woman in seeking to rise above economic dependence upon a single man for her livelihood, or by the incessant trumpeting of the glamour of escapist sex. None of these factors exist in the U.S.S.R., and the fact that organized, large-scale prostitution, houses, pimps, call girls, etc., do not exist, is clear evidence that there is no inherent need for this on the part of either Soviet women or men.

In 1973, in a very sharp and sensible break with tradition, a pamphlet was issued, called *Love and the Law*, in an edition of 100,000. By deliberately taking off from utterly sensational situations, however rare, it was designed to reach that portion of the Soviet population which is least apt to read serious matters.

Three seventeen- and eighteen-year-old boys and two young women of the same age went out of town one summer evening. They built a fire by a riverbank and there was drinking. The girls danced around the fire and stripped. Maybe they had heard of the ancient folk traditions pictured in the Rublev film. But they did not desire sexual relations, and the relations that did follow with each of the boys were proven to be rape not simply by the girls' testimony but by the injuries they suffered, which experts testified were typical of those inflicted when physical resistance is offered. When an observer in court asked the prosecutor, a man, "You mean the boys will be convicted?" he replied, "You expect us to pat them on the head?" "But the girls got undressed themselves. . . ." "Certainly that doesn't speak very well of them, but they didn't want what followed, no matter how bad they might have seemed or perhaps actually were." "What about the state of drunkenness?" "Drunkenness not only doesn't mitigate but increases responsibility. If you can't hold your liquor, don't drink, and if you get drunk, you answer for what happens."

The prosecutor then spelled out the key issue: "The law punishes rapists, and does not cease to function even if the victim is not a model of virtue. Naturally, the court considers that factor in determining the sentence." "So the behavior of the victim also is of significance?" "Of course, but it does not eliminate responsibility for the use of violence. *Even if a husband is the man involved, he is answerable under that same law on rape.*"

A husband can get two weeks in jail for "gross behavior" toward his wife, simply on her say-so. Similarly, a man can get three to seven years for rape on the woman's say-so, with no witness needed. This does not mean that Russian courts ignore such realities as the woman who seeks to entrap a man into marriage, which still happens, or that they fail to weigh the credibility of the testimony of both parties, or that attorneys and judges are miraculously free of the prejudices that hang on among other human beings. But, as I pointed out in another chapter, the fact that one third of prosecutors, judges, and lawyers and one half of citizen juror-judges are women immediately makes a difference. Moreover, the notion that enticing behavior on the part of a woman excuses the man for acting against her will, or proves that he did not do so, which is the universal "out" in rape defenses in this country, is specifically rejected in the U.S.S.R., as the case cited above indicates.

After all is said and done, the bedroom is chiefly the preserve of the married. In the previous chapter, it was made clear that the overwhelming majority of women are married.

Why do they really marry? A number of studies can be cited, but the one I like best is from Kirgizia on the Chinese frontier in the heart of Soviet Asia. A beautiful Soviet feature film from there made about 1970, *Jamilya,* set during World War II, tells the story of the very first generation of Kirgiz women who tried to marry for love. In Jamilya's case, the entire village sets out to lynch her and the male outsider, also a Kirgiz, with whom she eloped against clan tradition.

Little more than a generation had passed when sociologists investigated Kirgiz marriage and reported their findings to a UNESCO conference in Moscow in 1972. Of 577 Kirgiz women responding on a collective farm, 57 per cent said they married for love, 15 per cent because of common interests, 5 per cent because of the partner's physical attractiveness, 5.2 per cent for material reasons, 3.5 per cent because of the post held by the spouse, 3.5 per cent due to parents' insistence, and 1.4 per cent for fear of remaining single. In short, *only one in seven married for reasons other than the value of the partner purely and simply as a human being.* Unfortunately, no age breakdown was given. I suspect that it was the most elderly wives, married when parental pressure and material considerations were the rule, who had accepted spouses chosen for them or who settled for a comfortable life or status through the husband's position.

Has marriage been disillusioning or the contrary? Forty-eight per cent say they are still bound to their husbands by love, one quarter say it is mutual respect, another quarter cite the children, the comforts of home life, the mutual assistance given by man and wife. Only 1.7 per cent stay together out of habit, fear of condemnation, or the like. Research showing highly similar findings could be cited for Russia proper.

I think it can be concluded that there is light at the end of the bedroom, and that when proper sex education is provided, it will gleam considerably brighter for the Soviet woman.

Chapter XIII
When Working Life Is Done

As my wife and I got into our rented Soviet car to leave the hotel on the outskirts of Novgorod, an elderly woman—short, neat, sturdy, wearing a simple black coat, her gray hair pulled back in a bun over a face both strong and kind—waved and asked if we could give her a lift. She had just missed the intercity bus to Valdai, a vacation town on the road from Leningrad to Moscow. She was going to visit her son and his family.

She rode with us for three hours. During our conversation, a good deal of her life story emerged. Because what she had to say was so meaningful and we didn't want to miss it, we took the risk of asking her if we could tape the conversation. Many people are mike-shy, in any country, but she agreed, and in response to a question, said she had been a teacher in a school of commerce. "And now I am retired on pension. I travel. One year in Moscow, another here."

We chatted about places we'd seen, and I said I'd been extremely impressed by a collective farm in Estonia. She said, "Today you can't tell a collective farmer from a cabinet minister by the way they dress. The peasants' everyday clothes now are like those they used to wear on holidays. For example, I work here, in this junior college. [Later it became clear how she could work and be retired.] Students come to it from the villages (We belong to the International Co-operatives Association. We train for work in the co-ops.). The students are better dressed than me. And their mothers and fathers are collective farmers. That's how things are now.

"Previously I taught in a village. Well, you know what a village was like. Things were bad. And now I go to visit it. Everywhere there are television sets and washing machines; anything you can think of."

I explained our interest in Soviet women. When I described the dissatisfaction of American women with inadequate male help at home, she said, "The same kind of thing happens with us. Particularly young people. They get married. The young woman regards herself as all set. But then it turns out that one has to prepare meals. . . ."

She wanted to know about America, and we said that although Americans have all kinds of material goods which Russians don't, we feel very insecure economically, particularly as we get older. To this she responded, "But with us—how to put it—with us many things go very smoothly. Today, if you want to, you work; tomorrow, if you don't feel like it, you don't work. You work where you like it. If you don't like it in one place, go to some other place. Study wherever you want to. Education is a big thing with us, oh what a big thing! Take me, for example; I was from the kind of family that needed the money I could bring home. I worked in a textile mill."

She had been a highly dependable worker, believed in the goals of the Revolution, and was active in the Young Communist League. Therefore she was given the extraordinary opportunity, at a time when higher education was very limited, of being sent to college for training in what was then, at the beginning of Soviet modernization, the most high-status of all fields, heavy industry.

"I went to the Moscow Steel Institute. I didn't know anything at all about that. At that time I was eighteen. I entered that college in 1931. I didn't like it there. It was hot, there was the noise of the machines. And it didn't appeal to me. So I went myself to the head of the institute and explained. I had worked in the textile mill for six years, and I wanted to study something I could bring back to that mill. And so they transferred me to the Textile Institute. So you see how

free things are with us." She was speaking in the context of
that time, when every student was a burden on the shoulders
of the working class she had left behind, and transferring from
one college to another meant a certain amount of tax money
down the drain, aside from the fact that even then higher
education was entirely free, and students were fed and housed
and clothed at public expense.

"But the knowledge came to me with such difficulty that
I couldn't see that anything useful would result or believe that
it would be interesting to me. I went to the head of *that* institute, and explained *this,* and *they* transferred me to the Co-
operatives College. And that's where I studied. That's how
things are with us. And while I went to school, they organized
instruction in the textile mill, where the workers studied a
basic technical curriculum. So I was assigned there. And I
began to teach. Then they sent me to a technical high school.
And so I was in both places.

"And then my son was born (in 1941, the year the U.S.S.R.
was invaded by Hitler). My daughter was still very young.
And it was very hard for me. And by this time the war had
begun. You know, everything was turned upside down. I
worked in a factory to which I was assigned. There were no
days off. And I taught in the junior college. You see how
things used to be." So she had had a brand-new infant on
her hands plus a seven-day-a-week factory job, plus a teaching
load!

"However, I went on teaching. But I continued studying,
and at forty-three I graduated from teachers' college. With
us, for higher education, there is a higher teachers' college.
Then I taught for six years. So you see, that's all a matter
of free choice. Whatever you want to do, that's the occupation
you go into.

"Ten years ago my son was drafted into the Army. And
my daughter moved away. She was going to college. And so
I was left all by myself." She never spoke of a husband, and
we preferred not to ask. But for her generation, for a husband
to have been killed in the war was commonplace.

"And so I made a trip to the capital, to Moscow." She
had been teaching fifteen hundred miles away, in Baku, Azerbaijan, a Soviet republic of Islamic heritage on the Caspian

Sea. "I told them: 'I am alone in the house. It is hard for me.' And where I was, it was like a little village. I had to feed the stove, cut the firewood. 'It is very inconvenient. Transfer me to where it will be easier.' They shifted me to Novgorod. And you know, I then had only two years to go to retirement. You see how it is with us! They provided me with a good room." Novgorod, with sixty thousand people, was utterly wiped out in the war, so that in 1960 a room for oneself for a person without family was very good indeed. "And so I worked the two years. My son, when he got out of the Army, came here to me. He said to me: 'It's too hard for you, Mama.' And so I retired." She was then forty-nine, for teachers may retire after twenty-five years' service.

"Now I've been on pension for eight years, but in the teaching collective it's just as though I'm in my own home. When I need the extra money, I work for two months. I work there every year. On September first [the opening day of school] I'm always there. With the young teachers, I am always with them. I feel right at home. And if you want to know how concerned they are for me: last year I made a trip to Moscow. My birthday came when I was there. And while I was there, at my daughter's, I received birthday congratulations from them. That's how attentive they are. That moved me so, that they had remembered my birthday, and that they located me in Moscow, and congratulated me. That's how things are here with us. So you see how tranquil life is. We live collectively."

Each time I listen to that tape, I think: a place to live no worse than that of millions of aged Americans, although during the working years our living standard is three times as high; a pension that by her standards is enough so that she feels comfortable with the extra provided by two months' work a year; money enough to travel to her children's homes and even to far-off Azerbaijan where she used to teach; children who apparently welcome her; a community of which she feels a part, not confined to elders; and of course absolutely free medical care and hospitalization, to which she has never had to make any direct contribution. I am close enough to her age to feel a bit of envy, despite an incomparably superior living standard so long as I can go on working and paying into whatever will supplement the pittance of social security.

There are Americans, including women, who commiserate with Soviet women for the fact that they hold jobs. During the working years it's hard—easier than one might think, because they have child-care facilities, but harder than it should be because most men don't share homemaking equally. But when working life is done, the picture is very different. Women outlive men in the Soviet Union by nine years on the average; here by nearly as much. In both countries the age difference at marriage between men and women in the generation now near or past working age was much wider than it is today. As a consequence, the number of years of life alone after the husband's death is equal to the difference in longevity plus the difference in age at marriage of husband and wife. In the U.S.S.R. there are 27,000,000 women on pension and 9,200,000 men. Most of the difference is due to male losses in World War II.

The most important facts for women are that they may retire at fifty-five (younger in many jobs), that a work record of only twenty years at all employment combined is required to qualify for pension (less under various conditions), and that pensions average 70 per cent of *highest* earnings! Very large categories are entitled to draw full pension plus full salary if they choose to continue working, and professionals, because their incomes are higher, may draw one half pension plus salary. What it amounts to is that society considers work beyond the attainment of pension age something like overtime, and therefore one is entitled to that kind of bonus. There is a ceiling on combined salary plus pension, beyond which no pension is paid, but it is very high in terms of maintaining a good Soviet living standard.

The most important practical meaning of the job-plus-full-pension provision is that large numbers of women who came into the labor force from the countryside with only three or four years of schooling before or during World War II, and who never upgraded themselves above the minimum wage, are able to double their incomes, attaining a living standard they never previously knew. For those in this bracket who do not or cannot continue working, there is no *reduction* in living standard, as the pension for persons earning the minimum wage at retirement is 100 per cent. (Life is very hard, however, for those who retired about fifteen years ago when the minimum was lower, are no longer well enough to take any work, and have no family to help them.) These provisions are much more meaningful to women than to men: a higher percentage of them stayed in the minimum-wage bracket both because of the lower value placed on educating girls in their peasant families before the Revolution and for some time after, and because the double burden of job and family kept many women from taking courses that would have entitled them to higher pay. Pensions are tax-free. About 400,000 retired people each year get free or reduced-cost accommodations at vacation resorts, the free ones going to those with lower pensions.

Our country has constant inflation, and the rate gets worse every year. Widows lose their homes as tax rates become more than they can pay, and pinch pennies on essential utilities and food in a desperate attempt to hang on. Medicare, never really free, is getting more costly all the time.

Soviet people who own their own homes, extremely modest as they are, have no mortgages. Building loans are for ten years—far in the past by retirement. Property taxes cease when one goes on social security! Apartment rents have been frozen for nearly fifty years, and are only about 5 per cent of income. Consumer-goods prices have been steady as an over-all index for twenty years, with minor adjustments down for one product, up for another. I have an older friend in Moscow, a rank-and-file journalist who earned an ordinary salary. He retired recently at sixty, the minimal standard age for men. His wife, who is younger, a laboratory technician on a low salary, is still working. Together, their cash income is $259 per month at the official rate of exchange. There are American economists who would have you think it is really much less, because they look at the very high Soviet prices for clothing or cars. But this couple has a three-room apartment in a well-built house on a fine boulevard twenty minutes from the center of Moscow by public transportation (which is excellent, and costs only five cents): housing and a location New Yorkers in their high-earning years would be quite happy to have. They have a modest country cottage close enough to town so that he was able, when I saw him last, to travel to it daily on a cheap suburban train to visit their daughter who was there with their grandchild. Their refrigerator is well stocked and there is cash in his pocket. When I visited him on no notice in 1973, he served me a hot meal from food on hand and sent a visiting nephew down to buy fresh bread and milk, European style.

Including this family, I know four Moscow couples of retirement age, although one husband continues to work as a writer and another as a professor. Two of the wives are retired from high-status salaried jobs: professor and editor. But the employed wife of my journalist friend is the most interesting because she confirms what the hitchhiking retired teacher had told us. Although she could soon retire at two thirds of her earnings, she would never think of quitting as long as her health permits. While her job is routine laboratory testing, people doing their Ph.D.s at the research institute where she works count on her to help with their dissertations. When they get their degrees, "she is the first they invite to the celebration." She has standing and prestige in her "collective" among people whose incomes are two and three times hers.

One day our rented Soviet car broke down outside a palace built by Peter the Great in what is now a Leningrad park. Except for one man, the small crowd, all past middle age, that gathered around to assure us everything would be all right, was female. As we waited, we learned that the palace was now a rest home for people with cardiac problems, some of whom lived there and some of whom came there to sleep when the day's work was done. Two women who told us their stories had been widowed in World War II. One said that every important document in her large factory had to pass through her hands, and she was phoned and kept informed even at the rest home. The second, who was Jewish, told us with pride that she was assistant principal of a high school, and her standing and salary were such that she received the highest pension permissible under Soviet law. She had chosen to work beyond retirement age and received both pension and salary.

Retired widows may live in one of a number of situations. The traditional one is with offspring. I know a four-generation family living in a single large and modern apartment in Moscow. Great-grandma, about eighty and still spry, helps her daughter at the family's summer cottage, but keeps silent in the presence of strangers, as Russian women of that generation were brought up to do. Then there are the grandparents, retired. In the working generation of the family I'm referring to, the wife is a technical translator, a profession very much higher in the Soviet earnings scale than here, the husband a satirist. The fourth generation is their schoolboy son.

Two generations ago such a family would have been patriarchal, with Grandpa the master. Today it is a traditional one only in that it lives under a single roof. If any one individual's interests and needs are considered more than any other's, it is the child's, and he is a little spoiled. The mother and her mother gave the impression of having a slight edge in making decisions about the household, in an easy and co-operative situation. The grandfather seems to take for granted that the household is the women's realm.

Of the half-dozen Soviet women I know who are retired or of retirement age and live in family settings, not one is in a patriarchal situation, which means that that was eliminated in the very first urban generation to marry after the Revolution. They conduct themselves as equals, although one may be aggressive toward her spouse and another yielding, depending upon the individual characters involved. I remember particularly one of these retired women challenging her husband's spoken grammatical usage, with two younger generations present, all of whom joined in the argument, although the husband is an active literary critic and author of a dozen books!

The breakup of the traditional family of several generations under one roof has been helped by an eased housing situation. Most often, for the older woman living alone, this takes the form of a room of her own, as with our hitchhiker. But there are also retirement homes. Bella Solasco, who was brought to the United States at fourteen and lived here for forty-five years, returned to retirement in the Soviet Union in 1955. In 1971 she moved into a model home for the aged in Moscow. It houses five hundred, each in a room with private bath, its own balcony and ample closet space. There are single and double rooms, the latter usually occupied by couples. The cost

of $133 per month (95 rubles) covers room and board, all
medical services and medicines, plus recreation such as movies
and concerts. The rooms are cleaned daily, and other free
services include personal laundry, the beauty parlor in the
building, soap and toothpaste. The building is on the bank
of the Moscow Canal, an area zoned entirely for recreation
and physically the most attractive in the immediate vicinity
of the city. An orchard next to the canal is on one side, and
a pine forest on the other.

There is a main dining room, a smaller one on each floor,
and room service if desired. Meals are planned jointly by a
dietician and a member of the elected pensioners' council.
There is a staff of resident physicians and nurses who are
on duty round the clock on each of the thirteen floors. (If
this sounds a bit much, it actually follows the long-established
pattern of Soviet schools, child-care centers, and merchant
marine ships with large crews, all of which have physicians
on duty. The Soviet medical profession, primarily female as
you know, is very much larger than our own.)

There are two floors for the bedridden, two to a room,
cared for by their own large staff. Another floor is a polyclinic
with a gym and physical therapy facilities. There is a library
of five thousand books, being cataloged by volunteer pensioners under a professional librarian. The youthful staff—nurses
and aides, office workers and cooks, waitresses—put on amateur dramatic performances. There are regular readings of fiction and poetry for those with failing eyesight. These are in
one of the two recreation rooms on each floor, with TV in
one and radio in another, although many residents have their
own sets.

Retired women living in this facility include a geologist,
a drama critic, and a surgeon. This is not a typical residence
for the aged, but the very best. It is specifically in things coming under the heading of social welfare that the Soviet Union
has made a superior record, so it is reasonably safe to predict
that such places will be generally available in a decade. In
her small hometown of Rezekne in the Latvian Soviet Socialist
Republic, Ms. Solasko found a home for the aged for 350,
with rooms "neat, light, spacious, and nicely furnished, . . . a
modern clinic, a medical staff, and a prescription department,"

and with workshops and gardens for those interested in and able to spend time in them. However, the overwhelming majority of pensioners do not live in retirement homes, nor do they wish to. Furthermore, their children do not desire to place them there, as the notion of personal responsibility for aged parents is extremely strong.

The difference between the position of the Soviet and the Western woman of retirement age was put most neatly by Ralph Nader in a criticism of the American situation. He said that American women are encouraged to stay home and are penalized later for not having worked, because a woman receives only a portion of a husband's social security when he dies; widows are often excluded from pension benefits either because their husbands did not sign up for survivor's benefit or because the option isn't available; women who do hold jobs get lower pensions because they have worked fewer years, and some companies force them to retire early. Soviet women, on the other hand, hold jobs, and therefore are not dependent upon survivor's pensions (which do exist for that small percentage who did not hold jobs). The size of Soviet pensions is not dependent upon the number of years worked but upon earnings.

Wide provision is made for retired women to keep both self-respect and the respect of others. Within the family this takes the form of caring for a grandchild or children while its parents work. Here we speak not of the professional woman whose grandchild constrains her, but of the factory, farm, or clerical worker for whom time might hang heavy. Since the retired grandmother has her own income, this is not a matter of buying room and board by baby-sitting. It is particularly interesting that Soviet studies show only a very small proportion of families in which the main burden of housekeeping is borne by the grandmother.

The same kind of child supervision can be done on a paid basis. I know a Moscow couple, she an office worker going to college at night, he a writer, who employ a retired woman as part-time baby-walker and helper with their two-year-old, so that the husband, who does the housework and shopping, can otherwise concentrate undisturbed. They pay her a salary equal to her full pension, so she now has a larger income than before retirement! She also gets two days off per week, and paid vacation, as the law requires for all houseworkers. In general, Soviet people employing houseworkers were amazed at the low rates paid in the United States. Not having unemployment or racial or sexual job discrimination, they do not understand the effects of these factors in driving down the wages of houseworkers. Extremely few nonpensioners are interested in such employment, and that pushes wages up.

While this nurturing function, whether in one's own family or outside, is performed chiefly by retired women of limited education and low skill, it is not confined to them alone. Another Soviet couple I know, the wife a biochemist, the husband a sociologist, share duties very much as in the previous case, but help with their child, who is of young school age, is provided by the wife's mother, a retired economics professor at Moscow University. That such women exercise real power in the family is revealed in some strange ways: many children of atheist parents are baptized when a religious grandmother says, literally, that she won't take care of a heathen. This was a mass-scale phenomenon until not long ago. Of course, it also explains why many children of both sexes grow up with traditional views of a woman's and a man's function: Grandma instilled them, and this is not at all beneficial.

The first generation of women with higher education has reached the age of retirement in significant numbers only in the past few years. Some do take on the nurturing of grandchildren, particularly after school hours. But this is not universal, nor do they regard it as a full-time undertaking, as do the retired unskilled in many cases, who worked only for the combination of the money and the respect it brought. Every effort is made to provide meaningful activity for pensioners, whatever their interest levels. Our hitchhiking teacher illustrated one form of that. Some train young workers or merely show them the ropes to make them feel at home. All apartment buildings have house committees, usually composed of such people. Many have "comrades' courts," unofficial tribunals of neighbors that people may turn to with matters too trivial for courts of law and that also are encouraged to intervene in situations that we might regard as private. While this offers another outlet for the elderly, sometimes the effects are negative when they apply traditional village mores. Newspapers have reported a man being "ordered" by such a body to marry a woman whose apartment he frequently visited, even though he denied they had had sex relations, and, in any case, marriage was entirely a matter for them to decide. Such an order has no legal force but it can make things quite uncomfortable. Of course, it can be quite positive in cases of drunkenness or child neglect, if the individual is not beyond the reach of shaming or supportive actions.

Women on pension are involved in citizens' committees to inspect operations in retail outlets, medical facilities, and child-care institutions. They participate in, when physically able, or advise on neighborhood plantings of apartment courtyards, a matter in which the overwhelmingly rural background of older women is both a distinct advantage and a source of genuine respect from city-bred juniors who don't know much about making things grow. They have lifetime access to the social activities of the enterprises at which they worked, quite ramified and elaborate in large industries or offices. The visiting committees that are part of the activities of fraternal societies in our country are regular functions of Soviet trade unions, to which virtually everyone belongs, so that lonely elders are not left entirely alone or thrown back upon their families for moral support when they are sole survivors or have no one in the given community.

The co-ed children's organization, Young Pioneers (there are no sex-segregated organizations), has such help to the elderly as one of its functions, and this is directed particularly at teachers retired from the school at which a troop is centered. But the most striking example in my personal experience of respect for a retired woman, and the self-esteem this maintained, occurred when I recently visited the offices of a Moscow borough government in the company of a group of foreign teachers of Russian. Heads of committees rose in turn to explain their functions. Most were female. One elderly woman was in charge of citizens' volunteer activities, very highly organized and involving a great number of people. When she finished, the woman vice-mayor, who was presiding, said, "She is a pensioner, but she helps us. And she receives

the maximum pension." This is the Soviet way of saying that
she had made maximal use of her potential in her working
lifetime and had thus earned society's most tangible thanks.
The pensioner glowed with pride at her words.

Chapter XIV
Women and Power

Catherine (Yekaterina) Furtseva was U.S.S.R. Minister of Culture from 1960 until her death in 1974. Before that, she was for six years the head of the Communist party of the city of Moscow, a post which in Russia gives one more power than the mayor of New York City holds over here. Politically, she has been the most prominent woman in the U.S.S.R. in recent years.

In our system a political party boss may be the power behind a city's scenes, but that is always looked upon as at least a little dishonorable, taking power away from the mayor. Not so in the Soviet Union, whose Constitution says: "The Communist party is . . . the leading core of all organizations . . . , voluntary or governmental." The party leader is responsible not only for government, which is run directly by the mayor, but also for everything else, including industry, since the economy is publicly owned. And Moscow alone, with one sixth the total industrial output of the Soviet Union, is a larger industrial "power" than all but the greatest West European countries, the United States, and Japan. It therefore has more industry, and certainly more scientific research institutions and personnel, than India, the largest country governed by a woman.

What kind of woman got to hold such posts in the U.S.S.R.? Furtseva was born in 1910, daughter of a textile worker in a provincial mill town on the Moscow-Leningrad railroad. She was of the very first generation of girls to attend a trade school, which enabled her to become a skilled worker, a weaver. She joined the Young Communist League at age fourteen when, in the year of Lenin's death, 1924, it issued a general appeal to people of the working class to join the party or its youth organization to carry on his cause. It was national news that year when a young woman was appointed *assistant* foreperson in the textile town that is the state capital of the area Furtseva comes from. So it is not hard to understand her loyalty to the system that opened a road to her which no blue-collar woman has yet traveled in any capitalist country.

In 1930, at twenty, she joined the party itself. In 1933 she entered the college run by the national airline, and graduated in 1935. However, her abilities as organizer and persuader had already become clear, and her only employment in this field was not as flier or technician, but as assistant head of political affairs in an aviation high school. It was the function of "political commissars" like the twenty-five-year-old Furtseva to make sure that government policy was adhered to, that young people of the blue-collar and peasant classes got preference in education and advancement, and also that such students were properly fed, clothed, and housed. That was not simple in those early years, when social classes with no previous experience in government were learning how to run a country for the first time in history.

Furtseva was still interested in pursuing an engineering career, however, and in 1937 she entered the Institute of Fine-Chemicals Technology in Moscow. She graduated in 1942. It was at about this time that she met her husband, Nikolai Firyubin, today a deputy minister of foreign affairs (assistant secretary of state), and therefore a long step below his wife in rank. They had a daughter, and a young granddaughter in the school of the Bolshoi Ballet.

Although she graduated in chemical engineering, she was immediately assigned to head the Communist party in one of Moscow's boroughs, a major job and certainly an extraordinarily high one for someone aged thirty-two. Moscow is the center of the Soviet chemical industry as well as of its airlines, of course, and her technical background undoubtedly helped her cope with her new responsibilities. When she entered that job in 1942, the U.S.S.R. was in a life-and-death struggle with Hitler, and much hinged upon the major product of the chemical plants in those years: explosives.

In addition to running a borough and raising a child, she was accepted as a student in the correspondence division of the Higher Party School, an indication that her potential for top leadership was recognized. She graduated in 1948 and in 1950 was elected Second Secretary—assistant chief—of the Moscow Party Committee. That post carries the responsibility for culture, education at all levels, and science, and in retrospect prepared her for the cabinet post she now holds.

She became a national figure in 1952, with election to alternate membership in the Central Committee of the Communist party. Two years later she became the "super-mayor" of Moscow and in another two years reached voting membership in the Central Committee. In 1957 she became the first woman ever to be part of the small inner circle that runs the Soviet Union, a full member of the party's Presidium, today called the Political Bureau. (There was none in the Lenin-Trotsky or Stalin periods.) She was also its officer in charge of cultural matters. But as one of those who wanted to go furthest with liberalization (the dissident writer Solzhenitsyn was published legally only when she held that office) and with wiping out the heritage of Stalinism (she was among those who spoke most strongly in public for the ouster of Stalin's remaining cronies in office), she was among the leaders who were demoted when a policy of less far-reaching change won out in a political battle. In 1960 she lost her seat on the party Presidium, becoming instead Minister of Culture in the government, in which her function was to execute policy rather than make it. This is still an enormous responsibility. The tremendous publishing industry, network of theaters, opera and ballet, performing arts, the financing of painting and sculpture and manufacture of reproductions, and higher educational institutions in these fields are in government hands in the U.S.S.R.—effectively, in her hands. Carol Channing found her "fascinating on her favorite topic, the arts."

Arthur Miller, who had a long private interview with her, was highly impressed.

Of the other women who are full members of the Central Committee of the Communist party, we have described in earlier chapters the biographies of two: Yadgar Nasriddinova from Central Asia, who headed one of the two houses of the Soviet Congress, and cosmonaut Tereshkova. In the executive branch of government, perhaps Domna Komarova ranks next after Furtseva in real responsibility, although officially she is only one of thirty-seven women who are members of the cabinets of the fifteen republics constituting the U.S.S.R. But as Minister of Social Security of the Russian Republic, which has slightly more people than the other fourteen combined, her actual stature is obviously greater. She administers the payment of pensions to twenty million people: retired blue- and white-collar workers, farmers, war veterans, and the disabled due to all causes.

Her department is no mere bookkeeping agency. It maintains the homes for the aged and disabled, caring for some 150,000 in her republic, and the sheltered workshops for blind and other handicapped persons unable to work in normal employment. Some disabled are directed to specialized sanatoriums and health resorts maintained by the ministry in various parts of the country.

The personnel of whom she is in charge train invalids in eleven special high schools and forty-two special vocational schools. Her department also has to find jobs for all persons partially incapacitated in any way, operate factories manufacturing all artificial limbs and other prostheses, orthopedic devices, and even the electric cars given some legless and partially paralyzed persons. The Social Security Ministry supervises voluntary societies of pensioners and the handicapped— the Society of the Blind, for example, with 250 training and manufacturing centers in her republic. Komarova's responsibilities extend to making and supervising complex co-operative arrangements with unions, employment establishments, and many other agencies, as well as with local and "state" governments below and the federal government above, because much of the work for which she answers is carried out through them. She is the "boss," directly or indirectly, of about 75,000 people of every conceivable profession, not only welfare workers, but factory managers and mechanics, physicians, lawyers, accountants, teachers, and scientists researching and developing prosthetic devices such as artificial hands controlled by body electricity.

I have deliberately listed first Komarova's duties not confined to women because of a peculiar tendency in Western writing to fluff off administrative responsibilities attained by Soviet women as being "relegated" to female matters. At the same time one hears the justified complaint that in the United States, government agencies of particular concern to women and especially to those in greatest need are headed by men lacking a woman's sensitivity to women's problems. In that connection it is fascinating that Komarova has described herself as "Minister of Women's Liberation." Her department is in charge of payments of grants to approximately a million unmarried mothers, to another million mothers of large families (usually married, but the benefits are paid to the mother), and, most important, of sick benefits to the fifty million wage-and-salary earners in that republic, of whom half are women. The point is that pregnancy and related disorders such as miscarriage have always been classed in the Soviet Union with illness of any other kind, something that became part of United States government guidelines only in 1972 and was not being universally enforced at the close of 1973. Some American employers still make maternity leave conditional upon a woman being married, and about 40 per cent are still deciding for the woman when to stop working during pregnancy and when to return afterward. Some have no sick leave provisions at all. While none of that applies to the Soviet Union, there are a thousand and one individual borderline situations in which the decision of government authorities can affect duration and amount of benefits. For example, maternity and all other temporary disability benefits depend not upon base pay but upon previous average actual earnings, which is almost always much higher, and correct calculation certainly makes a difference to the recipient. Komarova's department directs two thousand teams of doctors, disability specialists, and union representatives whose job it is to determine whether an individual is disabled, if so from what

date and to what degree, and therefore what level of assistance shall be given, and whether permanently or temporarily.
It also has a fair-hearings machinery for dissatisfied applicants,
pensioners or beneficiaries. She is the direct administrative
descendant of Alexandra Kollontai, who held the same post
in the first Soviet Cabinet, at a time when the staff, funds,
and facilities were the tiniest fraction of those of which
Komarova is in charge.

Leningrad is the Soviet Union's second largest city, with
four million people. Its deputy mayor is Anna Boikova. She
has opinions about the relative merits of the sexes, and doesn't
mind expressing them out loud. All three of her assistants are
women, one in charge of supplies to schools, kindergartens,
and children's after-school centers, one performing the same
service for libraries, museums, theaters, movies, and book-
stores, and one responsible for the construction of such facilities. To a visitor who expressed surprise at her choice of
women only, she replied that women are more energetic and
tactful than men.

At fifty-three she is the mother of a librarian daughter and,
through her, a grandmother. She relaxes by cross-country
skiing and the typically Russian folk hobby of mushroom-
hunting in summer. But literally no one of her generation of
whom I know has had a "normal" career of entry into a profession and regular promotions. As a Leningrader, the event
that moved her in the direction of her present post was World
War II. The mother of a young baby when the siege of that
city began, she was evacuated to a small town in the rear.
When it was discovered that she held a teaching certificate,
she was put in charge of its schools, at age twenty-two, with
the bland male-chauvinist explanation: "All the men teachers
are at the front." She had to organize food for the school
meals, wood for the furnaces, school books and equipment.

"But the hardest thing I had to bear was seeing the children
with tearful faces and their mothers becoming widows one
after another. At times I was ready to give up and tell them
I wasn't made of steel, that I'd had as much as I could take."

But there was obviously enough steel in her: she held on.
Returning to devastated Leningrad during the war, but after
the siege had been lifted, she found that her reputation for

getting things done had preceded her. The Communist party sent her to one of its leadership schools, and then appointed her a "secretary" (its title for executive officers) in one of the city's boroughs. Our biography of Furtseva provides some idea of her duties in that post.

In 1969, twenty-five women were second or third party secretaries (in no case first) of the Soviet equivalents of states. In both Moscow and Leningrad, there are women presently in such posts. The eleven female full or alternate members of the party's Central Committee, other than Furtseva, Nasriddinova, and Tereshkova, were chiefly "secretaries" at that level. Their responsibilities may be gathered from the biography of Ibodat Rahimova in the chapter on ethnic minorities.

Soviet city government as such offers a more familiar pattern to us than that of their state governments. Nadezhda (Hope) Chumakova is mayor of Riazan, a city of 300,000, a little smaller than Oakland, California. Her day in the office, beginning at 8:30, is naturally a succession of meetings. The utilities department reports on its work. Next the managers of factories describe how the children's hospital will be repaired out of the funds at their disposal. The oil refinery, the synthetic fabrics, and the ceramic pipe plants had each given the city a polyclinic. Other industries were going to build two schools. These enterprises, like all others, are publicly owned, but not by the city.

The female reporter for a Soviet national newspaper doing a feature story on Chumakova writes: "Things that men have not been able to get done, the woman who is the bright chief of this city has succeeded in brilliantly. Perhaps this is a consequence of the mayor's purely feminine practicality and prudence? She *is* a woman, and she can hardly fail to understand that the more work one puts into one's home, the more that home is loved."

Like relatively few other cities, Riazan employs an official city sculptor, then just graduated from the country's leading art school, and the mayor was worried that there was no apartment for him yet and he had to live in his studio. The reporter rhapsodizes: "Veritable woods of birch, maple, and linden are growing up between the apartment houses. The tree plantings come to a total of 1,125 acres! This was

Chumakova's idea, her taste, the mark of her individuality."
When Moscow had needed a huge quantity of fresh flowers
for some special event, it had appealed to Riazan to supply
them, and Chumakova had done so. That's quite a compliment, because the two cities are in the same climate belt.

The feature story continues: "The fact that the mayor is
a woman shows in yet another thing. As such, she already
knows that the 'emancipation' of women means to free them
as far as possible of the burdens of housekeeping." Chumakova had sent a team to a Soviet city exemplary for its
consumer-service industries, and on the basis of what had been
learned, Riazan's efforts for two years had been concentrated
on this problem. Combined barber shops and beauty parlors,
dry-cleaning pickup and delivery stores, laundries, and shoe-
repair shops had been opened on the grounds of all large
factories, so that women workers would not have to make
side trips on their way to or from work. Should husbands
share this? They should, and an increasing minority does, but
no one can force them. Locating such services in places convenient to work makes it easier for a wife to persuade her
husband to do this.

As mayor, Chumakova's concerns cannot be solely or even
primarily with matters pertaining to women. She discusses
with staff whether an underground rivulet should be put into
pipes or a lined channel, what materials should best be used
in the city's building projects, where a war monument would
be sited. "She has the ability to win from higher authorities
the things the city needs." To persuade technical personnel
of her views, she bones up on the pertinent engineering literature and books on urban services.

Perhaps the most remarkable thing about Soviet women in
posts of high responsibility is that they are sufficiently taken
for granted that I learn of many of them not from articles or
other published sources that point them out, but simply by
coming across names with the female ending in the Russian
language, or with feminine first names, or actually by random
conversations with strangers seated at the same table in Moscow restaurants. It is in such ways that I discovered that N. P.
Makarova is Chief Justice of Moscow State, Nadezhda Troyan
heads the Soviet Red Cross and Red Crescent, Lydia Chupak

is the paid chairperson of the 28,000-member Moscow postal workers union, Zoya Mironova is a Soviet ambassador to the United Nations, Z. Israilova is Vice-President of the Uzbek Republic (her surname means that either she or her husband is Jewish), Rosa Aldahrova heads the work of Congress (the Supreme Soviet) between sessions (not a technical worker, but chairperson of the Permanent Commission of all its committees), Margarita Nikitina heads the enormous operations of the Central Board of Medical and Preventive Treatment of Mothers and Children in the Health Ministry. I could go on indefinitely.

Most women in office, like most men, are not in the executive or judicial branches but the legislative, which are largest. How does one get nominated to the Congress of the Soviet Union? Olga Tadysheva was elected to the current Congress at age twenty-four. She represents the Mountain Altai Autonomous Region, which borders the Mongolian People's Republic. She looks Chinese, but is surprisingly urban, although she is a shepherd, one of eight children born to a woman shepherd. Her father had been seriously wounded in World War II and died of the consequences a few years later.

Tadysheva did so well in boarding school that she might even have gone to college in Moscow, but her burdened mother, her friends, and her love for the mountains all kept her at home. An Altai shepherd takes thousands of sheep to pasture with only a dog for company, and today bottle-feeds hundreds of lambs. Olga Tadysheva also cares for thirty cattle. She carries a rifle for protection against predatory animals.

It was the very severe winter of 1968 that put her on the road to Congress. Snow buried the pastures, and shepherds had to dig the roads out by hand, haul loads of hay to the valleys, and gradually clear tracts for grazing. Locally, it was front-page news that not one of Tadysheva's animals died. Elected to a regional youth conference, she made a powerful speech. Why, she demanded, should the mountain areas be so cut off? They, more than anybody, needed more radios, books, and newspapers, more visits from touring musical groups and theater companies. And what about lecturers on world affairs, space flight, the latest fashions? She emerged as

spokesperson for the shepherds and cattle-raisers. This brought
her the nomination and the election.

There are 463 women in the two houses of the Supreme
Soviet, constituting 30 per cent in one and 31 per cent in
the other, as compared to less than 3 per cent in the United
States House of Representatives and not 1 in the Senate.
There were at least nine women on the Agriculture Committee of the 1974 Soviet "House of Representatives"; seven on
the Consumers Goods Committee; eleven on the Health and
Social Welfare Committee; seven on the Education, Science,
and Culture Committee; five on the Commerce, Service Industries, and Urban Services Committee; four on the Environ-
mental Protection Committee, etc. I write "at least" because
many ethnic-minority names are not identifiable by sex. In
the Central Committee of the Communist party, with 360
members, fourteen are female. That figure, low as it is, is now
the highest in the history of the U.S.S.R.

While Lenin believed in and practiced the advancement
of members of oppressed categories—ethnic minorities and
women—to highly visible posts so as to encourage the self-
confidence and strivings of such groups, the Central Committee members are elected purely on the basis of demonstrated
individual political qualities. In the prerevolutionary period,
there was never more than one female voting member, sometimes none, and sometimes not even an alternate. The body
was small at that time: about a dozen voting and alternate
members combined. The last four central committees elected
in Lenin's lifetime after the Revolution, 1920–23 (the conventions were annual), had *no* women at all, although that
body grew to fifty-seven in size. That was the period when
Leon Trotsky, in later exile very free in his criticism of Soviet policy toward women, was at the height of his political
power, in command of the armed forces, and a member of
the inner Presidium with Lenin and Stalin.

Immediately after Lenin's death in 1924, Claudia Nikolayeva, the printing trades worker described in our history chapters, was elected to the new Central Committee controlled
by Stalin. For nearly all the rest of Joseph Stalin's nearly
thirty years in power, the number of female voting members
was never more than two, and voting and alternate members

combined never over four. However, in the year before his death, 1952, when that body was enlarged to 235 members, it came to include seven women. Furtseva, the onetime textile worker, was one of those added that year.

How was it possible for a society to open its doors to women more widely than any other in job equality, control over their own bodies, higher education, child-care facilities, and entry into the professions, and yet have so few rise to the very highest level of political power? In 1927, a decade after the Revolution, women were less than one eighth of the Communist party's membership. In those years the party sought to recruit almost exclusively from the industrial working class and those who had demonstrated their loyalty by having fought physically in the Revolution and the civil war that followed. They were overwhelmingly male, as was the working class before the drive to industrialize, which had not yet begun.

The Great Beginning, a film of the 1930s, is to me *the* women's liberation film thus far. Vera Maretskaya played an illiterate young peasant wife of that day, when three fourths of the people lived in the countryside, and rural women had just been taught to read and write but as yet no more. The character she portrayed was a member of the large class officially recognized as *"poor* peasants," lacking even a horse to work the fifteen acres the Revolution gave them or a cow to provide milk for the children. For them, collectivization of farming—pooling their land and implements, with what little assistance the government could then give—was their only hope. But some of the men on her farm decided, as happened widely in real life, that since it was no longer their personal land to be worked, George should do it. Weather does not wait in farming, and the crop just had to be brought in.

Maretskaya's performance as the obedient young wife and mother, becoming increasingly distraught as she broke away from her household tasks to glance through the cabin window at the gathering rain clouds, torn between tradition and the obvious need of the moment, and finally rushing out to rally women and all who would help to go to the fields with sickles and scythes, is before my eyes to this day.

She was not kind, she was not gentle. She pulled people

physically who could not make up their minds, pushed men out of the way who ridiculed her. When the crop was in, the farm realized that the chairman it had was not the person for the job, and elected her instead. At this point, her husband, who had not objected to her activity to this point, left her and the village: "How can I take orders from my own *baba* [old lady]?" The scene between them, the poignancy of her love, her wavering but ultimate refusal to abandon the trust her fellow villagers had placed in her, is to me one of the great moments in cinema. I can think of none in Western film-making—certainly in that day—that treated love among the poor without condescension.

She matures in her post, but the sadness over her loss never leaves her, and she welcomes her husband back without hesitation when his wanderings have opened his mind. At the close of the film she is elected to the Supreme Soviet.

Women like her were elected to government, but not to top party leadership, which ranks higher in the Soviet Union, and which naturally consists of people whose membership is of fairly long standing. At the party's 1930 convention, only 7½ per cent of the delegates were women. I am impressed by the fact that the percentage of female members has increased steadily. By simple arithmetic, this means that the rate of increase of women in the party has been consistently higher, since the Revolution, than the rate of increase among men. More important is the fact that the ratio of women in *leadership* has risen faster than the rise in *membership,* indicating that as education and experience have been acquired, childcare has become available, and husbands have begun to give some assistance, women have gained elbow room. Thus, while the percentage of women members has not quite doubled since 1927, the percentage of women delegates to the national convention has trebled, and now *equals their share of the membership,* which it did not in the early years many Westerners have romanticized. More important, female representation now fully matches their proportion of the members not only at the club level but in county and city leaderships: 22 per cent. In 1972, 29 per cent of new members were female, the highest yet, while in actual numbers the single year's female *recruits* were equal to the entire female

membership a decade after the Revolution. Female membership now is *thirty times* as high as then.

The Communist party structure parallels and supervises
government at each level. The representation of women in
party leadership is much less than in government. Yet even a
comparison of women in Soviet city and county party leadership to those in government office in capitalist countries at the
same level, shows the situation in the U.S.S.R. to be seven
times as good as in Israel, which had a female Prime Minister
until 1974. However, in local councils there, only one member
in every thirty-three is a woman. That is the same ratio as in
state legislatures in the United States, our comparable bodies
in terms of relative population and government structure.
England, best in the West, has 12 per cent of women in local
governments versus 22 per cent in the Soviet Union (party),
and the United States and Israel have 3 per cent. In India and
Sri Lanka, with women premiers, female representation in
local government is even worse. In no capitalist country is it
significantly greater. West Germany has a total of two women
mayors, for example.

If one moves from party to actual government, the Soviet
picture becomes one of just about full equality by sex at local
levels. In 1973, 47.4 per cent of candidates elected nationwide
to village, county, borough, and city councils were women.
We have just seen that there is nothing remotely like such
figures in any capitalist country. Studies have been made of
the time members actually give to these responsibilities.
Among those who give little time, women give much less than
men: inequality in homemaking makes itself felt. But about
the same proportion of the deputies of each sex (one eighth)
manages to be highly active, and in this category women and
men give the same amount of time. Considering only these,
local government in the U.S.S.R. is really run by about
125,000 women and roughly the same number of men. What
do they do?

The power enjoyed by women in office ranges from grass-
roots matters, such as organizing sex education, to federal-
level control over culture at the other extreme. It is by no
means confined to matters concerning women, as I made clear
in describing females in authority in other chapters, nor is it

wielded only over them. When Arthur Miller interviewed Culture Minister Furtseva in 1969, there was a ten-foot table with, he guessed, two hundred manuscripts and books behind her, with slips of paper sticking out of them indicating marked passages, he assumed. He "knew that writers rather liked her—all sorts of writers, conservative and vanguard alike, more or less. The general feeling was that she cared about literature and was basically humane." But she had the power to decide, in pursuit of Politburo policy, that certain works should not appear or that particular passages had to be changed or cut out.

It is not only in government and party or management posts that women wield power. The largest of all Soviet organizations are the trade unions, with several times the total membership they have in the United States. Here one fifth of the members are women, there one half. In our country at the rank-and-file elective level, one trade union leader in twenty is a woman; there they are a majority: 56 per cent. In both countries there are fewer women at the top of the hierarchy. In the United States, with a hundred different national unions, each with an executive board, only thirty-five women serve on such boards, so the vast majority have no women at all. In the U.S.S.R. six hundred women hold such posts. Finally, at the very top, there are no women on the AFL-CIO national body, while over one third of the 140 members of the Central Council of Soviet trade unions is female. Western countries all generally resemble the United States in their union leaderships. For example, Dr. Shevach Weiss, of the University of Haifa, writing of Israel, finds that "for years now no woman has occupied any functions of importance on labor councils."

What do unions mean in reality in the U.S.S.R.? When the male manager of the streetcar barn described in the chapter about women workers talked about drivers' hours, phrases like this would pop out: "Say today she works, *with the permission of the trade union,* nine hours, then tomorrow it must be five." No overtime can be worked without union approval. The union leader (female) had every detail at her fingertips. As to vacation schedules, a particularly touchy problem in public transportation, which must function the year round, the manager said: "The management sets up a vacation schedule. The worker himself is consulted in setting up this schedule, and it has to be approved by the shop committee of the union. . . . If we in management desire to deviate from it in any way, we can only do this if we obtain the agreement of the shop committee of the union."

I wanted to know what happens if a worker has a grievance, and the union leader took off from a case in which management had imposed a penalty for violation of an operating rule: "The worker decides that was not right. He writes a complaint to the Workers' Grievance Committee of the Shop Committee of the union. And it decides the question: it invites the manager, it invites the worker, and it settles the matter. If it finds that the manager was wrong, it explains and says to him: 'you were wrong.' If it was the worker who was wrong, we discuss it with him and explain to him that it was he who was wrong and that the penalty was deserved."

I asked what other activities the union engaged in. The union leader replied: "The work of the union is directed toward improving the well-being of the workers: working conditions, safety skills, allocation of the financial resources of the enterprise [assigned for improvement of the workers' conditions]. "All this the trade union does. The kindergartens, the day nurseries, the summer camps, also belong to the trade union; distribution of free or cut-rate tickets to vacation or health resorts is a function of the unions. We also have a preventive-medicine hotel and treatment center in our enterprise. For it too, it is the union that grants admission. People get to stay there for a fixed sum [70 per cent below actual costs] and some entirely free of charge." (That is a matter of need: workers earning the minimum wage, having large families, etc.) "And, of course, the organization of socialist competition."

To my question about how union democracy is carried out, the union leader said: "The union decides everything. The committee is elected at a conference at which the outgoing leadership reports on its term of service. If a question arises that has to be decided at a general membership meeting, that kind of meeting will settle it. The executive committee reports on its activities to the workers. That's an absolute rule."

The manager spoke up at this point: "And we report to you." She rejoined: "And the members of management report to us on their work." He: "The committee has the right to call before it any executive, of whatever rank, including the manager. Then the union committee proposes some specific measures. It is then binding upon me to carry out that decision."

Another woman, the personnel manager, entered the conversation: "The union contract lists specifically what management is supposed to do during the upcoming year. When the contract is negotiated, the workers offer proposals—for example, to improve ventilation in such-and-such a place, or to improve lighting at another, or heat insulation. All this gets included, and then we are obligated to carry it out. And every six months fulfillment of the contract is checked out." The manager added: "At a general union meeting. And I can tell you that if I don't carry out the contract, I, as manager, am held to account. If the union committee finds that I am showing any disregard for the contract, it can issue a resolution not only here but can obtain a similar resolution from the city-wide committee of the union which would, in such a case, certainly impose some kind of penalty upon me. Moreover, the city-wide committee can demand that I be fired. It is my duty to reckon with the masses; I have got to listen to the voice of the personnel and must carry out rigorously the mandates it issues. If I don't, I am answerable to the trade union." (The union contract was posted on the carbarn walls.)

I was then told about the distribution of the year-end bonus, which is important as it is about a month's pay. My informants specified that "the bonus is distributed by the rank-and-file itself, with the participation of the union organization."

To the woman in the street—and at the controls of the streetcar—this is what power is all about. Money in the pocket. What shift one works. A vacation at the same time as one's husband, if you are married. Replacing a manager, if he or she is callous to workers' interests and, specifically, to women's. For example, in the streetcar system, it is a rule that women drivers get their vacations in summer if they have children, because that's when children would otherwise be unsupervised.

As I write this, I have before me two news items from the American press. Twenty-eight hundred telephone operators were on strike against a three-state company in the Midwest. When it had bought out Bell Telephone several years earlier, it cut their wages ten dollars a week, canceled sick pay and a medical plan. The women operators are forced to work over-time when an "emergency" overload situation exists. This happens often. The company refused to meet with union nego-tiators after the strike began, and explained its position very simply: "Operators are a dime a dozen. If you don't like the wages, quit and go on welfare." When members of the In-ternational Brotherhood of Electrical Workers refused to cross the picket lines, city officials denied them food stamps.

Another comparison. The United Farm Workers held its founding convention. Its constitution contains a provision say-ing that the *goal* of the union is to involve women equally in the union. There is a female vice-president. There were some women delegates to the convention. But the reality of farm labor in the United States is that, in November 1973, the lobbyist for the organization of employing farmers, the Cali-fornia Farm Bureau Federation, conceded to a legislative committe that preschool children are being taken to the field by parents, often under dangerous conditions. To Soviet women that would simply be horrifying. It hasn't happened there in nearly thirty years. Aside from government action to establish child-care facilities in agriculture, it is the women on the spot, in unions on government farms and in the boards of collective farms, who have exercised their power to get sea-sonal and now year-round child-care facilities established, knowing that that is government policy and it will support them.

As in so many other fields, so with respect to power, *Soviet* women *have* come a long way beyond any others anywhere. But thinking back to the data on their representation at the very top level in government and party, their attainment of full equality is still beyond the horizon. Direct male chauvin-ism is undoubtedly one of the reasons, as well as indirect con-sequences such as the time women lose in child-rearing, as this affects the accumulation of experience required in climb-ing to the top in any situation. In the words of Alexandra

Nichipor, currently Minister of Light Industry in the Soviet republic of Belorussia: "If a man changes his mind, nobody raises an eyebrow. If a woman does, they say: 'Well, what can you expect from a woman?'" Ms. Nichipor runs 112 factories, employing 140,000 people, in textiles, clothing, and footwear.

There is a legitimate question as to whether women actually desire power in numbers equal to men. Many do find satisfactions in the combination of a creative job plus child-rearing that men do not, because they remove themselves from the latter. But so long as chauvinist expressions such as the one cited above can even be heard, and so long as women who do or even might desire to move to positions of power are prevented from doing that, or even considering it, by the failure of men to share the burden of child-rearing, there can be no complacency. For those of us outside the Soviet Union, the question is only whether to regard anything short of complete equality as meaningless, or to consider the cultural and historical background in forming our judgments.

Chapter XV
And in the Other Communist Countries?

While this book is primarily about women in the Soviet Union, and while much comparison has been made of the lot of Russian women with that of their sisters in the United States, I think it is enlightening to compare their accomplishments also with those of women in other communist countries. This gives us two measuring rods with which to assess their attainments—that of a nation practicing capitalism, and that of a variety of nations applying socialism.

Human beings seek utopias. Before World War II, young people in the United States who hoped socialism was the solution to all problems pictured the Soviet Union in colors of very rosy red. After that war, a new generation of youth, characteristically impatient and unwilling to recognize that a social revolution can do no more than create the foundation for a new way of life, sought miracles elsewhere. Cuba is close to the United States. Fidel Castro and Che Guevara were more romantic figures than Hollywood or TV could ever fabricate. Women like Vilma Espin were active in the Cuban revolution and Americans were developing a guilty conscience about imperialism, so the ideals youth sought were pictured in their own minds as being realized in Cuba in the early 1960s. With respect to the status of women, this was helped by the fact that the suffrage movement in the United States was long past, the women's liberation movement had not yet emerged in the United States and Europe, and capacities for criticism were not too sharp.

Cuba is close enough to the United States to be visited without terrible difficulty, even when Washington put obstacles in the way. Spanish is a language known by a reasonable number of young Americans. "Brigades" from America went there at Castro's invitation to help cut sugar cane. And it soon became clear that, with the Latin *macho* attitude toward women complicating the problems of an underdeveloped country just emerged from semicolonialism, Havana offered no model for women's liberation.

A dozen years later, less than one quarter of women in Cuba hold jobs outside the home. With 43,000 children in child-care centers, "It's obvious," writes Ana Ramos, of Havana's *Prensa Latina,* "that this does not suffice to take care of all the children of working-age women." (In proportion to population, that's only one sixth as many children as are cared for in Soviet centers.) Ms. Ramos adds that with "standing in time-consuming lines, the insufficient number of workers' dining rooms, and the problem of transportation . . . , it's understandable why many women either quit work or are absent a great deal."

In 1965 the United States began to wage full-scale war in Vietnam. Our student rebellion at home was well under way and swelled to unparalleled strength in its opposition to that war. The heroism of the Vietnamese under napalm, white phosphorus, defoliation, and blockbuster bombs won the admiration of millions. Pictures of women antiaircraft gunners in North Vietnam, of female legendary heroes of the National Liberation Front who allegedly withstood the worst tortures the CIA could devise, of bombed, burned, and starving mothers and infants—all these converted sympathy into adulation. Achievements in the liberation of women were credited to the Democratic Republic of Vietnam; to which it had made no claim, and it could not possibly have accomplished them, given its cultural traditions and the fact that it had had no peace in which to reorganize society. The forced necessities of wartime were pictured as the realization of ideals, just as, forty-five years earlier, the equality of poverty called "war communism" in Russia had come to be regarded, even by some within that country, as the goal toward which they had striven.

With Vietnam as with Cuba, it was eventually realized that these were human beings and not a new race touched with the divine, and that they suffered the same disadvantages as any other agrarian Asian people. Le Thi Xuen, Deputy Chairman of the Women's Union of Vietnam (DRV), has written of such countries: "Only with the reorganization of small peasant holdings into large-scale socialist farms does the emancipation of women begin. The party has directed women's efforts into those spheres which are most suited to their physical abilities and their psychological and personal qualities." But considering the nature of Vietnam, the fact that by 1970 women were 37 per cent of all wage-and-salary earners meant that a tremendous stride had been made toward their independence.

North of Vietnam lies a country mysterious and unknown and large enough to impress Americans and Europeans. China has had over twenty years of peace in which to realize some of the promise of the Revolution. That is not long enough for the initial enthusiasm over the new way of life to settle down into acceptance of it as the norm. Aided by a language barrier far greater than that in the Soviet Union, by attitudes in the American press not innocent of a desire to find an ally against the U.S.S.R., and by restrictions making impossible private conversations by a foreigner such as I have had so many times in the Soviet Union, China has emerged as the current utopia, whether the subject is acupuncture or women's liberation. Yet, with respect to the latter, much Chinese legislation is copied almost word for word from that of the U.S.S.R. in 1950, less advanced than today's.

Chinese propaganda is much less responsible for the starry-eyed view of that country than foreign wishful thinking. The most revered woman in the People's Republic of China is Sun Ching-ling who, despite all her own accomplishments, is for historical reasons best known as the widow of the founder of modern Chinese nationalism, Dr. Sun Yat-sen. Writing on "Women's Liberation in China" in the official *Peking Review* in 1972, she set forth with absolute frankness problems beyond direct control by law alone:

"Today in our country there are people's communes in rural places where *women receive less pay than men for equal work* in production. In certain villages patriarchal ideas still have their effect. Proportionately, *more boys than girls attend school.* Parents need the girls *to do household work.* Some even feel that girls will eventually enter another family and therefore *it would not pay* to send them to school. Moreover, when girls are to be married, their *parents often ask for a certain amount of money* or various articles from the family of the would-be husband. *Thus the freedom of marriage is affected.* Finally, as farmers want to add [to] the labour force in their families, the birth of a son is expected, while that *of a daughter is considered a disappointment.* This repeated *desire to have at least one son* has *an adverse effect on birth control and planned birth.* A woman with many children around her naturally finds it too difficult to participate in any productive labour. Another thing hampering a workingwoman is her involvement in household work. This prevents many women from full, wholehearted participation in public services" (my emphasis; English from the original).

This does not mean that China has accomplished nothing, or little. What it says for China—and this is equally true for the communist world as a whole—is what I tried to make clear in the history chapters about the Soviet Union: that the present status of women is only in part a product of the principles and objectives of a new society. For the rest it is a reflection of two things: (1) where a particular country was, economically and culturally, when those new rules became its governing guidelines, and (2) how much time—specifically *how many generations and how many years of peace*—it has had to imbue people's consciousness with the new rules. That consciousness-raising cannot be accomplished only through education and propaganda. It requires the learning process of experience. Even that is dependent upon the degree to which the setting of that experience (urban-rural, industrial-farm) differs from the old.

Mme. Sun described a situation that is unavoidable in a country that continues to be four fifths rural, and has had only a quarter century in which to change people's thinking. The U.S.S.R. has had twice as long, and as its population is now urban in its majority, urban attitudes have a greater impact in the countryside than the other way around. Mme. Sun speaks of women receiving less pay than men for the same work. Not only is that not the case in Soviet agriculture, but we know that the number of farm wives who earn more than their husbands plus those whose earnings equal their husbands is greater than the number of husbands who earn more than their wives. That has a tremendous effect upon respect for women. Nothing remotely like that is claimed for China.

Mme. Sun writes that more boys than girls attend school, proportionately. In the U.S.S.R. it is the opposite, both in town and country, and that incidentally is the explanation for the fact that many rural wives earn more than their husbands.

Keeping girls home to do housekeeping instead of sending them to school hung on longest in the Islamic areas of Central Asia, within the Soviet Union; but that practice is long gone, as is the notion that it does not pay to send them to school, as their labor will be lost to the family when they marry. China charges a fee for high school (not elementary) education, as the U.S.S.R. did after World War II. The Soviet Union has not, for many years.

Mme. Sun's report that parents "often" ask for money from the bridegroom's family in exchange for their daughters continues to be true in rural Soviet Central Asia as well, but nowhere else in the U.S.S.R. There are no statistics in either case, because the practice is against the law in both countries. Rural consciousness in the Soviet Union has advanced past considering the birth of a daughter "a disappointment," because family income does not depend upon the sex of working children, as Mme. Sun says it does in China, where the heaviest loads are still hauled by hand, literally a man's job. Male children are still more desired than female in the U.S.S.R., however, in part as an unconscious carry-over from the time when it was sons who supported parents in old age, and when World War II wiped out the men. Unlike China, this preference is no longer significant enough to affect the birth rate in the Soviet Union, which is only one half as high as China's.

Families so large that mothers cannot participate in "productive labour," in Mme. Sun's language, exist in the U.S.S.R. only in Central Asia and Islamic Azerbaijan in the Caucasus.

These nationalities represent less than one sixth of the Soviet population, and among them it is one fifth of families that fall into that category of having five or more children.

Of all the matters of which she complains, there is one, but only one, that is still also widespread throughout the U.S.S.R.: the fact that the burden of housework and child-rearing falls chiefly on women and hinders their participation in other activities. As the social category of men who are most helpful (or least unhelpful!) in that regard is among the college-educated, partly if not largely due to direct pressure from educated wives, and as the number holding college degrees in China is as yet only a tiny fraction of that in the Soviet Union, it follows that this aspect of the family relationship has advanced less in China. The fact that all higher educational institutions were closed for about five years during the internal turmoil of the Cultural Revolution in the late 1960s will delay by that much the entry of larger numbers of women into professional occupations, and the progressive social effects this has within such families. Edgar Snow reported in 1971 that China *"may"* have 150,000 physicians (his emphasis). About one third, or some 50,000, are female. The U.S.S.R. has ten times that many female doctors. It is college-educated women who possess the confidence to insist that husbands share in the home. China has only a fraction as many of them as the Soviet Union.

Another negative consequence of China's disruptive period is that the mass organization of women, for which 76,000,000 members had been claimed, was simply dissolved. When it began to be rebuilt, in mid-1973, the Chinese press carried articles explaining why it was needed, and these were reported and quoted in the New York *Times* of May 27. Not only were women having difficulty getting equal pay for equal work, but they were having trouble simply in getting factory jobs at all.* The problem was that while the economic situa-

* Peking's official *People's Daily* admitted these things frankly in its editorial of March 8, 1973, translated in the pro-Mao New York weekly, *Guardian,* March 6, 1974: [There should be no more] "giving men and women unequal pay for equal work in rural areas, showing unwillingness to accept women as workers in some factories. . . . No factory should discriminate against women when

tion had unquestionably been improving for about five years, China in the twenty-fourth year of Communist rule had not yet succeeded in abolishing unemployment, which the U.S.S.R. had been able to do in its twelfth year. Where there is unemployment in any amount, those who already have jobs hang on to them, and those who don't can't get them. Industrial employment in China is traditionally chiefly male except in the textile industry.

As the key to the independence and equality of Soviet women has been the availability of both physical and mental work, and this is proclaimed to be the key in China as well, it is impossible to forecast when a fundamental change in status will occur there so long as unemployment exists. A similar problem obtains in Yugoslavia, the only other Communist-governed country that does not have full employment. In proportion to population, only one quarter as many Yugoslav as Soviet women are wage-and-salary earners, according to a report by a female Yugoslav scholar to an international conference of women from Communist-led countries in Moscow in 1970. The policy in Yugoslavia, Dr. Mira Mihevic said, was to slow the growth of employment, meaning that skill and education determine who gets a job. But it is the men who have more of both. This reflected itself in other respects. She reported "diminishing representation" of women in self-governing bodies, and referred to "this disparity . . . so damaging to women's social status," in the language of the Congress of the Yugoslav League of Communists itself.

There is a general similarity of policy among all Communist-governed countries with respect to women. Equality before the law in all respects is its chief feature. Also, there is the belief that emergence from confinement to the family is the key to liberation and therefore that paid employment is essential and equality in education is a goal to be sought. But there are also a number of points of difference among those countries. The most striking case is that of population policy. China is alone in seeking to hold its population down. As it has published no census results for many years,

recruiting new workers. . . . It is necessary to assign a certain number of cadres to take charge of work concerning women . . . and overcome the erroneous idea of disdaining such work."

firm conclusions are hard to arrive at. But the growth rate of "about 2 per cent" offered by Chinese officials in 1973 means about 15,000,000 additional people per year.

The problem is ruralism and tradition. Here, too, there is a direct parallel to Soviet Central Asia, the only part of the U.S.S.R. with a high birth rate. Rural women in mainland Asia have an abhorrence of abortion except when they become pregnant out of wedlock. Children are regarded as both a blessing and a pleasure, even if differently valued by sex. Men don't like the only contraceptive readily available everywhere *in the countryside* in both the U.S.S.R. and China: the condom. But in China there is an additional problem. A woman scientist, Li Hsiu-chen, the Health Ministry's chief expert on population, told a foreign correspondent in 1972: "Children in the communes can earn work points to swell family incomes." Physical strength is a factor in earning such points, according to economist John Galbraith after a September 1972 visit. This helps explain the preference for male children. In the Soviet Union the notion of child labor is horrifying today. In China, a much poorer country, every hand a family has working in the commune pushes it that much farther from the hunger line. Firsthand reports from China simply don't agree on whether abortion is available on the demand of the woman alone, as it is in the U.S.S.R. Seymour Topping, of the New York *Times,* wrote from Peking, June 27, 1971, that the husband's approval *is* required. More remarkable was the fact that *grandparents'* consent was needed until recently, for Han Suyin wrote (*Guardian,* October 17, 1973) that it "is no longer necessary." Grandparental prestige in China rises with the number of grandchildren.

Birth control information is not provided in China until shortly before marriage, and contraceptives are not sold to the unmarried, according to the *Guardian,* a New York Maoist weekly, on October 13, 1971. Despite much talk about abstinence, Edgar Snow, the friendliest American observer of China, with direct access to Mao and Chou, reported that while population growth had dropped below 2 per cent in 1966, "it shot up again during the cultural revolution. Millions of Red Guards went on 'long marches,' when the sexes more freely intermingled." It would have taken pretty universal intermingling to affect the national birth rate in a country of over 700,000,000.

Ruralism and tradition affect more than the birth rate in China. Before the dissolution of the women's federation, a Vienna reporter wrote: "I encountered women who had been equalized with men in every respect. . . . With Western cynicism, I inquired whether all this had caused the man to stop drinking and to stop beating his wife. . . . The lady president [of the All-China Women's Federation] assured me with a wagging index finger and a sad look that so far neither drinking nor thrashing had been eliminated. All educational efforts had failed due to the 'mulishness' of the men. 'The men laugh at us,' the lady president told me."

Now that the federation is being re-established, it is clear that changes in attitudes are still very much needed even in the most advanced parts of the country. Wuhan is a city of two and a quarter million with long and deep revolutionary traditions, site of the famous railway bridge across the Yangtse, and is accessible to oceangoing vessels. In short, it has maximum accessibility to new lifeways of every kind. Yet when women held a convention to elect a city committee for their revived organization in 1973, it was necessary to urge the members to struggle against the old ideas of "respecting men and despising women and regarding women as slaves and vassals." The report by the provincial radio service said: "We must oppose marriage by purchase and promote self-determination in marriage."

An article in the Chinese Communist party's central magazine, *Red Flag*, in 1969, titled "Rural Women Constitute a Tremendous Revolutionary Force," illustrates Chinese attitudes. Although women had helped out on the farm even in traditional China, the *Red Flag* article treated as noteworthy the fact that women in a particular agricultural production brigade had come out of their homes to help with the plowing. The article complained of the male belief that women are "absent-minded and careless in their work" and that male cadres are reluctant to recruit them for work. Women themselves were criticized for being conservative, superstitious, unwilling to study, and unenthusiastic about work. These male prejudices against women have long been outgrown in the Soviet Union, and the generation of farm women there that could be described as conservative, superstitious, and unwilling to study is now retired or on the verge of retirement.

Finally, the article complained that the child-care centers and social services that had long since been promised to free women for work outside the household weren't there. Members of the Society for Anglo-Chinese Understanding concluded that peasant women preferred their individual families to communal facilities, of which they saw fewer in 1970 than a decade earlier. Such centers do exist on a large scale in the cities. They are necessarily fundamentally custodial, with a few exceptions in each major city and model rural communes, because the staffs are usually untrained women whose qualifications are warmth, concern, and a minimal knowledge of hygiene. No schools for kindergarten teachers had been reopened by 1971 after the universal shutdown during the Cultural Revolution in 1966. Under the circumstances, it is not difficult to understand the motivation of a well-educated woman, one of author Barbara Tuchman's official escorts in a late-1972 visit, who has her child at home under the care of a housemaid.

It would appear that the women of China are at about the level of progress Soviet women attained within a decade or fifteen years after the Russian Revolution, to judge from Jessica Smith's 1928 description, *Woman in Soviet Russia,* or Ella Winter's *Red Virtue* in 1933. For example, of the thousand freshmen at Nanking University when it reopened in 1972, 27 per cent were women. (There are no nationwide figures.) That was the percentage of women in all of Soviet higher education in 1928, eleven years after the Revolution. But 1972 was twenty-three years after the Chinese Revolution. When that much time had elapsed in the Soviet Union, women were already 43 per cent, an incomparably better record.

Social welfare services in China are largely patterned after Soviet standards at the time of the Chinese Revolution, but don't meet their promise as fully. For example, a highly friendly dispatch reports that pregnant women receive fifty-six days off with full pay in *most* urban areas. No explanation was offered for the exceptions. There are no exceptions in the U.S.S.R., where the period of paid leave is now much longer. Chinese farm women are in the situation of their Soviet sisters a decade ago, when the individual collective farm provided what maternity leave it could afford. Today Soviet farm women are under the same coverage as nonfarm people, while in China the general rule is fifty days' unpaid leave, although in some communes women return to light work after thirty days. As the country is overwhelmingly rural, most women receive no paid leave.

As in the Soviet Union, employed nursing mothers place their infants in crèches on factory premises, and are given time off to nurse them. This permits women who must work to do so in that very early postnatal period, and is infinitely better than the situation in prerevolutionary Russia and China, and even in England a century ago, when women took their suckling children with them to work in the lint-clogged air of textile mills. Today the tendency in the U.S.S.R. is almost universally to take unpaid leave for a year, after the long paid leave runs out. During that year one's job and seniority is maintained. Women prefer this to placing a child in a nursery at that age.

Retirement for Chinese women is precisely the same as in the Soviet Union: at age fifty-five, which is five years earlier than for men; at age fifty for arduous types of work. In China the maximum pension is 70 per cent of earnings, in the U.S.S.R. 100 per cent.

Daily living is harder in China than the Soviet Union, just as it is harder in the U.S.S.R. than in the West. The reasons are economic. The wash is done by hand in China, as was the case in the Soviet Union a generation ago, and still is for many rural women. The U.S.S.R., which made 300 washing machines in 1950, now makes 5,200,000 a year; it made 1,200 refrigerators in 1950 and 4,000,000 in 1970; it made 6,000 vacuum cleaners and now makes 1,250,000. Mass production of home appliances has not yet begun in China. The easing of life for women represented by all this will be out of the question for China until its general level of industry is several times as high as it is today. There is another alternative, of course: getting the men to share in the home. But everything reported above suggests that that will be a longer and more difficult job in China, because its family traditions were even more oppressive than Russia's, and because the present ratio of rural to urban population is very much greater, with all the stagnation that implies.

Certainly Chinese law has sought to overcome this. In old China widows could not remarry, and when the Revolution granted them that right, there were many murders in the first decade of women who tried to take advantage of it. They were killed by "shamed" families, just as in Soviet Central Asia when women who took off the veil were killed. Women were virtually unable to initiate divorce in old China. Today their rights are equal with men's, and *they* initiate most divorces. Marriages were by parental arrangement and for financial consideration, and while we know that has not disappeared, every indication is that it is not the rule in the cities and probably not in the countryside any longer. The selling of female minor children is absolutely gone. Prostitution is claimed to have disappeared, and I have no doubt that it is very greatly reduced, but all experience elsewhere indicates that so long as any unemployment exists, some prostitution for reasons of want continues, however hidden. That was true in Russia until the abolition of unemployment in 1929. The hardships of World War II brought revival of marriage for financial considerations, if not prostitution.

All these factors together have given Chinese women, urban women in any case, and those on the advanced rural communes shown to foreigners, a dignity and self-respect commented on by all observers without exception. In addition, there is a degree of outright enthusiasm.

China differs from all other Communist-led countries in one respect that is not a matter of ideology but practical necessity. It seeks to reduce its birth rate, not too successfully thus far, and the others seek to increase theirs. The reason is an ugly one having to do fundamentally with the division of the world into hostile capitalist and communist military camps, and is the simplest proof that détente is good for women, everywhere. For purposes of war, China is alone in having limitless manpower. But North Korea finds itself facing South Korea, which has twice the population. North Vietnam faces South Vietnam, with almost identical population.

In Europe the situation was made clear with brutal frankness when, in 1972, NATO, the North Atlantic Treaty Organization military alliance, published a special study showing a widening population gap favoring it over the nations of the Warsaw Pact (Communist). It said that abortion is the chief reason for the decline in the birth rate of the Warsaw Pact countries in the preceding fifteen years, since the liberalization of abortion laws in Eastern Europe in the mid-1950s. Its population experts reported that 60 per cent of pregnancies were being aborted in Hungary, "probably the same" percentage in the Soviet Union, 44 per cent in Bulgaria, 36 per cent in Czechoslovakia, and 23 per cent in strongly Roman Catholic Poland.

To the NATO boast, a Soviet population scholar responded in a mid-1973 article: "As a certain demographer aptly put it, one needs many potential soldiers not to wage war but to avoid war."

Leaving the merits of that argument aside, the fact is that the East European governments have, with one exception, not interfered with women's right to control their own bodies. That's an understatement. They have provided well-staffed government clinics where abortion is available generally on demand, usually at virtually no cost. The one exception is Rumania, whose practice of going it alone, relative to the U.S.S.R., is in this regard not one that women can be happy about, irrespective of political views. Rumania illegalized abortion in 1966, bringing about a jump in the birth rate from 12 per 1,000 that year to 40 the next year. But women turned to illegal abortions and smuggled contraceptives, and by the first quarter of 1971 the rate was down to 20 per 1,000. (By way of comparison, it had been eighteen in the United States a year or two earlier, and about the same in the U.S.S.R.)

Even if the military consideration disappears, the East European countries, including the Soviet Union, will pursue policies aimed at increasing their populations. Just as China has too many people for its economic potential at present, the others have too few. The U.S.S.R. is virtually empty: it has two and a half times as much territory as the United States, but only a quarter more people. Small countries, industrially highly developed, like Czechoslovakia, are dependent upon imported raw materials and export markets to pay for the imports. This requires a labor force of calculable size. But some of these countries, Hungary and Czechoslovakia in particular, show virtually no population growth at all. The reasons are complex, but can be boiled down to the words of the nineteen-year-old Soviet woman in the previous chapter who regarded two children as a lot, three as too many, and thought four was "horrible." Yet she wanted to have *a* child, and raise it. She also wants to practice her profession as a literary scholar upon graduation.

My own belief is that the East European governments will be no more successful in boosting population than the Chinese in reducing it, and for the same reason: once means of controlling births are available, it is families and, above all, women who decide how many children there will be. In China, Soviet Central Asia, North Korea, and North Vietnam, they want a lot. In the bulk of the Soviet Union, and all of Eastern Europe (except, perhaps, Islamic Albania), they want few. And that's the way the birth statistics are going.

This is not a book about demography. But the different population problems of these countries help to explain policies that affect women's lives. They also help to explain the degree to which women control them, and make themselves heard. For example, Hungary in 1967 arrived at a law that seems to combine admirably the government's desire for more children with women's right to make their own decisions and, if they do want a larger family, to do so with least hardship. There a mother *who wishes to stay home to raise a child* gets a large monthly grant until the child is three. This time counts toward her retirement and other kinds of seniority, and her job is held for her. In 1970 Czechoslovakia adopted a somewhat similar law. In an earlier chapter I described the outraged response of Soviet women in the public press when a demographer proposed that the same law be adopted there. They wanted nothing that even *might* keep them away from work and thus prevent them from being up-to-date in a world of rapidly changing technology, affecting their chances of advancement to posts of greater creativity. But they were not concerned for their own, educated group alone. In their attitude toward child upbringing, they manifested a collectivist set of values that is more highly developed in the U.S.S.R. than in any other Communist-led country, probably because the educated professional group of women was itself raised in that way and is also the largest in proportion to population. Historian Maria Pavlova wrote as follows of the Hungarian measure:

Experience has shown that Hungarian women with a professional or paraprofessional education take little advantage of the grant and try to return to work sooner than others. It is the women who are doing unskilled and monotonous work, jobs that are not creative, who readily make use of this right, leaving work and giving all their time to their children. *Can these mothers bring up their children better than the nursery schools?* Will not such long breaks from work tend to restrict the education of women? *The revival, due to this measure, of prejudices about the need to bring women back to the family,* or the claim that women's labor is unprofitable [because of the inefficiency of someone entering and leaving the labor force, retraining costs, child-support grants, etc.] and the like, does do *definite harm to society.* I do not deny that the Hungarian experiment may be of significance for certain sections of women. It cannot provide the final solution.

However, she was approving of a North Korean law under which mothers of three or more children get eight hours' pay for six hours' work, and a system in East Germany in which two mothers share a single job. But as a Soviet article about East Germany pointed out, any arrangement in which a woman works less than full time hinders her chances of promotion to executive responsibility: "Who will appoint a manager or a chief physician who won't be on the job full time?"

The East European countries differ from each other in many ways. Some reflect different economic conditions: a richer country can finance more and better child-care facilities. East Germany may be the best in the entire communist world, and therefore the whole world, in that particular regard. But Czechoslovakia, which is almost as prosperous, has very few such facilities. The reason is that its child psychologists, and those of Hungary, have come to the very opposite conclusion from the Russians: they hold that institutional care, even if only during the day, results in children being less developed both intellectually and emotionally than those who have the undivided attention of an adult all the time. But then are women to go back to homemaking? What if they want both a child or children and an interesting job?

The combination of technological inability as yet to take all housekeeping out of the hands of the family even in the most advanced countries, and psychological inability to get men to share equally, has made it impossible to arrive at a solution that would guarantee to all women fully equal opportunities for advancement with men.

The East European countries differ widely in terms of what, for want of a better word, might be called puritanism, and in certain respects is unmistakably sexism. Poland, for example, has strippers, hired by a government entertainment agency. The purpose today is to extract hard currency from foreign tourists, particularly Germans. But the fact that the first strip show in Poland occurred in 1956, in the town of Częstochowa, which is a place of national pilgrimage to the shrine of the Black Madonna (so named because of its darkening with age), to me speaks volumes about the relationship between religious restrictions and the very phenomena they are supposed to restrict. Poland also has "hard-currency" prostitutes with easy access to hotels for foreigners. Rumania has nightclub acts of the old New York Fifty-seventh Street variety of the years before stripping became "respectable," but equally based on the female body as sex object. These are also aimed at the tourist mark or yen. East Germany has pictures of nudes of opposite sex face to face in magazines, within the written concept that sex relations are normal human activity so long as they don't become the chief concern of life to the exclusion of everything else. East Germany also creates no difficulties for unmarried persons living together or simply spending a night together in a rented room. The Soviet Union makes it very hard, but also has virtually no prostitution. East Germany and other nearby countries have matrimonial ads in their papers, which Russians regard with revulsion. Czechoslovakia and some others have computer dating bureaus, which some writers advocated in the Soviet press, but which were not accepted there.

The differences in all these East European matters (so as not to create a misunderstanding, I'd like to specify that abortion policy varies from country to country, but only Rumania forbids it), and in divorce law, have a variety of reasons. The simplest, which should be obvious at this point, is that each makes its own policy. It is not made for them by the Soviet Union. There are the economic reasons of which I have spoken. There are differences in national psychology. The Czechs, for example, as their movies show, have a deliciously earthy sense of humor. Religious differences, even though the majority of these peoples are today atheist except for Poland, play an important role, as everywhere.

A most important basis for difference is recent history. The countries that fought on Hitler's side (East Germany, Rumania, Hungary) or essentially had socialism imposed upon them (Poland) react differently from those that regarded the U.S.S.R. as an ally or that had genuine spontaneous revolutions. The mores of an *imposed* system, regarding prostitution, for example, do not quickly sink into the culture.

All, however, have a commitment in principle to equality for women, shared in theory but not in practice by Sweden. That is immediately evident from the statistics on women in positions of achievement. Some practice policies of placing women in highly visible posts—the Cabinet, for example, or the Central Committee or Political Bureau of the Communist party—to a degree that the Soviet Union does not. But it seems to me that the overriding criterion for determining the freedom gained by the mass of women from dependence upon men is permanent and guaranteed entry into the labor force at all levels of earning capacity, assured by free access to higher education, giving them their own source of income and maximal ability to decide whether to live with a man or not. The Soviet Union leads all other countries in percentage of women employed and in female share of the labor force. In the U.S.S.R. women are 51 per cent of the wage-and-salary earners and 52 per cent of working collective farmers; in Rumania 47 per cent of the gainfully employed, including agriculture, and 30 per cent of wage-and-salary earners; in Bulgaria 43 per cent of wage-and-salary earners; in Poland 38 per cent of wage-and-salary earners in the socialized sector (farming is largely private). In the Soviet Union 88 per cent of women of working age are gainfully employed, nearly all full-time, or students; in East Germany 79 per cent, of whom one third have three-quarter-time jobs; in Hungary 67 per cent are employed. And the overriding criterion for the advancement of women in the mass is their share in the student body of higher educational institutions and, more importantly, their share in employment in the professions. There, too, the U.S.S.R. leads the world. For students, the percentages are: U.S.S.R. 49, Bulgaria 45.3, Hungary 44.5, Cuba 40 in colleges and 50 in universities, Poland 42, Yugoslavia 40, Czechoslovakia 38, East Germany 34, Mongolian People's Republic 32 (this was the most completely illiterate and underdeveloped of all countries now under Communist rule, and its women were the most oppressed), China 27 (in one leading university; no nationwide data), North Vietnam 12 (before U.S. bombing began in 1965; no wartime data, or postwar as yet). For Albania, the one Maoist country in Europe, I have found no statistics. However, in a 1973 speech, its Premier said: "Atavism [throwback attitudes] weighs heavily on the mind and conscience of women with their feeling of submission to men. . . . The educational and cultural level of women in general is still low. . . . The backwardness of women in vocational qualifications is felt everywhere, but it is felt especially in the countryside." They need to struggle "to free themselves from the shell of their inferiority complex toward men."

When one considers only engineering and technology majors, i.e., excluding education, medicine, and the humanities, there is much sharper differentiation. The Soviet Union is in a class entirely by itself, with 38.3 per cent of such students female. Next comes Cuba, with 28.5, followed by Poland and China with 20 and Czechoslovakia with 17. No other country in the world has even 10 per cent, East Germany coming closest with 8.6, followed by Sweden with 6.4.

Among women already practicing professions, the U.S.S.R. is also beyond comparison. Alone in the world, a majority of its employed college-trained professionals are female. In other East European countries, the figure runs about one third.

But in terms of understanding the problems yet unsolved,

and where to probe for solutions, the deepest comprehension by a top leader in the communist world is that of Premier Pham Van Dong of North Vietnam, in an interview with the Danish newspaper *Information,* in 1972:

"Full equality on the economic and political level is one thing, but the way things are done in the home is quite another. *In many of the societies where women have achieved political and economic rights there are women who are extremely capable and knowledgeable who nonetheless feel they are in an inferior position with regard to men*" [emphasis mine]. He was obviously speaking of Communist-led countries, because communists do not believe that women truly have political and economic equality in others. "Our women work far harder than the men all day long. If you compare the work and productivity of men and women, you will find that it is women who contribute the most. They are thus also the ones who are producing the conditions for full equality.

"Your women are correct to maintain that the struggle for women's liberation must be carried out *along with* the economic, political, and cultural struggle. *Women's liberation does not automatically come about with taking control of the means of production.*"

Epilogue

Film critic Rex Reed has the following passage in a review of *Hearts and Minds,* which he calls "the best film at the 1974 Cannes Festival." The film is a Columbia Pictures-financed documentary of the war in Vietnam; Reed says that company refuses to show it to the American people for fear of making political enemies (San Francisco *Chronicle,* June 23, 1974):

> There is one horrifying scene in a Vietnamese brothel in which two GI Joes proudly display the wounds they have in-flicted on Vietnamese women, then lie back while the girls sat-isfy their sexual appetites as they tell the camera, 'Boy, if our girl friends back home could see us now!' Quick cut to film clips of old Bob Hope movies in which Hope gathers two Oriental cheesecakes to his bosom and winks: 'Come here, you slanty-eyed chinks!'

Nothing in that passage could be written about the Soviet Union. It is impossible to pick up a major American news-paper any day of the week without reading about some fault of the U.S.S.R., gathered either from its own press or by cor-respondents there, or reported by recent émigrés. As I write these words, one of the most extraordinary publicity cam-paigns in my memory, participated in eagerly by all our mass media, was reaching a climax. Its purpose was to imprint upon the minds of Americans—and of the noncommunist world in general—the notion that the concentration camps of the Stalin era, as described in Alexander Solzhenitsyn's book *The Gulag Archipelago,* are the typical and permanent image of Soviet society.

But none of the small army of professional accentuators of the negative about the U.S.S.R. (maintained literally at the American taxpayer's expense—Congress appropriates the money) on Radio Free Europe and Radio Liberty in Munich has ever been able to circulate a passage about Russian brutalizing of women comparable to that quoted above. One reason is that the racism and male chauvinism of the aforementioned film cannot be found in anything that Soviet movie-goers have ever seen. More important is the fact that no one has accused Soviet soldiers of rape or of its systematized equivalent—patronizing brothels staffed by the female victims of war—*in this entire generation.* Many of their fathers and uncles did it when they took Berlin thirty years ago. An American raised in Moscow has told me of his best friend, a Russian, confessing to him in a Dostoevskian night of soul-searching that he had raped a German woman under the impact of the horrors he had seen inflicted by Germans upon Soviet people of both sexes in the four years of war he had somehow survived. But the very fact that to him it was a lapse from communist morality—that is how he conceived it—indicated that he did not regard those actions by the enemy as justifying what he had done.

In the generation and a half since then, the Soviet government has imposed its will by military occupation twice, in one week of fighting in Hungary in 1956 and essentially without violence in Czechoslovakia in 1968. Accusations of rape or establishment or encouragement of brothels have been absolutely absent from the immense literature of condemnation of those Soviet actions in the West, and even from newspaper articles of the time, which were not exactly marked by scholarly objectivity.

The Soviet Union claims it has developed a "new human." In this sense, at least, it has. One of the ways in which it has done so is reflected in another reason why that Rex Reed passage would be impossible in the Soviet press. That press sim-

ply would not print, and never has in the thirty-five years I
have read it daily, a description of women by any Russian
equivalent of "cheesecakes" or of Orientals as "slanty-eyed
chinks."

In the course of this book I have presented innumerable
examples of the ways in which Soviet reality falls short even
of its own ideals as far as women are concerned, never mind
the goals set by certain Western feminists that may not be
accepted in the U.S.S.R. On the other hand, I spelled out in
the chapter on professional people my own discomfort at my
discovery that the United States is actually slipping backward
insofar as women's admission to the higher realms of occupational achievement is concerned.

I have recently received a copy of a letter that illustrates the
contrast between the real situations of women in the two countries more poignantly than any scholarly weighing of data possibly can. It was sent to *Ms.* magazine, which chose not to
publish it, by a young woman born in Colorado and raised in
California. She writes:

> I lived in the Soviet Union (Moscow) for three years between
> 1969 and 1972. Prior to that, from 1965 I had visited the
> U.S.S.R. three times. More recently I visited there from July
> through November 1973. I was married to a Soviet citizen and
> have two young children, the older of whom (seven years) went
> to Soviet nursery schools. . . . My father is Jewish, born in pre-
> revolutionary Russia, and my mother is U.S.-born, but of Ger-
> man ancestry.
>
> My husband and I separated in 1972 and I returned to live
> in San Francisco. . . . I am faced now with raising my two chil-
> dren without the help of a husband for many more years to
> come. This is not an unusual position for a woman in either the
> United States or U.S.S.R. I have tried to do my best by my chil-
> dren in the United States these past two years, but now I am
> certain I will have more success if we return to Moscow. . . .
> I want my children to learn music, participate in sports clubs,
> go to summer camps, be bilingual. All these opportunities will
> be free of charge to me there. I want to continue my university
> education. I can do this in the U.S.S.R. In that country there is
> no such thing as paying for education. It is all free. There is no
> such thing as unemployment. I will have a job at a salary I can
> support my family on while going to the university in the eve-

nings. My children will be well taken care of at the nursery (round the clock, if I want it,) and at school and after-school activities and study sessions.

I, as a woman and as a single mother, will be more free to determine my life and the life of my children in the U.S.S.R. than I am able to do while living in the U.S.

The letter-writer, whom I know, is perfectly aware of the imperfections of Soviet society. She experienced male chauvinism in her relationship with her husband. As she writes elsewhere in the letter, she did once hear an anti-Semitic remark on the job in Moscow. The ideal of civil liberties in which she believes is American, however much our reality may differ from it. But the years of her adult life have been divided about evenly between the two countries. And, based on real experience, her choice, as a member of the female half of humanity and of its very large single-mother subgroup, is the Soviet Union.

Whatever choices some individuals may be able to make in moving to any country from any other, it is obvious that the solutions for the overwhelming majority must be found in their native land. I hope readers find in this book material from which to draw conclusions about the solutions to be sought in our own country.

Bibliography

Space permits listing only books about Soviet women and directly related themes and those providing international comparative information, plus sources on the theory by which efforts to liberate women in the U.S.S.R. have been guided. (For the same reason, it is impossible to list articles used.) For serious Soviet research, in English, see the translation journals *Current Digest of the Soviet Press, Problems of Economics, Soviet Anthropology and Archaeology, Soviet Education, Soviet Law and Government, Soviet Sociology, Soviet Studies in History, Soviet Studies in Literature,* and *The Soviet Review.* My information on American women comes from a long list of books stimulated by the women's liberation and feminist movements of recent years and from articles listed in *Women Studies Abstracts,* 1972 and 1973. I have also drawn heavily on American and Soviet newspapers.

English-language Sources

Bochkaryova, Y.; and Lyubimova, S. *Women of a New World.* Moscow: Progress, 1969. (The only history of Soviet women in English; authors are veterans of women's movement.)

Brown, Donald, ed. *The Role and Status of Women in the Soviet Union.* New York: Teachers College Press, 1968.

Buck, Pearl. *Talk About Russia with Masha Scott.* New York: John Day, 1945. (Recollections of young peasant-born Soviet schoolteacher married to an American.)

Dodge, Norton, ed. *Women in the Soviet Economy.* Baltimore: Johns Hopkins, 1966. (Thorough but outdated.)

Engels, Friedrich. *The Origin of the Family, Private Property and the State.* Moscow: Foreign Languages Publishing House, n.d.

Field, Alice Withrow. *Protection of Women and Children in Soviet Russia.* New York: E. P. Dutton & Co., 1932.

Gadzhieva, S. *Dynamics of Change in Position of Dagestanian Women and the Family.* Moscow: Soviet Sociological Association, 1972. (Women of an ethnic minority.)

Galenson, Marjorie. *Women and Work: An International Comparison.* Ithaca, N.Y.: School of Industrial & Labor Relations, Cornell University, 1973.

Gasiorowska, Xenia. *Women in Soviet Fiction 1917–1964.* Madison, Milwaukee, and London: University of Wisconsin Press, 1968.

Geiger, H. Kent. *The Family in Soviet Russia.* Cambridge, Mass.: Harvard University Press, 1968. (Major data is a full generation old: Soviet World War II refugees and German ex-prisoners of war in the U.S.S.R. The Soviet family has changed immensely since then.)

Ginzburg, Eugenia. *Journey into the Whirlwind.* New York: Harcourt, Brace & World, 1967. (Memoir of persecution in Stalin period.)

Gordon, L.; Klopov, V.; and Gruzdeva, R. *Stages of Life Cycle and Mode of Life of a Working Woman.* Moscow: Soviet Sociological Association, 1972.

Gruber, Ruth. *I Went to the Soviet Arctic.* New York: Viking, 1944. (Through feminist eyes.)

Halle, Fannina. *Woman in Soviet Russia.* London: Routledge, 1933. (Feminist viewpoint.)

———. *Women in the Soviet East.* New York: E. P. Dutton & Co., 1938.

Hobbs, Lisa. *I Saw Red China.* New York: McGraw-Hill, 1966.

Jacoby, Susan. *Moscow Conversations.* New York: Coward, McCann & Geoghegan, Inc., 1972.

Kanaeva, I. *Some Outlooks in Family's and Dwelling's Development.* Moscow: Soviet Sociological Association, 1972. (Poor translation.)

Katasheva, L. *Natasha. A Bolshevik Woman Organizer.* New York: Workers' Library, 1934.

The Diary of Nina Kosterina. New York: Crown, 1968. (Born 1921; her diary covers 1936–41.)

Kharchev, A. *Marriage and Family Relations in the U.S.S.R.* Moscow: Novosti, 1965. (Trends.)

Kollontai, Alexandra. *The Autobiography of a Sexually Emancipated Communist Woman.* New York: Herder and Herder, 1971.

Komarova, Domna, ed. *Social Security in the U.S.S.R.* Moscow: Progress, 1971. (The editor, a woman, is Minister for Social Security in the Russian Republic, U.S.S.R.)

Lenin, V. I. *The Emancipation of Women.* Preface by Nadezhda Krupskaya. Appendix by Clara Zetkin. New York: International, 1966.

Lenin on Women's Role in Society and the Solution of the Question of Women's Emancipation in Socialist Countries. Moscow: Soviet Women's Committee, 1973. (Forty-nine fact-filled speeches on present status of women in eight Communist-governed European countries, Cuba, North Vietnam, North Korea, Mongolia, the PRG of South Vietnam, Guinea, India, the Arab countries, South Africa. Solid data in most cases.)

Mace, David; and Mace, Vera. *The Soviet Family.* Garden City: Doubleday & Company, 1963. (From standpoint of leading marriage counselors.)

McNeal, Robert H. *Bride of the Revolution: Krupskaya and Lenin.* Ann Arbor: University of Michigan Press, 1972.

Madison, Bernice Q. *Social Welfare in the Soviet Union.* Stanford: Stanford University Press, 1968.

Marx, Karl; Engels, Friedrich; Lenin, V. I.; and Stalin, Joseph. *The Woman Question.* New York: International, 1951.

Patai, Raphael, ed. *Women in the Modern World.* New York and London: The Free Press and Collier-Macmillan Limited, 1967.

Rowbotham, Sheila. *Women, Resistance & Revolution.* New York: Pantheon, 1972. (To conclude her section on Russia by saying that women have been "silenced by the revolution" is to be very misinformed indeed.)

St. George, George. *Our Soviet Sister.* Washington, D.C., and New York: Robert B. Luce, Inc., 1973.

Selivanova, Nina. *Russia's Women.* New York: E. P. Dutton & Co., 1923.

Shulman, Colette, ed. *We the Russians: Voices from Russia.* New York: Praeger, 1971.

Sidel, Ruth. *Women and Child Care in China.* New York: Hill & Wang, 1972.

Smith, Jessica. *Woman in Soviet Russia.* New York: Viking Press, 1928.

——. *People Come First.* New York: International, 1948.

Sonin, M. *Changes of Occupational-Qualificational Structure in Woman's Work and Family.* Moscow: Soviet Sociological Association, 1972. (Strongly liberationist male.)

Stafford, Peter. *Sexual Behavior in the Communist World.* New York: Julian Press, 1967. (Only ignorance of the rural 45 per cent of the Soviet population can explain statements like: "there is virtually no social stigma attached to divorce" in the U.S.S.R.)

Strong, Anna Louise. *I Change Worlds.* New York: Garden City Publishing Co., 1937.

Sullerot, Evelyne. *Woman, Society and Change.* New York and Toronto: McGraw-Hill, 1971. (The best of all international-comparison books.)

Tatarinova, Nadezhda. *Women in the U.S.S.R.* Moscow: Novosti, 1966.

Tchernavin, Tatiana. *We Soviet Women.* New York: E. P. Dutton & Co., 1936.

Terent'eva, L. N. *Ethnical Process and the Family.* Moscow: Soviet Sociological Association, 1972. (Study of ethnically mixed marriages.)

Timbres, Harry; and Timbres, Rebecca. *We Didn't Ask Utopia: A Quaker Family in Soviet Russia.* New York: Prentice-Hall, 1939. (Very important; the best and most human description of small-town Russian life in the industrialization years; much about women.)

Titma, M.; and Kenkmann, P. *Family as a Factor in Socialization of the Personality in Socialist Society.* Moscow: Soviet Sociological Association, 1972.

Trotsky, Leon. *Women and the Family.* New York: Pathfinder Press, 1970. (1936 prediction, in *The Revolution Betrayed*, excerpted here, of "inevitable new growth of prostitution," is one of many examples of political bitterness resulting in highly inaccurate analysis.)

Volkov, A. *Changing of Woman's Position and Demographical Development of the Family.* Moscow: Soviet Sociological Association, 1972.

Weaver, Kitty. *Lenin's Grandchildren: Preschool Education in the Soviet Union.* New York: Simon and Schuster, 1971. (Excellent; both eyewitness and scholarly; lively.)

Winter, Ella. *Red Virtue. Human Relationships in the New Russia.* New York: Harcourt, Brace & Co., 1933. (The classic on Soviet women in that period; splendid.)

————. *I Saw the Russian People*. Boston: Little, Brown & Co., 1945. (Women in World War II.)

Women in the Soviet Union: Statistical Returns. Moscow: Progress, 1970. (Essential tool in any serious study; abbreviated version of Russian-language volume.)

Yankova, Zoya. *Changes in the Structure of Women Social Roles in Developed Socialist Society and a Family Model*. Moscow: Soviet Sociological Association, 1972. (Poor translation; author is the leading Russian family sociologist, somewhat conservative.)

Yurkevich, N. *Women's Labour at the Industrial Enterprise and the Stability of Marriage*. Moscow: Soviet Sociological Association, 1972. (Values, housework situation, happiness evaluations; liberationist outlook. This is a twelve-page summary of his book.)

Russian-language Sources

Abramova, Aleksandra. *Okhrana truda zhenshchin*. Moscow: Profizdat, 1972. (Protective laws.)

Academy of Sciences of the U.S.S.R. *Sem'ia kak ob'ekt filosofskogo i sotsiologicheskogo issledovaniia*. Leningrad: Nauka, 1974. (Critique of American family sociology; Soviet findings on socialization of individual by family and society, on family disorganization, on family as source of children's values in U.S.S.R.)

Arenshtein, Aleksandra. *Rannim moskovskim utrom*. Moscow: Moskovskii rabochii, 1967. (Fictionalized biography of revolutionary Sofia Smidovich and her husband.)

Beliakova, Anna; and Vorozheikin, E. M. *Sovetskoe semeinoe pravo*. Moscow: Iuridicheskaia literatura, 1974. (Law school textbook on Soviet family law.)

Beliavskii, A.; and Finn, E. *Liubov' i kodeks*. Moscow: Sovetskaia Rossiia, 1973. (Sensationally frank case studies of rape, prostitution, property squabbles in inheritance, divorce, marriage brokers, etc., in the U.S.S.R. today.)

Belova, Valentina; and Darskii, Leonid. *Statistika mnenii v izuchenii rozhdaemosti*. Moscow: Statistika, 1972. (Women's opinions on family size; use of contraceptives.)

Berezovskaia, S. *Trudiashchiesia zhenshchiny—v sotsialisticheskoe stroitel'stvo*. Moscow: Sovetskoe zakonodatel'stvo, 1931. (Male resistance to bringing women into industry, upgrading them, and giving them management posts, in first dozen years after the Revolution.)

Bestuzhevki v riadakh stroitelei sotsializma. Moscow: Mysl', 1969. (Postrevolutionary constructive careers of women who graduated from a college for women before the Revolution.)

Chechot, D. M. *Sotsiologiia braka i razvoda.* Leningrad: Znanie, 1973. (Divorce in U.S.S.R.: latest statistics, trends, reasons for, duration of marriages before divorce, nature of family life in such marriages: distribution of duties, etc., effects of divorce on children.)

Darskii, Leonid. *Formirovanie sem'i.* Moscow: Statistika, 1972. (Rates of marriage and childbearing.)

Emel'ianova, Elena. *Revoliutsiia, partiia, zhenshchina.* Smolensk: Smolenskii Gosudarstvennyi Pedagogicheskii Institut imeni Karla Marksa, 1971. (The women's movement 1917–25, based on archive research; highly positive evaluation of Kollontai.)

Fainburg, Z. *Vliianie emotsional'nykh otnoshenii v sem'e na ee stabilizatsiiu.* Moscow: Sovetskaia Sotsiologicheskaia Assotsiatsiia, 1972. (Research into effect of emotional relations within the family upon its stability.)

Iovchuk, M. T.; and Kogan, L. N. *Dukhovnyi mir sovetskogo rabochego.* Moscow: Mysl', 1972. (Sociology of the Soviet worker; specifically denies that the family is the prime source of motivation of the employed married woman with or without children.)

Iurkevich, N. G. *Sovetskaia sem'ia.* Minsk: Belorusskii Gos. Universitet, 1970. (Frequency of orgasm in women; reasons for divorce; homosexuality; male help in home; equality in family decisions; exciting debate with other Soviet scholars on the family.)

Kantorovich, Vladimir. *Glazami literatora.* Moscow: Sovetskii pisatel', 1970. (Observations of essayist-journalist of deep perception and utter honesty, profoundly committed to women's liberation.)

——. *Zametki pisatelia o sovremennom ocherke.* Moscow: Sovetskii pisatel', 1973. (Sample chapter heading: "From the 'glass-of-water' theory [of sex relations] to 'the mawkishness of a pastor.'" Beautiful, beautiful, beautiful!)

Kharchev, A.; and Golod, S. *Professional'naia rabota zhenshchin i sem'ia.* Leningrad: Nauka, 1971. (Sociology of employed woman re family; conference recommendations to improve status of women in all aspects.)

Korolev, Iu. A. *Sem'ia, gosudarstvo, obshchestvo.* Moscow: Iuridicheskaia literatura, 1971. (Public opinion stronger moral force than pressure of law, but law is necessary; prohibition of May–September marriages undesirable; marriage counseling needed; realities of child-support payment situation; religion and marriage.)

Leningradki: Vospominaniia, Ocherki, Dokumenty. Leningrad: Lenizdat, 1968. (Reminiscences, feature stories, documents of Leningrad women, 1890s to date. What the Revolution has really meant.)

Morozova, Vera. *"Privlechennaia k doznaniiu . . ."* Moscow: Molodaia Gvardiia, 1970. (Biographies of revolutionaries Maria Golubeva, Claudia Kirsanova, Concordia Samoilova, Rosalia Zemliachka.)

Orlova, Nina. *Pravovoe regulirovanie braka v SSSR.* Moscow: Nauka, 1971. (Soviet laws on marriage and their history, by legal scholar.)

Petrov-Maslakov, M. A.; Derankova, E. B.; Maizel', E. P.; and Poskalenko, A. N. *Sovremennye protivozachatochnye sredstva.* Leningrad: Meditsina, 1973. (IUDs and the pill of foreign and Soviet manufacture; results of Soviet IUD in 3,500 women; pill side effects; advice.)

Problemy byta, braka i sem'i. Vilnius: Mintis, 1970. (Twenty-six sociological papers on problems of home life, marriage, and the family.)

Riurikov, Yuri. *Tri vlecheniia.* Moscow: Iskusstvo, 1968. (Relation between sex and love; the world literature from Kama Sutra on; criticisms of sexless and vulgarly sexed Soviet writings in poetry and fiction and nonfiction; civilized, powerful, sophisticated; fine stylist.)

Soviet Sociological Association; and Institute of Social Research. *Dinamika izmeneniia polozheniia zhenshchiny i sem'ia:* XII International Seminar on Family Research. Moscow: Nauka, 1972. (Fifty-one sociological papers, in Russian and English, in three volumes, including updating by same authors of many in *Problemy byta, braka i sem'i,* above.)

Stasova, Helena. *Vospominaniia.* Moscow: Mysl', 1969. (Memoirs of oldest woman Communist leader, who lived to ninety-three and was alert and active until her death in 1966.)

Tolkunova, Vera. *Trud zhenshchin.* Moscow: Iuridicheskaia literatura, 1973. (Elimination of nepotism rules handicapping female employment and advancement; maternity leave raised to 100 per cent of pay and discrimination between union members and nonmembers abolished; pension benefits favoring women; updates Abramova, above.)

Umurzakova, O. P. *Sblizhenie byta i traditsii sotsialisticheskikh natsii.* Tashkent: Fan, 1971. (History, accomplishments, problems of women of largest Central Asian people.)

Vorozheikin, E. M. *Semeinye pravootnosheniia v SSSR.* Moscow: Iuridicheskaia literatura, 1972. (Most detailed treatment of Soviet family law.)

———. *Brak i sem'ia v SSSR.* Moscow: Znanie, 1973. (Brief update of Vorozheikin, above.)

Zakharov, M. L.; and Piskov, V. M. *Sotsial'noe obespechenie i strakhovanie v SSSR.* Moscow: Iuridicheskaia literatura, 1972. (Handbook of social welfare and social security laws, including sick leave, retirement, temporary and permanent disability, assistance to mothers, trade union and government-agency contest and court recourse.)

Zhenshchiny goroda Lenina. Leningrad: Lenizdat, 1963. (Earlier volume of reminiscences and biographies of Leningrad women, including those who suffered at Stalin's hands.)

Zhenshchiny i deti v SSSR. Moscow: Statistika, 1969. (Two hundred pages of statistics on Soviet women and children.)

Zhenshchiny v SSSR: Statisticheskie materialy. Reprint from *Vestnik Statistiki,* No. 1, 1973. Moscow: Statistika, 1973. (Twenty pages of updating of statistics in previous title. Many sharp changes, so 1969 source should not be used without checking this one.)

Index

minority women, 173, 174–75, 179, 181–82, 189, 197–98, 199–200; and male psychology, women on, 206–23; and marriage and the family, 224–52 (*see also* Family, the; Marriage); professional women and, 126, 128–30, 134–35, 138–39; protective legislation and, 112–23, 138–39, 311, 316; rural women and farming and, 160, 167–71; and sex, 253–73 (*see also* Sex attitudes and behavior; Sex roles); spokeswomen on, 204–23; and women in positions of power, 303–4

Mamedova (woman oil painter), 142–43

Managers (executives, leadership, management), women and, 124–40 *passim*, 163, 287–304 (*see also* specific aspects, individuals, jobs, kinds); ethnic minorities and, 176, 177–78, 180, 198–99, 201

Manual trades, women and, 110–12. *See also* Physical work, women and

Manufacturing (production), women and, 92, 102

Maretskaya, Vera, 148, 297–98

Marriage, 26, 121, 224–52; and children, 224–52 (*see also* Childbearing; Children; Mothers); in Communist countries outside the Soviet Union, 309, 316; and divorce (*see* Divorce); and employment among women (*see* Employment); ethnic minorities and, 176–77, 181, 182, 194–96; and the family, 224–52 (*see also* Family, the); forced, 14, 176–77, 182; and housework (*see* Housework); minorities and intermarriage, 194–96; post-Revolution, 55, 70, 71–72; pre-Revolution, 12–16, 26–27; sex attitudes and behavior and, 253–73; sex roles and, 224–52; spokeswomen on, 205, 206–23; statistics, 240–41, 273; weddings, 242–45

Marx, Karl, 4, 153, 247

Marxist Revolution, women and, 30–43, 44–63, 64–73

Masevich, Professor Alla, 84

Maternity leaves and benefits, 5, 6, 114, 116–19, 121, 122, 123, 139, 291

Mechanical trades, women and, 106–7

Medical care: profession, women in, 75, 79 (*see also* Physicians, women); retired women and, 277, 282

Melamud, Grunie, 192

Menstruation, 266, 267

Metal refining, women and, 101–2

Mihevic, Dr. Mira, 311

Milkmaids, 78–79, 217

Mill, John Stuart, 21

Miller, Arthur, 290, 300

Minimum-wage laws, 113, 114

Minorities, ethnic women. *See* Ethnic minority women

Minuhin, Dr. Esther, 192

Mironova, Zoya, 295

Mohammedans. *See* Islamic heritage, Soviet minority women of

Mokil, Sarah, 148

Mongolian People's Republic, 322

Monich, Zinaida, 162–63

Morality, sex attitudes and, 253–73

Moscow, 14, 55, 58, 72; City Council, 92; Institute of Economic Engineers, 86–87; women in positions of power in, 289

Moslems. *See* Islamic heritage, Soviet minority women of

Mothers (motherhood), 114–19 (*see also* Child-bearing; Children; Pregnancy); aid to, 114–19, 121, 122, 123 (*see also* Maternity leaves and benefits); marriage and the family and, 224–52 (*see also* Family, the; Marriage)

Ms. magazine, 326

Mukhina, Vera, 141

Mushroom-gathering, 74

Music, women and, 132, 148–51; composers, 132, 150–51, 192

Music to the Songs of Yiddish Poets, 192

Nader, Ralph, 283

Nakedness (nudity), puritanism and, 255–56